CRIMINAL *of* POVERTY

Praise for *Criminal of Poverty*

"Something inside all of us will awaken when we read this book and bear witness to the excruciating plight of our generation's poor. With unflinching courage Lisa Gray-Garcia brings the raw events of her childhood to the page. She decenters us with her searing images of destitution and blows us away with her resolve to beat it. We are not the same after reading this hellish tale of a young girl's struggle to survive."
— Yannick Murphy, author of *Here They Come*

"*Criminal of Poverty* lays bare the devastating effects of inheriting a life of poverty, as well the real redemption and power in finding your voice."
— Michelle Tea, author of *Rose of No Man's Land* and *Valencia*

"Tiny's indomitable spirit comes to life in her amazing story of poverty and homelessness, reaching into and teaching our hearts and minds. With her flawless descriptions of the pain of living in the margins of the richest country in the world, she opens up an important window onto a reality looked upon by many but truly seen by few, augmenting our capacity for empathy and action in an area so in need of social change. Bravo Tiny, for your gift to us all! Punto!!!"
— Piri Thomas, author of *Down These Mean Streets*

"Most books on poverty or the poor are written by people who have never been really poor, or are individualistic tales of a bootstrap pull that separates the (once) poor person from society as a whole. Tiny, a.k.a Lisa Gray-Garcia, has written an eloquent, graceful and refreshingly humor-filled book that tells a story which places poverty in a larger social, spiritual and political context. It challenges the reader to let go of clichés and catch phrases about the poor and homeless and see a population of struggling, hard-working survivors who can work miracles when given proper support. It also is a compelling love story of a mother and daughter who surmount hurdles and climb out of pits that would defeat many, while building ladders and twining rope so that others can join them in their ongoing efforts to bring more and more people out of the quagmire of relentless poverty, hunger and hopelessness."

— devorah major, author of *where river meets ocean* and *Brown Glass Windows*

"In America we prefer not to see our poor. Only if we turn determinedly away can we maintain the illusion that we are not all responsible, not all culpable. Lisa Gray-Garcia won't let us avert our eyes. With style and verve she hauls our unwilling attention to what matters. If your heart is unmoved when you finish this memoir, then it's made of stone."

— Ayelet Waldman, author of *Love and Other Impossible Pursuits*

CRIMINAL *of* POVERTY

GROWING UP
HOMELESS
IN AMERICA

by TINY, aka LISA GRAY-GARCIA

CITY**LIGHTS** FOUNDATION
SAN FRANCISCO

Cover design by Yolanda Montijo
Book design by Elaine Katzenberger
Typesetting by Harvest Graphics
Photos and cartoons courtesy of author's collection
Poem on page xx by Tiny

Library of Congress Cataloging-in-Publication Data

Gray-Garcia, Lisa.
    Criminal of poverty : growing up homeless in America / by Tiny,
aka Lisa Gray-Garcia.
        p.   cm.
    ISBN-13: 978-1-931404-07-5 (alk. paper)
    ISBN-10: 1-931404-07-0 (alk. paper)
    1. Homelessness—United States. 2. Poverty—United States.
3. Gray-Garcia, Lisa. I. Title.
    HV4505.G835 2006
    362.5092—dc22
    [B]
                                                        2006018783

Visit our website: www.citylights.com

City Lights Books are published at the City Lights Bookstore,
261 Columbus Ave., San Francisco, CA 94133.

To mi hijo Tiburcio, my sistah Swan and my Mama Dee, without whom there could be no me.

acknowledgments

There are so many folks to thank, and this is surely not going to be an inclusive list. For anyone who I haven't called out individually here, please know that your support and scholarship and love keep me going!

First, my mother Mama Dee, for giving me life, for her insight, her refusal to ever give up, her art, her humor, her beautiful smile, her resistance; my editor Elaine Katzenberger at City Lights, without whom this project would NOT have happened; the Tres Jennifers: Jennifer Navarro (y Milo), Jennifer Harris and Jennifer Swan (y familia), for being fantabulous artists, writers, compañeras, sistahs y hermanas por vida; the Po' Poets Project, welfareQUEENS, *POOR Magazine* Board of Directors for being my fellow revolutionary poets, writers, poverty scholars, partners y familia fo' lyfe; Jewnbug (y Solomon y mama), Mari Villaluna, Laure McElroy, A. Faye Hicks, Dharma, Tracey Faulkner, (mama & daughter resistors)Vivien and Jasmine Hain, Aldo Arturo Della Maggiorra, Joseph Bolden and Charles Pitts; other *POOR* staff & family: David Smith, Miguel "Muteado," Ashley Adams, Roxanne Trade, Giovanna Barela and family, Anna Morrow, Oji Elliot and Estrella, Connie Lu, and Alex Cuff, Digital Resistors, POOR Press authors and families: Byron Gafford, Marvin Crutchfield and his family, Marlon Crump, Jane Dickens, Ace Tafoya.

Mary and Willie Ratcliff, Marie Harrison, J.R. and the *Bayview Newspaper* for being my other family and always being there, and for being the baddest Black Newspaper in the West!; Osha Neuman for being the baddest civil rights attorney that ever lived, a great writer and artist, and my true father/uncle and friend; Leroy Moore for being one of my inspirations, a badass revolutionary journalist, Po' Poet, my brother and Tiburcio's uncle.

Ingrid DeLeon (y Jorge) for being my mama's friend, mi hermana, Tiburcio's tia, and PNN's first reportera; Barry Schwartz for being one of my best friends, *POOR*'s friend and the best daddy in the world!; James Tracy for being there and being such a dope organizer and brilliant poet; Paul Boden for teaching me new ways to swear every day, helping out *POOR* whenever the Coalition on Homelessness was a little less broke than we were and for being a radical fighter for the rights of people in poverty; Applied Research Center, Gary Delgado and family for helping *POOR* when we weren't gonna make it and doing all that you do in racial justice organizing.

Jean Ishibashi (ISH) for being one of the few teachers who truly understands community learning; Dan Gottron for being *POOR*'s amazing webmaster; Will Oleson for helping out no matter how poor *POOR* got; Ben Jesse Clarke, Jeff Perlstein, Andrea Buffa and all the Media Alliance staff for keeping media real!; Fred Pecker and ILWU Local (6) for being there; Marissa Kunz for her beautiful artistry on the Po' Cats and *POOR* online; Diallo McLinn for his art and his friend-ship; Jaclyn Pace and David Baal, for their art and support; Susan Sandler, Olivia Araiza, Valentina Velez-Rocha from Justice Matters for all the work they do and who saved me y mi familia from more grinding poverty; Cathy Rion for giving *POOR* her dope development skills; and William Romero for being my other brother. Inkworks for taking a chance on *POOR*; Eddie Camacho for his amazing art and talent; La Raza Centro Legal; Homeless Prenatal Program; Center for Young Women's Development; Tenderloin Housing Clinic; PODER; Just Cause; POWER; Hospitality House; Mesha Irizarry and the Idriss Stelley Foundation for resisting police brutality and speaking up for unheard families; devorah major and Piri Thomas for inspiring me; Chance Martin and *Street Sheet*; Terry Messmen and *Street Spirit*; the American Friends Service Committee; the National Association of Street Newspapers; and Ed Willard, who helped this almost homeless (again) mama out.

Michael Foley and Anthony Janigian, for loving me and helping me and *POOR*; David Hamlet, for kicking down his unbelievable administration skills to *POOR*; Roma Guy, for being *POOR*'s donor and supporter; all the *POOR* donors and Race, Poverty and Media Justice Interns and volunteers, and all the youth, adult and elder poverty scholars who fight and struggle every day in every way, no matter how hard it gets.

And many thanks to the San Francisco Arts Commission, whose support enabled me to finish this memoir and to fund the welfareQUEENS workshops.

contents

preface

Camping citations up by 255% in San Francisco . . .
One out of every seven families are at-risk of homelessness in the U.S. . . .
In 2003, the number of Americans living in poverty rose by 1.3 million . . .

It's illegal is to be homeless in America. Poverty is a violent crime. Like thousands of unheard, unseen, very low and no-income children, families and individuals living in poverty in America, I have been incarcerated for those crimes. I am a criminal of poverty.

This is my story, my mother's story and my grandmother's story—three generations of poor women in America. It focuses on the criminalization of poor families, poor women, mothers and children, through the telling of one family's struggle with poverty and homelessness.

My story also illuminates the root causes of poverty through the story of three generations: my grandmother, an Irish immigrant, teenage mother and battered woman in pre-New Deal patriarchal America; my mother, a mixed-race child surrendered to foster care, a survivor of abuse who tried for many years to escape her childhood torture until one day the struggle became too great; and finally me, a daughter raised by a poor single mother who lived "one paycheck away from homelessness" until finally there was no longer a paycheck to keep us housed, a daughter whose duty it was to keep my family alive by any means necessary, a daughter who was home-schooled in the school of hard knocks.

But this is not a rant about what I didn't have (typical school-system education, traditional family structure, material wealth)—I will forever be grateful to my mother for giving me the best life she could, for giving me strength, intuition, art, her trust and, above all, the intellectual means to understand my situation and develop a pedagogy of poverty.

Rather, this is a condemnation of a system that values independence and separation—children from elders, mothers from children, parents from school systems—rather than interdependence, community, support and care giving. This is a condemnation of a system that makes it hard for all parents to thrive, for poor parents to simply survive, for poor women to raise and care for their children, and for children to help their parents. A system that doesn't support people who need help, whoever they might be, and instead sets up a pecking order of the deserving and undeserving poor. A system that pits the poor against the poorer.

We poor folks have bought into that same belief system; we rarely recognize the root conditions of systematic oppression that have brought us to where we are. We are ashamed of our "mistakes," we are ashamed of our poverty and too often we are ashamed to ask for help. So, after we have finally lost all hope, tortured by our internalized shame and our psychiatric diagnoses, floundering in shelters, SRO hotels, in our cars or on the street, then we arrive at the point where someone else is deemed better qualified to make "our decisions" for us: "They're too sick to be on the street"; "That child should be in foster care"; and on it goes.

"We need to clean up this neighborhood." When we hear those hygiene metaphors we need to be conscious that the human beings who are being "cleaned up" and "cleaned out" are people of color, poor, homeless, youth, elders, someone functioning with a substance abuse problem, living with a mental illness or other disability, living in a car, migrant day laborers, etc. Or they could be people whose work is not recognized as work, such as panhandlers, street newspaper vendors, recyclers, and/or workfare workers. These people, if they happen to be dwelling, sitting, sleeping, and/or working in a neighborhood that's undergoing gentrification/redevelopment, will be targeted by the police for harassment, abuse, arrest, and eventually incarceration.

The clearest example of this process was the "clean-up" of New York's Times Square under the mayoral administration of Rudolph Giuliani. In the 1990s, while HUD was reducing its overall budget by 90%, and simultaneously demolishing housing projects and exchanging housing for mostly useless and unredeemable Section 8 vouchers, Mayor Giuliani launched his Clean-Up New York campaign. He began with a proclamation, "Panhandlers, peddlers and prostitutes must be cleaned out," making a public link between sex-workers, unlicensed vendors, street artists and panhandlers. He presided over a racist, classist effort to purge the city of any visible trace of its vast number of poor and low-income inhabitants in a push to create a Disneyfied, tourist-friendly city. Giuliani's "clean-up campaign" was so successful in achieving that goal that it became the model for cities across America as they strove for more tourist dollars, redevelopment money and real estate increases.

Cities like San Francisco, Atlanta and Sarasota have followed suit. Homeless people, poor intergenerational families, youth of color, migrant workers, these are always the first to be "cleaned out." The shelter systems to which they are remanded are usually run by large corporate developers who get million-dollar contracts to provide beds and some kind of integrated case management services. The whole system then operates like a pseudo-jail, with nightly piss-tests, integrated welfare/workfare at slave wages, most of which must then be used to pay for the homeless person's bed, and a tiny cash grant which barely covers luxuries like aspirin or toothpaste.

Shelters, however, are still not truly incarceration. Poor folks actually get jailed for many reasons, most of which have to do with simply being poor. Crimes of poverty can include violations for the act of being homeless and/or very low-income in America, such as camping on public property, blocking the sidewalk, recycling, loitering (which can include sitting while homeless), and in my family's case, sleeping in a vehicle or driving with expired plates (Driving While Poor). Other crimes of poverty might fall into the category of the "undeserving poor," for example, a family barely subsisting on welfare is convicted of welfare fraud for lying on a form to receive medical care or extra food stamps, "crimes" that many poor parents get accused of. These and other crimes of poverty and homelessness are increasingly common all over the United States, especially in cities like San Francisco with its scarcity of affordable housing and high-speed gentrification, redevelopment and subsequent destruction of low-income communities. The experience of being put in jail for crimes of poverty can destroy a person's mental and physical state so entirely that one can lose the strength to go on about the business of survival as a poor person or, even worse, a poor parent.

Mine is a story of survival, common to many families subsisting in poverty in the United States. Like many of my sisters and brothers in the third world, it was necessary that I work to support my family, rather than take part in a formal education that makes no allowances for the erratic schedule of a working/ houseless child. Contrary to Western capitalist standards where healthy families are made up of individuals whose personal advancement and fulfillment are considered paramount, I am honored that I could help my family, that I could help my mother, and like poor children all over the world, I am aware that without my help, she would not have made it. In our pathologically self-centered modern society, where we are all expected to survive and prosper in a cut-throat economic system that does not provide child care, housing, healthcare or a good public education, mine is not only a story of survival but of triumph. And above all it is a call for vision and clarity: the denunciation of the oppressive system that drives people into poverty and keeps them there, and the recognition that first and foremost all people deserve whatever help they need.

This poem is honor of mothers
homeless mothers and poor mothers
low-wage mothers and no-wage mothers
welfare mothers
three-job-working mothers
immigrant mothers
and incarcerated mothers

In other words
this poem is honor of
INS-ed with, CPS-ed with and
most of all system-messed-with mothers

This poem is in honor of all those poor women and men
and yes, I said men, 'cause don't sing me that old song
about gender again

Who fight and struggle
and steal and beg in every crevice
and corner to keep their kids in a bed
Who dress and feed with tired hands
Who answer cries over and over again

This poem is in honor of those
mothers who deserve to be coddled
and loved
fed and protected
instead of criminalized
marginalized and rarely respected

Who can barely make it, but always do
and still raise all the world's people
like me, you and you

Can I get a witness?
This poem is in honor of mothers
who can barely make it, but sometimes do
and still raise all the world's people
like me, you and you

Dee and Lisa at the Redondo Beach house by the ocean, before the divorce.

CHAPTER 1

the end of innocence

"I can't breathe here . . ."

These were the largest sidewalk squares I had ever seen. My mother and I were stranded on one, holding onto each other for dear life. I was eleven years old. We were in downtown Los Angeles—the Rampart district, on the edge of the Crenshaw area, famous for graffiti, police helicopter chases and opaque landscapes filled with ancient alabaster apartment buildings, immense streets and sidewalks.

"I can't take that job . . . I can't breathe here . . . I've got to get out of here," her words came out in tense clumps.

I couldn't stop myself from focusing on the size of each cement square. As she spoke, they seemed to grow larger, and the thick foundation of the apartment building in front of us seemed to stretch and bend, threatening to curl over us. I only heard parts of her words, and after several minutes it was just the consonants jumping up and down in the atmosphere.

"But couldn't you just try it for one week?" I begged, trying to appear nonchalant, my desperation dangling in the silent, white-brown afternoon air. I looked up, hoping for some sky, some hint of blue or a tip of cloud, but I found only the usual omnipresent glare, a sky color specific to Los Angeles, generated by the reflections off of windshields, chrome bumpers,

1

sunglasses, apartment windows, billboards and the bottoms of airplanes.

I tried again, "You need this job, it might be the last one you get." While she pondered this momentarily, the parts of my stomach that were drowning in an admixture of adrenaline and acid came up for air. "We're not going to make it without that job. We have no savings, what about the rent?" Despite my efforts to keep it from happening, fear was seeping into my voice.

"But you know I can't breathe in this smog. I just don't know . . ."

My whole body searched for something else to say, knowing so well, so perfectly clearly that if she did not take this job, if she did not get out of the house *now*, get back to normal immediately, then life would change for good, not partially or just for a while, but completely, irreversibly and forever.

"Lisa, I don't know what to do. Maybe I can get a job in Santa Monica. The air will be better there. I know jobs are competitive in West L.A., but . . ."

As she spoke, we both continued to shrink, hovering together on the sidewalk while an exhaust-filled breeze began to circle and expand above us, swaying the fronds of the dusty palm trees. That day was the end of things previously lived: innocence, goofiness, dumb ideas, eleven-year-oldness. That day was the end of life as I had known it. And like all endings, it was actually a beginning: the beginning of crisis, terror, impossibility, extreme poverty and vicious cycles. Yet, as is often the case, beginnings are never very clear and endings are even fuzzier, so we went home to initiate what became an odd sort of schedule, a schedule to change things, an impotent form of desperate networking with no network.

Even when my mom was working things hadn't been "normal," from a conventional American perspective, i.e., two parents, a stable home, steady income, etcetera. My father had divorced my mother when I was four years old, threatening her with a custody battle if she ever demanded child support, and so we were always poor. My mother struggled constantly with the isolation and desperation of being a very low-income single parent. Still, I thought she was an excellent mom, one who protected me, taught me and mentored me. I was always included in the complex discussions and strategies necessary to keep both of us alive, which I loved. We were completely entwined co-conspirators.

One of our most hopeful times had been when my mother got the job she had just recently lost. She had been a social worker/case manager in a Catholic group home for emotionally disturbed adolescent girls, a position that was created with a government grant. The nuns took a chance on my mom, a newly minted social worker with no work experience, and after one year my mother had become highly respected for her innovative techniques. Implementing an approach that is now referred to as "family restoration," she attempted to keep each family she worked with intact, using a team approach that included extensive advocacy and support. By her second and last year there, she had become a team leader of teachers, therapists and house managers. Her position was terminated when the funding ran out, and now, a few months after she'd been laid off, she was physically ill and emotionally distraught, caught in a complex web of phobia, conflict and poverty.

We lived in a dilapidated apartment building located on the edge of Hollywood, barely touching the border of Hancock Park, a remnant of old money and faded glamour. As you stepped onto Rossmore Street—what Vine became once you crossed Melrose—you entered a lush, green, tree-lined, non-Los Angeles peace that filled your nostrils and chilled your eyelids. If you didn't look back, you could imagine that you were walking in some wealthy gated community, but if you turned around, you faced the corner of Melrose and Vine, nexus of Hollywood hopes, broken dreams and desperation.

I straddled these disparate worlds with a daily visit to Winchell's Donuts, at the corner of Melrose and Vine. Back when my life had made sense, I would stop in at Winchell's on my way to school, taking a quick detour to acquire a plain old-fashioned, enjoying the hustle and excitement of being a kid in a city too large and tense to notice you. After my mother got laid off and I no longer went to school, my visits to Winchell's became one of a series of patterns that I established in my attempt to hold on to some semblance of order. I wasn't familiar yet with the notion of reading newspapers or drinking coffee, but I was able to go there and buy something, to get out of the house and partake in some sort of normalcy.

Our apartment was art-deco-huge with incredibly high ceilings, wall-to-wall carpeting and floor-to-ceiling cream-colored drapes. Our landlord, who also owned the Rossmore Hotel that had housed none other than Mae West herself, explained to us that Errol Flynn had had our apartment built for his girlfriend, and so we were really quite lucky to get it at only $390 per month. I didn't know who Errol Flynn was, but I hoped it would rival my friend Cindy McCoy's status of living in the building where the Hillside Strangler used to rent an apartment.

One day while my mother was still working, we bought a small orange cat at the local pet store that catered to the wealthy people in Hancock Park. My mom, orange cat and I lived happily ever after until my mother lost her job, at which point a lethal admixture of cat dander, wool carpeting and smog began to slowly suffocate her, causing her anxiety to be compounded with the onset of severe asthmatic symptoms.

"A blossom fell and very soon I saw you kissing someone beneath the moon . . ."

Ever since my mother bought the Nat King Cole tape, she played it eight hours a day. His buttery voice coated the yelling that emanated from our apartment.

"Lisa, you have to help me get out of here!" That's how it would begin, and then she'd hand me enlarged handwriting thrown across a lined piece of paper, "Call them."

Sometimes I'd sneak out onto the fake balcony/fire escape that extended delicately by peeling wrought-iron tendrils over the five-lane intersection. I watched people going to and from things, things that seemed to have a beginning and an end, 9:00 to 3:00, 8:00 to 5:00.

"But what about going to school today?" I would sometimes ask.

"You can't go today. You can't leave me alone. You've got to help me get out of here!"

"Here" was an amorphous concept, depending upon her level of depression that day or week. Sometimes it meant the actual apartment—it had been ten months since she'd lost her job and three months since she'd been out of the house. But more often "here" meant the whole city of Los Angeles, or even the entire continent.

In the first few weeks after she was laid off, my mother called my school to get permission for me to come in late or be absent for a few days at a time when she needed my help and absolutely couldn't be alone. But the school system didn't allow for anything outside of the accepted norm, and family health crises, homelessness or the need for a child to work weren't on their list of valid reasons for a child to miss school. Eventually they began to threaten my mother about my truancy and so she just stopped calling them; I was quickly forgotten, just one more child with a "difficult" life in the massive L.A. Unified School District. A few years later when we were in the throes of homelessness my mother tried to re-enroll me, but the location of our parked car was not their idea of a proper home address. My mom gave up completely after that, though according to her it was not the end of school, it was just the end of "their" school.

I was now enrolled in the school of hard knocks, learning to take over tasks that my mom's depression made her incapable of handling; basic adult things like balancing a check book and paying bills, making medical appointments and taking care of the car registration became my responsibility. I had to teach myself most of this, and as our poverty increased the tasks got harder, including eviction preparations, bank-ruptcy and creditor evasion, not to mention launching a microbusiness at the ripe old age of 13.

"If I could just get out of this place, maybe I could get a job, maybe I could breathe. Lisa, you've got to find me a therapist. What if we move to Mexico, will there be medical care there?"

And then there was the most challenging and labor-intensive job of all, one that began in that apartment and continued for the rest of my mother's life: I became her caregiver/advocate. In the beginning, and often in later years, this entailed an endless number of phone calls to seek help or some kind of advice or information. Different calls were always on the list depending upon her focus that day—to get employed again, maybe volunteer, to try school, to become less isolated—but almost consistently the quest for a therapist would be part of the plan. We had no money except her meager unemployment that would run out very soon, and there was no free therapy available that we could find, so this, the most important of needs, was left unmet.

The Reverend Jim Bond of the Peace and Freedom Church would appear on the list at least twice a week. He had shaken our hands once at a seminar called Becoming One With Your Political Correctness.

"Hi, I'm Jim Bond. Welcome. Here's our program."

My mother believed that if someone acted helpful you should take him or her seriously, take them up on their implied hospitality.

11:22 A.M. Tuesday:

"Hi Reverend Bond, it's Lisa. Just calling to check if you know of any low-cost therapy resources in the area?"

"Therapists?" an audible gulp.

"Yeah, for my mother."

"Oh."

6

11:40 A.M. Thursday:

"Hi Reverend Bond, it's Lisa. Just calling to check if you know of any graduate schools in the Seattle area? My mother wants to go back to school."

11:37 A.M. Monday:

"I thought you loved me, you said you loved me . . . we planned together . . . to dream forever . . ." Nat was whispering in the background.

"Hi Reverend Bond, it's Lisa. Do you know of any good volunteer resources in the Canada area?"

"The dream has ended, for true love died . . ."

"Also, are there any free therapists in that area?"

"Lisa, can I ask you a question?"

"Yeah, sure."

"How old are you?"

"Eleven."

"Aren't you supposed to be in school right now?"

"Oh nooo, school's already over for me. You see my school starts at 6:00 A.M. and it's over by 11:00."

"That night a blossom fell and touched two lips that lied . . ."

7

CHAPTER 2

origin stories: grandmother

Life was never easy for my mother and me. My father left us when I was four, but he really left before I was born, venturing out into the night to consume large amounts of unknown substances, preparing for his future role as a disillusioned, wealthy psychiatrist. When he finally abandoned us for good he used his birthright of money and social standing to intimidate my mother, and after a bitter, debilitating divorce she was left with no alimony, minimal child support, and almost no personal resources to pull together a life for the two of us.

But my mother's story of struggle didn't begin there. It began with the systematic torture of a mixed-race orphan girl in a series of foster homes, a childhood so horrific that she suffered from severe post-traumatic stress syndrome to the end of her life. She was an illegitimate love child, the product of my Irish grandmother's liaison with an Afro Puerto Rican high-stakes gambler. My grandmother, an impoverished teenage immigrant from Liverpool, was too poor and too ashamed to care for her illegitimate daughter and she gave her up to foster care. My mother's poverty, my mother's mother's poverty and my poverty, an unending chain of isolated poor women with no resources, no family, no support, and no luck.

My grandmother, Helen Josephine, was one of eleven children born to an extremely poor family who lived in the Irish ghetto of Liverpool, England. Her story was told to me many times by my mother, who had gotten it in bits and pieces during the few times she reunited with her mother as an adult. These bits of stories were coupled with my mother's scant memories from the days in Philadelphia when my grandmother would visit her at the orphanage.

But the largest source of Helen Jo's story came from my mother's half sisters, whom my mother didn't even know existed until her fourteenth birthday. It seems Helen Jo had already abandoned three children in desperation before ending up in Philadelphia and getting pregnant with my mother, and this first group of children—two girls, Jan and Margie, and one boy, Earl—saved up their money as young adults and hired a private detective to find their mother. When they did find her, and found out about my mother as well, they assumed my mother had been the cause for their abandonment, and so their relationship with my mother was always problematic. But they all shared an intense love of story and scandal, and in those times that they did manage to connect there were many hours of gossip and conspiratorial recanting of the "horrible story of Helen Jo."

Something happened when Helen Josephine Elizabeth McMurphy was thirteen years old. It has never been clear in the vague stories that were passed down—maybe it was a rape, maybe just the violence of poverty. Whatever the cause, the custom in those days was that poor Irish Catholic girls who were pregnant, or considered at-risk of pregnancy, like Helen Josephine who was quite well endowed and considered a provocation, were sent away by their families to a convent. There they would learn to do manual labor and gain the basic skills to perhaps find work as a domestic who could earn and add to the family's income.

But Helen Jo's family's plan was oddly foiled, since the nuns were captivated by the tiny girl with the hourglass figure, with her black hair and wide eyes the color of fresh coal, and they took her under their wing and painstakingly taught her the "King's English," working with her for hours on her elocution and the proper pronunciation of consonants. It's not clear what, exactly, the nuns had in mind for Helen Josephine, though my grandmother maintained throughout her life that she was being groomed to become a Shakespearean actress. It's not clear either why suddenly, after two years at the convent, the nuns summoned her one day and told her to pack her bag and get ready to "go out on her own."

"Come here dear," Sister Maria caressed young Helen's soft face, "You must fulfill God's destiny for you to become someone very special. Just be careful and work hard and you can become anything you want."

"But I don't think I'm ready, Sister," Helen Jo whispered.

"Well, we can't keep you here any longer, my dear," and with those fateful words they handed Helen Jo a small purse filled with a tiny bit of money and her birth certificate.

The day my grandmother left the convent she had only the one pair of lace-up boots she had on her feet and the dark stiff woolen coat she wore on her back.

"Goodbye dear," Sister Maria walked her to the massive front door of the convent, opened it slowly, and gave Helen Jo a little shove of encouragement. The large door swung closed behind her with a deep harrumph.

Somehow, she managed to make the voyage to New York, traveling across the Atlantic "to be on the stage," as she would say to my mother and which my mother would repeat to me with a sardonic smile playing at the corners of her mouth. The contents of the nuns' coin purse had barely covered her steerage ticket, and then within two days of her arrival in Manhattan she met up with a man whom she would marry within the course of a few short weeks, her "plans" changed forever by that desperate decision.

"Ya stupid mick, have you burned my dinner again?" her husband's fury rumbled down the dark narrow hall, reaching out to her like the sharp claws of a deadly animal. Since losing all his money in the crash of '29, he had forbidden the use of any electricity in the house. After dark the only light in the house was the soft glimmer emanating from a lone streetlight outside the kitchen window.

She gazed at the line of cooking pots hanging above the stove, their bright copper bottoms gleaming in the darkness. When they were newly married, on her fifteenth birthday with her husband nearing his forty-fifth, her mother-in law had brought the set of pots and pans to the house, proclaiming loudly, "I hope you'll be able to use them dear, I know you aren't used to such nice things. I know your family barely had indoor plumbing."

"Ya goddamn stupid mick, how hard is it to make dinner?" his voice dragged her tired mind back to the moment, "If your head wasn't on your shoulders, you'd lose it."

The sound of his steps shook the floor. His feet, like his body, were wide. His head and face were long, topped off by a solid brush of dark red hair.

"Get out of here you idiot!" his huge hand came crashing down, throwing her to the side of the room, "You can't do anything right. Why did I get stuck with an ignorant mick like you for a wife?"

She tasted the warm redness in her mouth; her hands shook as she reached for the pan, her thin fingers trembling. He was coming at her again.

"Do ya think I'm going to stand for this? I can send you back to that hole you came from, with all the rest of your lowlife relations!"

She held on tight—it would have to be now, if he came any closer.

"Aah, what the hell. I'm too tired to deal with the likes of you tonight," he turned and lumbered out, the floor resuming its foreboding quake.

Her head began to throb. She clutched the thick handle and began to stand up carefully, moving very slowly. She needed two hands for the heavy pan as she walked across the hardwood floors that she'd spent endless hours polishing to a high shine yesterday. "You stupid bitch, you think this is clean?" and then a clenched fist crashed into her face and then another and another. Hours later she had awakened, slumped over in a pool of her own blood in the darkened hallway

She stepped slowly out of her slippers, feeling the floor with her toes. The pan felt solid in her hands—it would be tonight, it had to be tonight, now, while things were quiet. She sank to the floor, swallowing screams, Please someone help me—good God what am I to do?

"You're a stupid mi– just like your mothe–" he was drunk by now and his insults grew in volume, dropping consonants from every other word like dry leaves. Soon he would get up to deliver a beating, as he did every night.

She felt the metal fly from her hand. And then there was no sound, the voices left her. He was quiet. Just a faint whisper from the gramophone, *"It had to be you . . . wonderful you . . . I wandered around and finally found somebody who . . ."*

No one was ever sure why, but when Helen Jo ran out into that cold New York night, fleeing what she thought was a murder scene with no money, no support system and no immigration papers, she headed for Philadelphia. In fact, she hadn't killed her husband, though an admixture of alcohol and a hard conk on the head with an iron frying pan did render him unconscious until far into the next day. The three children woke up to find their father slumped over in his favorite chair the next morning, and discovered that their mother was gone.

My mother told me this story several times, always with a mix of sorrow and admiration. Sorrow for the collective sadness of the children left behind in that house and admiration for Helen Jo's final and resolute act of desperate rebellion. And then the story would pick up again with my grandmother's arrival in Philadelphia and her fateful meeting with the man who would become my mother's father.

"Miss, you must be cold. Would you like to wear my coat?"

"Oh no, that's all right. I'm fine."

"What's a pretty little lady like you doing out alone at night?"

He was tall and thin, with kinky black-brown hair, dark skin and eyes like smooth pieces of brown suede, and even on the cramped, freezing Philadelphia-bound bus he seemed to swagger as he looked deep into Helen Josephine's eyes. He had started talking to her as soon as she ran breathlessly onto the bus wearing a thin winter coat and carrying no luggage, the strands of her long black hair like small birds taking flight. His voice was smooth, like butter in a warm pan, melting into her ears and soothing her fear.

"Where are you headed, little lady?" he began.

This question caused a tremor in her heart—she had nowhere to go and no one she could tell. Her husband had never allowed her to have any friends or money; she'd never had a job in the United States and he had never signed the papers to finalize her citizenship. She had absolutely no idea where she was headed; she only knew that she was running.

"You know, I'm a professional singer and I'm on way to the top—I'd love to take a beautiful little lady like yourself along with me," his voice came back to her and she listened, let it calm her. She let him go on talking all the way to Philadelphia, barely responding but slowly letting herself become convinced.

"Well sweetie, this is my stop. Why don't you come with me and I'll set you up in a nice little room out of this cold?"

She nodded and followed him off the bus and down the dark street. He walked fast, grasping her hand tightly and pulling her along with him, *"Forget your troubles c'mon get happy,"* a honey-glazed tenor rolled from his mouth, spreading slowly across the bitter night sky. He sang as he walked, each step crunching down into the thick snow. My tiny 18-year-old grandmother walked numbly by his side, her small boots leaving child-size footprints.

She lived with the honey-voiced man for several months in a dark corner room of an old hotel in downtown Philadelphia. She awoke each day alternately overwhelmed by his sweeping charm and terrified at being there at all. He would leave each morning with a soft kiss to her forehead, and after he left she would circle the room in a thick haze wondering where she was and how she could leave. Sometimes she would walk outside and get lost in all the people, loud cars and towering brick buildings. The only thing that calmed her were her moments with Saint Patrick and Jesus as she sat with the small ceramic statues at the tiny altar she'd built in secret behind the dresser. Each day as she walked the streets she would pick up some little thing— a flower, a piece of shiny glass—to place at the tender feet of her minute Saint Patrick statue and the even smaller likeness of Jesus on the cross which had come from her mother's house. As she did this she would pray for forgiveness—there were so many things she had done wrong, so many things she must do to absolve her sins, and it terrified her to think of them.

Sometimes he would be gone overnight, sometimes only for a few hours. When he came home he would sail into the room bringing flowers and candy and promises of million-dollar singing contracts.

Eventually she began to feel a life growing inside of her. She said nothing, and as she became bigger and weaker she stopped eating. She needed to punish herself—she needed to suffer for her sins. One day as she knelt asking Saint Patrick for forgiveness she collapsed.

She woke up in a hospital several days later—he was leaning over her, "Honey, baby why didn't you tell me? That's so beautiful, we have a little child. You know I'll do the right thing. Let's get married. We'll have a big wedding, my family will love you. Everything will be fine." He held her close and she felt him breathe in and out and, for a second, she lost herself in his dream.

Then she shook her head quietly from side to side. "No," she said. She could not marry him, or anyone else for that matter. "But honey, what do you mean?" a rush of words flowed from his mouth. She watched his lips move and his eyes plead, and she nodded her head absently until he finally stopped.

Two days later they returned silently to their small room with a tiny infant girl. She put the baby in a small wooden bassinet and then lay down on her bed without saying a word. He changed his shirt and within minutes he was gone. She shuddered as the door shut behind him. With his departure the baby began to cry

Hours turned into days, but she refused to move. The baby cried and cried, but she never got up to give it any care. He came home to find the infant almost blue. "Oh my God, she's almost dead! Honey, what's wrong?"

But Helen Josephine gave no reply—only staring ahead blankly. He picked up the baby and rushed it to the hospital.

A week later he returned with the infant and a very small old man barely taller than Helen Josephine. "Let me see my little daughter-in-law," the old man proclaimed loudly in a voice thick with other worlds.

The tiny old man limped into the room. He was wearing a full-length camel hair coat that trailed on the ground. His shoes were old and scuffed and his hat was too big for his head. He walked over to Helen Josephine, his eyes two shining black puddles peering out from under folds of dark brown skin. "Pobrecita, let me see if I can help," he murmured.

After that the old man came over every day with a bag of groceries. He warmed the milk and prepared the bottles, he rocked the baby to sleep, bathed her and changed her diapers. He cooked meals for the young mother and told her stories about his struggle to come to the U.S. from Puerto Rico as a poor immigrant; he complained about his "ingrate sons." Once in a while he would stop to ask a question—usually about her family, sometimes something simple like if she was hungry— but she never responded, continuing to stare straight ahead or act as though she was sleeping. His son rarely stayed there anymore, and eventually he just stopped coming by at all.

After almost a year had passed, Helen Josephine got up from her bed one morning very early, looked around the room as if she was seeing it for the first time, got dressed and walked out the door. As the door shut the baby began to cry, letting out a scream that woke the entire building. The landlady of the building came in to see what was wrong. She found the little baby alone and carried it downstairs with her.

Two full days later Helen Josephine returned to the room with a new hat and some news. "I got a job," she told the old man as he stood at the sink washing the baby. "I got a job, so now everything will be okay."

"Really, well that's a relief," the old man chuckled, "We thought you were dead."

From that day on Helen Josephine awoke before the sun was up, got ready for work, took the baby—whom she had decided to name Mary Jo—downstairs to the landlady who had agreed to watch her in the mornings for a few cents a week, and went to work.

The old man would come every day at 1:00 to pick up the child and take care of her until 6:00 when Helen Josephine would return. As she settled in he would boil a pot of loose tea for both of them and stare carefully into his teacup in preparation for a "reading" by Helen Josephine.

"You know Helen, you're really good at this. I know a lot of people who would like to know their future. It might be worth a few bucks!"

Eventually more people started to come into their little room "to hear their fortunes" told by Helen Josephine. On any given night there would be up to ten people crouched together around a small table wedged tightly into the middle of the room. The attendees were mostly older men, sons of immigrants all, born in red-lined Irish, Italian, Puerto Rican and Jewish ghettos—not too far from their indigenous roots to still believe in magic, but far enough to worry about the future of the stock market in the rapidly dying capitalism of the Depression. Several of them would blur the lines between psychic and mistress, looking lasciviously at the attractive single mother who held two full-time domestic jobs and still barely had enough money to buy groceries. This group included Maxi Rosenburg, who also had a penchant for little girls and would come by at 4:30 each day, sending the old man home so he could molest little Mary Jo under the guise of "helping out with child care."

One day the old man fell ill, and when Helen Josephine came home the baby wasn't in the room, only a befuddled and partially dressed Maxi Rosenburg alone under the covers.

"Where's my baby, and why are you half dressed?" she screamed.

"I don't know sweetheart . . . I don't know anything any-more," Maxi answered blankly.

"Where's my baby?" Helen banged on the landlady's door.

"The old man never came to pick her up. I had to miss work because of you. I can't take care of this child, Helen. You're going to have to put her in a home if you can't find someone to watch her. But it's not going to be me, I have enough to do. You should've thought of that before you spread your legs for every Tom, Dick and Harry you meet."

There was no one who could watch the small girl, and after two days missed at both jobs Helen Jo was going to be fired. Within a few days, one-and-a-half-year-old Mary Jo was shipped off to her first foster home.

18

CHAPTER 3

origin stories: mother

From as early on as I can remember my mother would tell me horrible stories of sexual, physical and emotional abuse, the neglect, starvation and torture she endured at the many foster homes she lived in as a child. My mother rarely cried and she never let anyone hug her; instead she would tell her horror stories like someone recanting a case study for their dissertation. Her eyes would become dark and her voice would drop, and she would return to the terrified place of a scared child while remaining the cogent adult in the retelling. Sometimes she would vow to pursue a lead on a torture victims' support group or she'd declare her intention to write a book because she thought her experience was "like the case of Sybil," a severely mentally ill woman whose story had been made famous by a best-selling book and movie.

But she never really did anything about all that pain except tell me the stories, her voice trailing off, going alone into a place where I couldn't reach her. Sometimes, if she would let me, I'd hold her hand and try to comfort her, tell her everything would be okay. Most of the time I would just cry for her, my tears falling where hers could not. And I would vow to her and to myself that somehow, in some way, I would make as much as I could okay for my mom, no matter how long it took me.

The story that always began and ended one of these sessions was of her time at Marguerite Leland's home, where she was placed when she was four years old.

"May we help you?" a towering female figure draped in a dark red and navy blue velvet dress inquired in a deep New England drawl.

"Are you Mrs. Marguerite Leland?" her mother didn't wait for a reply as she continued breathlessly, "I need to leave my daughter with you. I can't keep her anymore, I have to work. I have nowhere else to take her. I can pay five dollars a month as soon as I find a job—please."

The large woman towered in front of them, huge green eyes glaring out of a wide white face, "What is your name?"

"Helen Josephine McMurphy, and this is little Mary Jo," she answered, reaching deep into her throat for her best appropriated "King's English" accent, masking her usual clipped, Liverpudlian Irish inflection.

"Irish, eh?" the tall woman threw back her thick silver hair, "Well, I'm not a charity, so if you can't pay she'll have to work. These are hard times, everyone is having trouble. Oh, and please call me Marguerite."

Helen Jo had gone dress shopping to find the perfect dress to present little Mary Jo to this, her most recent foster home. In the last three years she had been sent to three different families— they always started out well but inevitably something would go wrong. The situation with the last family, Mary's favorite, had seemed like it would last forever, until one day the eldest daughter, who was mentally disabled, decided she wanted to perform a sexual act on Mary, one she had experienced when she was raped herself. Little Mary, only three years old at the time, almost died of asphyxiation under the sheer weight of the massive girl, but before she was completely suffocated the mother came in and found them. Within days Mary Jo was gone from that beautiful farmhouse, which always remained in her memories, filled with the sounds of laughter and happiness.

In the first six months of her stay with Marguerite everything was wonderful. It turned out that the Lelands wanted to create a family and Mary Jo was to become the perfect little girl of Marguerite and Johnny Leland. To that end Marguerite used to dress her up in beautiful outfits and take her along on weekend trips to the Everglades, to the Rockies, to Niagara Falls. In every picture they appear as the idealized American family, little Mary Jo in Shirley Temple curls, Johnny Leland in a tan gabardine suit and Marguerite dressed in some flowing '40s floral print dress, a scowl dancing at the corners of her dark red lips.

"Get down, GET DOWN!!" One morning as Mary Jo came downstairs for breakfast, Marguerite was hiding behind a couch to avoid the gunshots flying through the room. "Johnny's shooting at me," Marguerite whispered through clenched teeth as she grabbed Mary Jo by the hair, pulling her down so tightly, it almost hurt.

In twenty minutes it was over. The house fell into a deep silence. Johnny stood up, tucked his gun in his jacket, put on his hat and walked out the front door. Marguerite and Mary Jo watched him from the window as he strolled down the long walkway to the front gate. He opened and closed the small white door in the picket fence that marked the edge of Marguerite's property without looking back or even turning his head.

Marguerite refused to leave her room for several weeks after Johnny left the house. There were no more dresses, Shirley Temple curls, trips or even report card reviews. The family was over as quickly as it had begun, and Mary Jo's role as pretend daughter was no longer needed.

One dark, grey winter day a month or so later, Marguerite walked Mary Jo through the house and surrounding acres of land as if it was the first time Mary had ever seen it, telling her in a disembodied voice, "Your mother hasn't sent any money for your board and I can't afford to keep you for free, so you'll have to earn your keep if you are to stay here anymore." With that, Marguerite began to read off a list of chores, strenuous tasks far beyond the abilities of a five-year-old girl: the marble staircase must shine like glass, all hardwood floors need to be polished, pots, sinks, fine china and drawer after drawer of heavy silverware need to be washed, scrubbed, shined and polished. Flowers, trees, and all of the grass would need to be mowed, picked, pruned and weeded and Mary Jo was to start immediately.

If any of these tasks was not finished or accomplished to Marguerite's satisfaction, Mary Jo was beaten with a board. Most days it seemed there was some task not done "just right," and so most days the whoosh-whack of a wooden board smacking against flesh and the subsequent sound of a small child crying could be heard in the large house.

A few days after the tour of the property, food simply stopped being available. No plate was ever set again for Mary Jo, though elaborate meals were served for Marguerite's many guests. Breakfasts with sausage, rolls and toast, lunches with sandwiches piled high with meat, cheese and lettuce, dinners of pasta, chicken, pot roast, vegetables and salad, but nothing for Mary. To stay alive she stole the cat's food when she could.

Eventually Mary learned it wasn't safe to ask for things, to hope that life would change or even to think much at all. In fact, the only safe thing to do after she finished the chores and got her beating was to sit for hours in one place and rock back and forth.

Four years passed filled with days spent just sitting alone on the back step all afternoon and into the night. It was easier to stay there quietly without moving or thinking. Way after dark, the elderly woman who rented a room at the top of the stairs would open the back door and whisper out to Mary Jo, "Come to bed," sometimes slipping her a piece of bread.

My mother stayed in that house with Marguerite for five years altogether, until she was nine years old. Years later, with the help of therapy she realized how those years had left her in a constant state of anxiety and that she had suffered most of her life from post-traumatic stress syndrome. There were also physical repercussions from the starvation and the resulting malnutrition, which had long-term effects on her body, including a mouth full of bad teeth and a heart condition that eventually led to her premature death.

After a social worker finally intervened, Helen Jo came to pick my mother up, and when they arrived at my grandmother's tiny room in the basement of a brownstone in North Philadelphia, neighbors and friends clicked their teeth at the emaciated girl for many days, "She looks like she's been starved! What's wrong with that woman, not feeding the child?"

Although my mother's suffering was obvious, there was never any intention on my grandmother's part to keep her at home. Later in life, my mother would understand that there was really no way she could have, being an undocumented immigrant with no child care and working two full time jobs just to scrape by, but my grandmother's constant rejection caused her a deep and lasting pain. But the thing that she always said hurt the most was the fact that instead of registering horror at my mother's condition, Helen Jo actually took Marguerite's side, blaming my mother and accusing her of being incorrigible and a "great inconvenience."

"It will be five dollars a month, paid on the first. Don't *ever* be late Miss McMurphy, otherwise we'll have to turn your child back over to the State. Do you understand?"

Mary Jo gazed up at her mother's tired face as she pulled up the corners of her mouth, taking special care with all of her consonants. "Yes, of course, I understand dear, I will never be late. I have two jobs now and I'm also working for the landlord to keep the rent down. You're all wonderful people to take in my little girl and I won't let you down." She continued with an endless string of promises about her integrity and praise for the wealthy benefactors who were so kind as to run this orphanage and take in poor girls like Mary Jo.

As Helen Jo sat with the director of the Philadelphia Home for Needy Girls she knew that this fine upstanding woman could

23

not think badly of her for being a poor Irish immigrant woman with a bastard child and no family, because after all she didn't speak like a poor Irish girl. She spoke as the nuns had taught her to, enunciating her words properly. My grandmother never lost hope in the illusion of respectability. She believed that if you acted like you had "class" people would believe that you did, and you could thus attain respectability in their eyes. This ability to use elocution and vocabulary to move between worlds, to attempt to reach beyond one's class status of poverty and crisis, was practiced by my grandmother, passed down to my mother and also, eventually, to me, as a crucial survival mechanism.

After her mother finished the appointment with the director, she buttoned Mary Jo's coat saying, "I'll see you as soon as I can." She left her 9-year-old daughter on the street in front of the Home and walked quickly into the afternoon sunset.

Mary Jo watched with terror as her mother scurried away into the darkening afternoon sky. After she left, a group of children from the neighborhood found her, "Hey little girl, are you the new orphan? Are you the new orphan?" "Hey little girl! Cat's got your tongue? Can't you talk?" "I think she's deaf. She sure is funny lookin', like a little nigger!" "Nigger lips! Nigger lips! Can't you talk?" "Can you fight? C'mon, stand up, poor little deaf and dumb orphan girl can't talk, can't move," and they circled around her until one of the boys stepped forward and proclaimed, "I think we need to help her 'cause she can't move herself!"

Mary Jo, catatonic with fear and with too many silent screams in her head from the years of abuse mouthed the words, "Please don't," but no one could hear.

After a few more minutes of yelling, squealing and circling they picked her up, carried her onto the playground and put her into an empty trashcan. Later that night the janitor found her there, afraid to move a muscle in case someone would hear her.

"A mixed-race child"—that's how each sentence began when the social workers at the orphanage described my mother in

their reports. *A mixed-race child, Mary Jo is always hungry, she could be anemic. Mary Jo, a mixed-race child, was asking for shoes again today. When her mother, Helen Josephine, visits she doesn't display very much affection toward her daughter.*

The Philadelphia Home for Needy Girls was a study in early philanthropy. It sat on hundreds of acres of beautiful, fertile farm land in the Pennsylvania countryside which had originally belonged to a trolley magnate who endowed the estate to run an orphanage for white "parentless" girls (perhaps this was the reason for the constant reminder about my mother's "mixed-race" status). The institution was known for its supposed "progressive education" practices, run by a former settlement worker who trained under Maria Montessori herself. They purported to connect school and home in a way never done before by any educational institution. In fact, what was most significant was the amount of the work required from each child who lived in the home.

Each day at the orphanage began with a rooster, a bell and chores. There were everyday chores: washing, dusting, polishing, scrubbing and shining; once a week chores: egg collecting, cow milking, butter churning and baking everything from cakes to bread; and then there were seasonal chores.

Winters and anything close to the holidays were filled with every imaginable type of roasting, toasting, baking and broasting. While one pie would bake, another crust would be rolled out. One group of girls would be mixing and whipping chiffon and fresh cream to top the bread pudding and apple crisps, while another group would be skinning, dicing and washing all the fruit and piling it into big pots for the pie maker. Apples would be pressed and boiled into cider, cinnamon sticks boiled and crushed for fresh spice.

The desperately hot summer months were filled with hours and hours of sweat-filled canning. Peaches, pears, apricots, apples, blueberries, strawberries, rhubarb, and then there was jam and ice cream to be made.

All in all, the home produced almost everything its residents

25

consumed, wore and slept on by converting the large student body into a highly productive, well-organized machine.

Nativity plays, Easter services, church choirs, dancing around the Maypole, parties and holidays that would rival the best Bing Crosby movies, all of this was meant to prepare the girls for living out the perfect American dream. These candy-coated dreams were planted in the developing minds of poor parent-less girls without the means to achieve them, and they would both propel and haunt my mother for the rest of her life.

My mother lasted four years in the orphanage, a four years that she remembered fondly, notwithstanding the intense labor required and the ongoing discrimination she endured from three racist staff members. She remained an advocate for life of well-run non-punitive institutions for kids, rather than what she saw as the other option: unchecked abusive foster homes.

After the orphanage she bounced around to a few more foster homes, and then ended up for a while with her mother again in Helen Jo's tiny apartment in North Philadelphia, where she fueled her love of Hollywood movies. After pretending to go to school every day, my mom would hop on the streetcar to go see a movie, reveling in the fantasyland of MGM musicals. One day, one of the neighborhood pedophiles almost whisked my mom away, but she was saved by the watchful eye of the "village," the African American, Irish, Puerto Rican and Polish families who all took part in raising the neighborhood kids. They interceded by physically grabbing my mom and taking her home and severely beating up the pedophile who had almost successfully lured my mom to his apartment with promises of candy and comic books.

After that incident she was shipped off to more foster homes and more abuse until she ran away for good. She landed back on my grandmother's doorstep where she began to hang out with a group of "bad" kids, who spent their days sitting in a broken-down car and drinking. It was this last foray into trouble that made my grandmother decide to send her out west to live with her eldest daughter, who had recently "found" Helen Jo again after her own journey of struggle as a teenaged single mother of two.

Although she lived on the outskirts of Pasadena, my mother's half-sister was determined to enroll my mother in the extremely white, wealthy Pasadena school system, sharing the belief that the key to success in moving beyond your class position was to surround yourself with "better" people. My mother proved to be quite adept at "fitting in," and she appropriated her classmates' realities, clothes, lifestyles and attitudes so well, in fact, that six months after leaving Philadelphia as a mixed-race bastard with a thick accent and the demeanor of a tough, street-smart "rocker chick," she had metamorphosed into a preppie who hung out with all the beautiful people. It was then that she became "Debbie," shedding the poor, Irish-immigrant moniker of Mary Jo and birthing what she envisioned as a new, white, middle-class self. With nary a trace of her Philly accent left on her tongue, she wholeheartedly believed in her new identity, and that's when my father entered the picture, a "respectable" boyfriend whose romantic attention was another part of the American dream that looked like it was coming "Debbie's" way at last.

CHAPTER 4

origin stories: mom & dad

My father was the descendent of colonial politicians, son of a frustrated Hemingway-wannabe entrepreneur and an intellectual suffragette. His was a life of extreme privilege and extreme insanity, one common to wealthy American bohemians living out their eccentricities in beachfront mansions. Into this strange American family walked my mother, a sexy, mixed-race "exotic," the embodiment of all that was other. They dated while she was still in high school, living out her newfound sorority mythos, and while my father was between high school and college, spending his time surfing and contemplating his array of college choices. She was happy with him because he seemed brilliant, as well as "three inches taller and three years older," the edict set down by her appropriated Pasadena sorority standards. He was happy with her because she was everything his pseudo-rebellion demanded, an unfamiliar exotic whom his family would never want him to know or accept. After a summer courtship that included watching my dad surf for hours and then listening to his arguments and essays on capitalism and art, with a hefty dose of English literature and poetry thrown in for romantic juice, they were separated for the next few years—my dad going off to Reed College in Oregon and my mother left behind to finish high school, where she would ultimately end up in a sad spiral downward into punctured mythologies and smashed illusions.

Desperate to believe her own lie of an appropriated identity of race and class privilege, my mother blindly followed the lead of her wealthy, white Pasadena friends. At the end of her senior year, a series of dismal SAT scores and failed sorority rushes at UCLA was capped by a rare incident of drunkenness at an end-of-summer party, and the rich and beautiful girls decided that my mother was a bad seed, someone who never should have been allowed into their clique in the first place. She was summarily excised from her "friends' " lives, their privilege and their plans, and was set adrift without an authentic idea of her own about who she might be or what she might do. Life post-high school had abruptly become a vista of endless days of confusion and solitude.

At this point my mother floundered, sitting immobilized in front of the TV on the shredded couch of her last foster home deep in the City of Industry, a smog-infested suburb of Los Angeles. For hours upon hours, my mom and her last foster father watched WWF wrestling, but though the very poor, very kind Alfred Rodriguez and his Hawaiian wife Minnie loved my mom's company, they knew that an 18-year-old girl needed to be out of the house doing "something."

So after a year of my mom's WWF watching, her worsening smog-induced asthma and too many potato chips, Minnie Rodriguez "found" my mother's mother, who was working as a live-in maid in the Berkeley hills in Northern California, and she sent my mom up to stay with her. In later years, whenever my mom would tell the story of the Rodriguezes her eyes would cloud and her voice would become soft. That was the last time she ever saw them, because as she would tell it, Alfred got cancer and, as a working poor man with no health insurance, he fell into horrible debt, and to save his wife from further poverty he committed suicide by driving his broken-down painting truck onto the train tracks that ran across his little street.

The cold mist and constant breeze in Northern California made for clean air that my mother could actually breathe, and it flooded her confused mind and filled her with a renewed energy. Within weeks of her arrival in the Bay Area she had become a part of it all. Donning a black beret, with her long hair in a thick braid she soaked up the rain and fog and the hipster attitude of the Berkeley streets, spending her days working as a manicurist in the financial district and taking night classes at a community college in Oakland, hanging out late to attend rallys sponsored by the Black Panthers.

She had been corresponding with my father the whole time he was away, and two years into her life in the Bay Area he began to plead with her to join him. At this point he was struggling with the hell of medical school, discouraged and on the verge of dropping out. Still unsure of what to do with her life, she eventually agreed. My grandmother, in her one act of motherly concern, insisted that they actually marry rather than just live together, and so they were married in a civil ceremony with no friends or family present, after which they immediately moved to St. Louis where my father was attending the University of Missouri.

They lived in St. Louis for four years, surviving on literally pennies a day—a meal could be made of fried soy beans, though there could be no heat in a Missouri winter. This extreme austerity plan was instituted because my dad didn't want to ask his parents for financial help, and it took a severe toll on my mother and on their relationship. When my father's schooling was finished, they moved back to California, where my father would become an intern at Camarillo State Mental Hospital and where my mother would work as a volunteer and a lay counselor.

I was born in the hospital on the grounds at Camarillo, and though the birth had been difficult and draining and my mother pleaded for some recovery time, three days later we all boarded a plane and flew to Hawaii where my father would proceed with his psychiatric residency at a hospital on the island of Oahu. It worked out well, since my father could surf in his free time and my mother was adopted by a large native Hawaiian/Phillipino family—she finally had found a community and was making some close friends. For the first time in her life she was putting down roots, and she was heartbroken and resentful when my father insisted upon moving back to California at the end of his residency.

By the time they landed in Redondo Beach, things between them had deteriorated to the point where our home was a place of anger—both repressed and expressed, sometimes violently. I was only a toddler then, but I remember the fear and sadness, the fighting and the tense silences. It was from this home that my father finally ventured out one night to abandon us for good, and the end of their marriage ushered in the beginning of our years of poverty and isolation, my mother and I alone with no family or friends to help us.

CHAPTER 5

origin stories: a very young tiny

We lived at the edge of the ocean, my father, mother and I. My memories of that time are always at night, backlit by fog, tinted by rays of moon glow. Our nineteenth-century Victorian sat on a hill above a crashing sea. The house tilted precariously on the edge of a little patch of grass and a maze of gnarled ice plant, reaching out like a finger over the glimmering waves.

My room was small but tall, like a distorted corner in an *Alice in Wonderland* story. The walls and the curved Victorian windows seemed to reach up into the sky beyond where my four-year-old eyes could see. Every night before I went to bed I would peek at the sea, which always seemed to be busy doing so much—waves crashed to meet their shore deadlines, the phosphorescence busily recreating itself, the lobsters and clams, sea-anemones and sharks all caught up in their complicated ocean schedules. I was afraid to gaze too long for fear that one of the ocean people would notice and become angry with me for spying and decide to kill me so that I wouldn't reveal their secrets.

But the fear that permeates those memories doesn't come from the ocean, nor my room with the large cartoon-like monsters who convened in the uppermost corner of my ceiling—I had a scratchy blanket to take care of them. It's a filmy memory of the nights that were played out downstairs between my perpetually wet-suited dad and my increasingly desperate mom.

It all began when we moved there. My mother had taught herself to be the perfect wife: dinner was on the table at precisely 6 P.M., a juicy rare roast beef, boiled potatoes, green salad, and a bright green or dark red vegetable, things that I've never forgotten because I couldn't have any of them. For the first three years of my life I had horrible food allergies and was relegated to a nauseatingly watery rice cereal, delicately served in a beautiful antique bowl with a large silver spoon. I never understood in my toddler head why I was only allowed the rice cereal soup while my mother and father delighted in bloody carnivorous feasts.

At that time my father was slowly but surely having a mental breakdown. He hadn't really wanted to be a psychiatrist; his real love was reading and writing, and he'd wanted to be an English professor, but that was not the will of his parents who had made it very clear that they expected him to attain power and money, preferably through a career in medicine.

To this end they had "accepted" my mother, though they wouldn't let her mother, my grandmother, enter through the front door of their palatial beachfront house because she was "shanty Irish," unworthy of anything more than the servant's entrance (she worked as a maid). But they had realized early on that my mother was willing to devote herself unconditionally to the whims of my very odd father and facilitate his successful graduation from seven grueling years of medical school.

After finishing medical school and his residency in Hawaii, he began a successful private practice in Redondo Beach, chosen for its good surf and proximity to Los Angeles. This was when the brief period of very rich times began for all of us. I was enrolled in an expensive Montessori school, my mother designed her own clothes, mostly dashiki's and muumuu's, and had them hand-sewn. I wasn't old enough to remember much about this time except that everything was really big, big televisions, big stereos, big tables and most of all big toys.

Back then, my cousin Annie was always present at our dinner table, another example of the generations of very poor women in my family. She was there because she and my mother loved each other dearly, and of course, because there was always a good meal and Annie was always hungry. Annie was pretty in a small brown animal sort of way. She was all of 92 pounds, and this was not because she was anorexic. Rather, she had been starved as a child due to the severe neglect of her poor, withdrawn mother, my aunt Jan.

Annie's mother, my mother's older half-sister, would disappear for several days at a time when Annie and her younger sister were growing up. Jan would leave the girls in an assortment of California micro-shacks that were endemic to areas like Pomona, City of Industry and San Bernardino. The paint was perpetually peeling and there was never any furniture, but the worst thing was that there was rarely any food in the house. In good times Annie and her little sister would concoct food simulations like "vinegar sandwiches," which consisted of a two pieces of white bread drenched with vinegar, or if they were lucky enough to have some ketchup in the house, the delicacy of a "ketchup sandwich" could soothe a hungry stomach for a while. In spite of all this, everyone loved Annie's mother. Sometimes the most harmful people can also be the most charming, and Jan never meant any harm. She just couldn't stand to become dependent on anyone or anything, and saw it as the utmost form of failure to receive a "hand-out," such as welfare or food stamps. Jan had been beautiful once, but she'd lost her teeth before she turned 21, which meant she always had to hide her mouth when she talked. She never had much use for food herself and survived on a steady diet of cigarettes and coffee, which colored her thin face a pale yellowish gray.

Annie was always happy to be at our dinner table. She was in awe of my father, the handsome, rich doctor, who was always "accidentally" getting out of the shower whenever

Annie happened to be using the toilet. This furthered Annie's admiration of my father, as he was apparently well endowed, and Annie was somewhat obsessed by the size of a man's penis.

As the years passed, the basic niceties and appropriated conformities between my father and mother were replaced by furtive glances, loud clanks of dishes, whispers behind doors and subsequent slams until the house became permanently divided. The division was accentuated through music. My father was a fan of Don McLean, Bob Dylan and any other folk singer type, while my mother favored rock-and-roll and rhythm-and-blues, with a heavy dose of disco and salsa thrown in. These musical camps were blasted at each other across the house in place of normal conversation. My mother, who had given up dancing due to my father's disdain for it, began to take it up again with a new vengeance. My father, on the other hand, began what he and his equally insane friend called "rescue operations" of large luxury boats (sailing for dinner cruises and the like) that didn't want or need rescuing, which didn't seem to matter to my father. He would leave the house for his self-appointed harbor duty to the tune of some plaintive ballad, with a *20,000 Leagues Under the Sea*-like set of harpoons, goggles and fish tackle, murmuring, "Godspeed."

I was never clear on what, exactly, was the last straw for either of them, or if there even was one, only that things grew more hateful, more violent and more tense with each passing day, culminating in a huge fight during which my father broke my mother's arm, the police came and then they left, and then my parents separated for what seemed like a very short time.

My father bought FBI-quality tracking devices in an attempt to catch my mother in the act of cheating on him while they were separated. This was a precursor to the case he would make against her in their extremely painful and bizarre divorce proceeding where he brought in her dressmaker to testify that my mother was having miniskirts made, which proved her status as an unfit mother.

My father didn't actually want to have custody of me, but

for some reason he was determined to harm my mother as much as possible while also avoiding any alimony or child support payments. This experience was terrifying for my mother, as she was really no match for my father's heavy-handed tactics and high-priced attorneys. He knew the worst thing he could do to her was to take me away, and so he set about doing that at all costs. In the end, some of my mother's friends testified on her behalf and she was awarded custody, but she was left with a bleeding ulcer, a minimal child support settlement, an order to sell the house for almost nothing, and a fear of ever entering the courts again.

The mini-chapter of privilege, comfort and security in my mother's life was over, and in its place a bloody wound of pain, betrayal, and fear opened, one that would never properly heal. As for me, at four years old I wasn't really sure what had happened; I just wanted my mama to stop crying.

CHAPTER 6

on our own

With very little transition time, my mother rented a broken-down houseboat for us to move into. A rather small live-aboard in the harbor in Redondo Beach, it was all she could afford with the meager child support check and no job or other source of support. It was an ancient two-story houseboat that seemed like it had been built in the time of the Swiss Family Robinson, with a massive, rusty mast, creaky stairs, a broken toilet, and a foot of water in the hull that we had to drain with a saucepan each morning so as to be sure we wouldn't sink. But of course, these things didn't seem like problems to my 4-year-old mind. I thought the boat was the most wonderful place in the world, and what an amazing mother I had who had brought us from that odd house we'd been shipwrecked in to this amazing house that swayed with the tide and communed with the fish, algae and waves.

My days were spent commanding a troupe of fellow harbor kids. I was the leader in a complex game that began with the creation of a story and always included a search-and-destroy mission, mystery, spy plan or some other exciting kid process that made absolutely no sense at all. It was one of the best times of my life, spent in the pursuit of sheer fun.

Each after-school adventure began with me perched on the

top of one of the square fire extinguisher boxes that sat at the end of each slip, concocting that day's story while I spoke to the core members of the team, three 5- to 6-year-olds soiled with the sheen of sweat and the film of school dust, their eyes shining with the endless possibilities of our next "mission." There was Bobby Sandler, whose dad was an alcoholic fisherman who supplied us with endless stories of when he was "a fisherman in the Sahara." Most nights of the week he would stagger home at 3:00 A.M. from the Dock of the Bay Bar & Grill with a different woman each night, promising that she was the one he'd been looking for all along to be a mom for his son. Felicité Marcus was a Haitian girl whose parents, a beautiful French-African mother and a green-eyed fisherman father, had been married and divorced six times and had traveled several times around the world. They fought daily about whether to stay or to leave for France, yelling about which one of them would kill the other and which weapon they would use. And finally there was my best, saddest friend, Cindy, who lived with her father on a boat littered with used Budweiser cans, with no refrigerator and a barely working toilet. Her mismatched clothes were always soiled and/or torn and her shoes never fit right. Cindy was always slightly afraid and maintained an expressionless gaze, frequently asking me if I thought her mother would ever come back.

"The people at the end of this dock who live in the yacht are actually the owners of the *whole world*, and they're planning to blow up the harbor tonight before they leave because they don't want anyone to know who they are or what they do. You see, there was a crash last week in the middle of the ocean and everyone thought it was a storm but it was actually a bomb they planted in the hull of another yacht that was trying to get their power. And they didn't just hurt all the members of the crew and the other rich people, they hurt all the fish and animals with that bomb," I whispered the last sentence for effect.

"Ooh," the team let out a thrilled sigh.

"So what are we going to do?"

"We have to sabotage their plans."

"What if we get caught?" Cindy whispered. She was always afraid of getting caught.

"Cindy, you know we never get caught."

Nights (before my strictly enforced 9:00 P.M. bedtime) were a silly blur, filled with my mother's series of disgruntled but hilarious English-rocker-style boyfriends who were constantly "fixing" the boat—one could usually be found dangling precariously over the bow in full mod attire, swearing and spitting in a proper cockney accent. I'm not sure if my mom was having as much fun as I was, but I didn't think about it very much really, since I was only four years old.

The bizarre and wonderful boat that went nowhere only lasted for one summer, ending in what would become historically known as Dee and Tiny's first eviction. We were evicted from the yacht harbor because our boat wasn't new enough to be docked there, one of several evictions issued that summer to old houseboats that belonged to poor people with nowhere else to go. It seemed that live-aboards didn't create the proper environment for the sailor-class the harbor was hoping to attract.

Our next move was to a small stucco duplex in lower Redondo Beach, a solidly lower-middle-class area known for its racist police force, plethora of oil rigs and the perpetual stink of natural gas.

The duplex, painted a dark, mustard brown, was owned by a boyfriend of Annie's, and so she was paying very low rent and could pass on a similar deal to my mom. The small building sat forlornly on a cul-de-sac, and there were exactly nine things on that street: an oil rig that perpetually rocked up and down, in and out of the tired earth; three houses with weak-eyed, underfed dogs and weak-eyed, underweight, poor white kids; two houses with brightly dressed, perfectly groomed Latino children and the sweet smell of tamales wafting out from the broken screen doors; an old-man house with a gnarled man who never seemed to leave his dusty window except to threaten the neighborhood kids with his shotgun; a tiny elementary school with a cracked asphalt playground; and a mortuary, the neatest, nicest building on the street.

I later learned that my mother had her first bout of agoraphobia in that house. Every day when I came home from the little elementary school's meager kindergarten she was there, not there like a stay-at-home mom but there like she was stuck, caught by the threads of the shag carpet, unable even to dance her way out.

Dancing always carried my mother and me in and out of happiness. All my life, I was schooled in dance at the wild heels of my mother. My dance "lessons" began in that Redondo Beach duplex. Each day after school I witnessed my mother performing a fascinating mix of body contortions, moving across our living room floor to an extremely loud recording of Little Richard or some other driving rhythm. She never talked about her daily dance sessions, she just did them, as one would perform a sacred unspoken ritual. And no matter how depressed or hopeless she was, for that magical hour as Little Richard, Sly and the Family Stone, Donna Summer, and other favorites played on the stereo, her life and problems, reality and desperation melted away into a beautiful world of blood-boiling, heart-racing, old-school rhythm-and-blues, gospel, rock-and-roll, and disco.

It was at this point that Czatar Rudolph (aka, Rudy) entered her life. Rudy was a "refugee" from communist Hungary, but Rudy wasn't one of those privileged Europeans, educated, sophisticated, scholarly. Rudy was Eastern European ghetto communist, a 99-cent-store-shoppin' petty criminal, a domestic violence perpetrator with full-on pimpin' '70s platform heels, wide-flared jeans, shiny shirts and a big golden fro. I suppose he would have been considered a fox back then, but I just thought he was mean and stupid, partly because he was, but mostly because he represented competition for my mother's affection and, even more important to me, her attention. I had just turned five years old and wanted to be the only thing in her world.

My cousin Annie was holed up in the back unit of the duplex in the throes of her own version of agoraphobia. "I'm not leaving the house till my hair grows long, hon," she would say in her most seductive little girl voice. She lived on free cheese and the kindness of strangers. Or, to be exact, the kindness of her long-suffering, endlessly annoyed boyfriend. Her tiny house faced a very large yard filled with yellowish grass, bits of chicken wire and fragments of dented car parts, the ground thumping every five seconds when the oil rig that shadowed the yard would enter its well.

At first it was wonderful between my mother and Annie, but eventually my mother's love turned into a desperate dependence. Days and nights of darkening depression made her increasingly needy, which was completely intolerable to Annie, who had no reserves of strength to care for anyone but herself and was barely holding her own self together. One terrible day, I came home from school to find my cousin screaming at the top of her lungs in a shrill, bloodcurdling tone, "Get away from me, Debbie! GET AWAY!" Her lips were drawn over tightly clenched teeth, and she emitted a low, menacing growl. The scream and the growl were common to all of the overworked and overwrought women in my family, prone to extreme bouts of dark anger, calling forth in those moments all of their collective years of pain and torture. A deafening silence filled with unspoken vows of revenge was established between my mother and Annie, and life in the little house became even more tense and uncertain.

My mother's sheer desperation was transformed into a determined focus. She decided that she would finally finish school; after ten years of serial dropouts and false starts, she would get her Masters of Social Work against all odds, and she would look *fine* in the process. While the destructive Rudy scenario played out against the backdrop of Annie's rejection, she busily applied to graduate schools. Six months later she managed to finesse her acceptance into a graduate program in social work at Fresno State University with some resourceful storytelling and sans the math part of the GRE exam.

My mom spirited away in an Angela Davis fro, with her collection of hand-sewn, hand-dyed dashiki-esque dresses and a cosmetically distributed tan. The effect was devastating, she looked like a mixed-race queen, rocking fierce tropical colors and revolutionary possibilities. Well, she was from L.A. where it was enough to look like a revolutionary—you didn't actually have to be one. In this cloud of appropriated radicalism, we landed in Fresno.

But in Fresno you couldn't really rock the "sort-of revolutionary" thing. For a person of color, Fresno was all about blending in. Fresno was a hick town with a college thrown down in the middle of it, and the only radicalism that existed was the United Farm Workers movement—brown power/black power were only just getting started. The San Joaquin Valley, dripping with the fresh juice of grapes, the luscious, omnipresent scent of apples, apricots, alfalfa, cherries and lettuce, took to things "in due time" and the rest of the world would just have to wait—it may have been the mid-'70s and the world outside was blowing itself up, but so what, there were crops to harvest and mini-malls to build, and besides, how much could you really think about in 106-degree weather anyway? Consequently, the two African American radicals on campus resented my mother for what they perceived as her attempt to "pass" as a white person when it was clear to them that she was black. And the white people were nervous around her because she was clearly only half-white and identifying, even if only stylistically, with a radical like Angela Davis, well, that was just plain crazy.

Suffice to say she toned everything down within about five months, not because she was intimidated—that would be giving up, and my mom never gave up, even when it would have been easier or more pleasurable to do so. No, it was because she couldn't work the fro, do her homework, hand-wash the dashikis *and* get to an 8 A.M. class on time.

"Her parents are D-I-V-O-R-C-E-D." My life in Fresno, at least for the first six months, was another kind of hell. My par-

44

ents were divorced, a fact that had meant little or nothing in Los Angeles where almost all of my friends' parents had been divorced, or for that matter had never even been married. But in Fresno, every introduction, every conversation or casual exchange began with the announcement that I was the child of divorced parents, proving that somehow I was surely strange. In Fresno, and in fact the whole San Joaquin Valley, it seemed that everyone was married. It didn't matter that most of these married people were rather frightening in their extreme conventionality, or their front of extreme conventionality. Replete with bubble hairdos and polyester matching suits for both men and women, the bottom line was that they were *married* and therefore had a church-sanctioned family in the eyes of God, and therefore—in the limited logic of kids—they were normal.

But of course, in the end we were kids, and divorced parents or not, I was almost six and they were six, and so we had fun. In Fresno this meant a new kind of fun, a variety of which I never had before or since: this was country fun. Trees, rivers, streams, farm animals, fields, meadows, straw, lakes of all shapes and sizes, hot nights with micro-flies filling your nostrils and gallons and gallons of lemonade.

Although my mom was surviving on less than $300 a month in child support and financial aid, she managed to provide me with healthy food which she taught me to cook— she'd taught me to make my own breakfast at the age of four but I now graduated to the wonderfulness of making dinner. She was able to pay the rent and buy me the requisite Fresno-esque school clothes so I'd be able to sort of fit in to the rural-meets-strip-mall style that dominated the Fresno school district. I loved my life with her then. She laughed a lot, studied a lot and teased me a lot. She was spending her spare time with Palestinian college students who lectured her about Allah and what was wrong with America while flirting with her mercilessly. She also managed to do some in-school work with the UFW movement, a project befitting her as-yet-unidentified raza soul. And she began to collaborate with a very sweet African American church-going man who used to invite us to a tiny one-room church in Modesto (a nearby town even more hick-like and farm-filled) where my mother could fulfill her need for some of the best down-home gospel that we'd ever hear in our lives.

In later years, my mother would always bemoan the loss of the tight-knit community she had found in graduate school. We would talk for hours about what had made that experience fulfilling, yet at the same time boring. She had people with whom she shared an intellectual kinship, the excitement of what she was learning, and an internship at the local mental hospital for the criminally insane.

And yet, even with all of those focused activities, along with the Palestinian guys and the African American man-friend, it was no match for the exciting, dangerous and vindictive Czatar Rudolph who was waiting, always waiting and cheating in the smog-filled cavern that is Los Angeles.

"Come back, Debbie," he would whisper to her on his visits from L.A., his golden fro framing his angry scowl in the afternoon sun that swept across the Fresno landscape. "Come back so we can be together," the whisper and the plan would trail off slowly, like a snake hypnotizing his prey, readying for the strike.

So at the end of the two-year graduate program we headed back to the murky and insecure world of Rudy, the San Fernando Valley and no job prospects. There was something new and lost about my mother in this time. The sad reality is that my un-parented, poverty-stricken mama never had any role models for success, no advice on problem solving as the problems arose, no ideas on how to make plans for the future, no support for setting goals. She had taught herself to survive, but was never taught to thrive. And if one takes a break from the terror/excitement/challenge of sheer survival, there can be a void of emptiness, a black hole of confusion and anxiety, a void easily filled by the challenge, excitement, and endless impossibility of the Rudy's of the world.

CHAPTER 7

the valley

Whitsett Boulevard was smack dab in the middle of the brown-gray L.A. suburb called the San Fernando Valley. Just north of Hollywood, it had originally been designed as a bedroom community for the stars, but they had all gone many years ago, leaving it like a forlorn one-night stand.

Our apartment complex was a study in soiled pastel stucco. Like a giant slice of birthday cake that had sat for too long in a bakery window, its soft greens, pinks and yellows were covered with dust and soot and its long-ago landscaped hedges were filled with weeds, used paper cups and dried snail tracks. The view from the slatted windows was distorted by mineral deposits and grease.

Our neighborhood bordered a wealthier part of the valley filled with mid-sized, tree-lined homes with nary a sidewalk in sight. In L.A. they measure the wealth of a neighborhood by the existence of sidewalks, and for some reason the richer the area the more sparse the sidewalks will be. Obviously, it has something to do with cars, garages and lawns. Suffice to say, every area we lived in had plenty of sidewalks, no lawns, hardly any trees and a lot of alleys. But we did have delis and little restaurants featuring the cuisines of all cultures, styles and communities: Vietnamese, Salvadoran, Cambodian, Mexican, Greek, Italian and some of the best Jewish delis anywhere.

For me that year was all about After School. Eight years old, I had just started the third grade and I was the original latchkey kid. At 3:00 P.M. on the nose every day I would run home with my two best friends after making a short stop at the nearby Jewish bakery, filled with fresh baked hamentaschen and cheese danishes to die for, still crisp, still warm.

I ran home with my luscious danish, filled with plans for the strange urban games I invented each day to play with my new urban friends. All of my friends were nerdy smart kids, the sons and daughters of poor immigrants, and they all had big plans to go to college and lift their families out of poverty. We understood each other that way, since as far back as I could remember my dream had been to make my mother happy—and in the American capitalist sense that meant to buy her a house and a car, one that worked and was preferably new and shiny, like none she'd ever had—and perhaps most importantly, my amorphous plan was "to take care of her." This had begun with my mom and Annie's half-joking, half-real request, "Hon, are you gonna take care of us when we're old and crotchety?" My answer was always an adamant *yes*, with the idea in my head even then that it shouldn't be any other way.

One of the games we played was called Steps, and it entailed walking slowly up the side of the forbidden Safeway delivery ramp and then running down the other side. Of course, in this and all the games there were the requisite paroxysms of laughter, common to silly 8- and 9-year-olds. The other games were all about me, my cat, the radio and our empty apartment. I loved afternoon talk radio because it meant the apartment wasn't quiet—I was terrified of silence. My games were elaborate tableaus involving my cat, the houseplants, all the inanimate household objects that were around and my mom wouldn't miss, and a variation on a concept involving me as the Head Administrator of a large agency or advocate for many people in need.

That one short year in that extremely unattractive apartment complex was one of the best years of my life. My mother was in a horrible abusive relationship with Rudy, and we were barely surviving on the child support from my dad and what she could get from Rudy once in awhile. Her position as a marginalized, unsupported single mother was now fully locked in place, culminating in the humiliation she experienced when she had to apply for welfare and was put through all kinds of drama which made her feel worthless and "undeserving" of any public assistance. And yet I was happy; she loved me, provided food for us, paid the rent (I guessed), and to me it seemed as though all was well.

At the end of the year we left the Valley and Czatar Rudolph in a flurry of possibilities. My mom had gotten a job, and now everything was going to be great. My mother wouldn't have to worry anymore, or more importantly, she wouldn't have to take all that crap from the welfare worker anymore. We were on our way to better things, and since my mom was excited, so was I. Of course, I was sad to leave my friends, especially my rich Jewish friends who had decided by the end of that year that I was the only poor white shiksa who was fun enough to invite to all the coolest parties, catered by Baskin Robbins and other tasty corporate logos. Their faux friendships, filled with the promise of future Bat Mitzvah invitations—and more importantly, more free food—had inspired me to start lying about what part of Hollywood I was actually moving to ("You know, the rich part," I would say). By this time I had learned most of what I needed to know about L.A. party skills: fake laugh, superfluous conversations that held little content, and of course the compliments that meant little and were spoken as fast as a mouth could humanly move. Without really intending to, I was preparing myself for life as a superficial L.A. pre-adolescent, but more interestingly, I was unwittingly participating in a family tradition of identity "trading up."

We moved to Los Angeles, Hollywood to be exact, and my mom began work at what was to be the job of her life. She'd been hired as a case manager/social worker at Catholic group home for troubled girls, and this would be her very first professional experience. It was a huge challenge, one that the skills she'd learned in grad school had only partially prepared her for.

At first she had to adjust to simply working with other people. Having had no real working experience until then, she wasn't very versed in organizational diplomacy, and early on she was deemed "unsuperviseable." This just meant that she had some very strong beliefs and innovative ideas that didn't always meet with the approval of the nuns and the Catholic hierarchy that managed the home, but with the help of a therapist she was seeing at the time she managed to pull herself out of that dangerous label and incorporate some teamwork practices into her work. She became one of the most-loved social workers there, and though it was mostly the youth and families who truly appreciated her efforts, some of the younger, more conscious nuns also appreciated my mother's innovations and dedication to her work.

For the first summer at her job she was truly terrified. For someone already suffering from severe anxiety, a big move to a new apartment, a new neighborhood and a new job was a huge challenge to face on one's own. This is no doubt why at this point I began to be integrated into her everyday activities. It began with me accompanying her to her job each day and hanging out in the convent's yard area, something I actually loved. This wasn't really new, since I'd gone with her to several of her grad school classes because she couldn't afford child care in Fresno. But this was a little different. I began to take on the role of her personal manager, making sure she had all her things together the night before, helping her avoid the dreaded lateness write-up that she was prone to getting due to the chaos in her mind and in our lives.

That job lasted two and a half years, and those were some of the most hopeful times of our lives. When the funding was cut for her position, the lay-off came down on us like a six-ton hammer, leaving everything shattered in its wake. My mom showed me the flimsy slip of pink paper that had flattened our hopes and killed her budding self-confidence.

Her newfound coworker friends advised her to try to get another job immediately, and she blindly sent out resumes. She acquired all the proper reference letters and scoured the want ads. She went to interview after interview, and six grueling months later she got a call back. Someone finally wanted to hire her, but by then it was too late. By this time she was well into a complete breakdown, psychologically, physically and financially. Joblessness, isolation and the fear of impending homelessness had left her paralyzed, crippled by the fear of too many unknowns, her worsening asthma and deep depression.

CHAPTER 8

mexico

"Lisa, I think we might be able to survive longer if we move to Mexico. We only have $2,000 left. But that's also why I don't know if we should make the trip, it's a big risk . . ."

"Of course we should," I chimed in quickly, "and besides, it's a lot cheaper to live there, and maybe you could get a job easier in Mexico." I was 11 going on 30 and every decision we made together was fraught with the fear of its drastic implications.

"But what if we don't make it?" she asked, the pen hovering over the lined paper as she considered the priority of today's calls.

"What have we got to lose? We might as well take the chance," I replied.

Somewhere between completely giving up and extreme desperation, my mother had started to believe that we could hold on a little longer on the tiny bit of money we had left if we went to Mexico. Being poor in a third world country seemed to make more sense for two people who were completely alone, and more importantly, it was easier to think about trips across the border than it was to drive across town for an extreme agoraphobic like my mother. I happily agreed, thinking anything was better than this, and that maybe my mother would meet a boyfriend, which would make everything easier.

We pondered every possible hostel, school program and

employment opportunity in cities from Oaxaca to the Yucatán, until my mother was finally convinced that *maybe* we would *try* to go.

"Call United, Continental, TWA, Aero Mexico, reserve every afternoon and evening flight for the next five weeks, to Mexico City, Guadalajara and Mazatlán." The concept behind my mother's multiple reservation program was that because it was so difficult for her to make a trip at all with her fluctuating health—sometimes her asthma was so bad that she couldn't breathe—compounded by the difficulty she had in getting anywhere on time, that if we booked every possible flight, we were bound to make one of them.

After several days of making reservations, I developed a travel-agent voice, simple and to the point without the use of gratuitous prepositions or adjectives, "One adult, one child, round trip to Mexico on flight 234." I usually got travel-agent discounts, or at the very least, was spoken to as an adult. Somewhere between the fourth and fifth week of this, we gingerly boarded Flight 164 at 6:00 P.M. to Guadalajara, Mexico.

"She'll thrill you and she'll kill you . . . She's got Betty Davis eyes . . ."

I could barely see through the thick sheets of sticky rain streaming across our windshield as decade-old American hits blasted from the radio. It was our first night in Guadalajara and my mother had rented a small red car with our last remaining shred of credit. We circled the city what seemed like a thousand times, joyously confused by jet lag, hunger, and excitement, surrounded by the tall caramel and taupe buildings that seemed to be in an odd state of complete decay and antiquated perfection.

We halfway looked for street signs (there were none) and sort of glanced at a map—both of us aware that at the moment we stopped being lost we would have to face reality and then the moment of pure magic would end. The tiny car swayed in the hard rain and our tires barely tasted the road.

The buildings seemed to curve and sway in sync with the music, acting as our muscular dance partners on the glimmering asphalt.

"*Guadalajara . . . Guadalajara . . . Guada . . . la . . . jar . . . a*"

We checked into a rather expensive hotel, planning to spend one night and then move to something cheaper. But for folks who have lived in poverty for much of their lives the idea of roughing it doesn't hold much appeal. So try as we might, we couldn't seem to leave the Holiday Inn Guadalajara. My mother was loathe to fraternize with or even speak to the other American tourists, and we immediately made friends with all the hotel's maids, busboys and waiters.

"Tiene cansado?"

On our second night in Guadalajara we were packed into a 1969 Chevy Camaro going 92 miles an hour on our way to three wedding parties (the favorite Saturday night entertainment). My mother began to ask our newfound friends, Isaias, Roberto, Miguel and Diego, whether or not they were *cansado* (tired) which we were gringo-certain meant "to be married" (*casado*), to which each and every hombre strenuously replied, "NO!"

We squealed in reckless abandon when Isaias accelerated the shining red machine, and we got quiet when he slowed down to a cruise, our hungry faces kissing the warm night air of the wondrous state of Jalisco.

Soon after that night, my first crush walked toward me down the street one day in the Zona Rosa district of Chapalita. I had a pink mohawk, which no one in Mexico understood or wanted to understand, with many an hombre telling me, even though I was only 11 years old, that if I changed my hair to something normal they would love to marry me—my mother fended off the multitude of contingent marriage proposals with stories of my future plans to join the convent. When I saw my first crush walking down the street with a jump in his step, wearing a studded leather jacket and three earrings, I fell in love, and seven hours later my mother and I were in our first club, listening to extremely loud, *rock en español*, punk rock, new wave, and *banda* music.

At approximately 1 A.M., the crush, whose name was Miguel, and his family strolled into the club. From young *niños* to the *abuelo* and *abuelita*, each family member twinkled with imminent group laughter. They took turns loving each other with their eyes, teasing each other with their easy jokes and implicit support. My mother and I tasted their family-ness like a forbidden piece of chocolate cake, drank its nectar like alcoholics in the midst of prohibition. We sat on the edge of their group joy and felt, for brief luxurious moments, like we were a part of them.

At 2 A.M. the family's band, "Sombrero Verde" went onstage. The rhythm and the possibilities coursed through my head. My feet, which lived to move to a beat, any beat, propelled me toward the dance floor, lighter than they had ever been before or since. I was lifted off into a world of sound and heat existing just above the neon-lit floor squares. I danced my Billy Idol-like solos to every tune Sombrero Verde played. The music was goofy hotel-rock, but it didn't matter—we were a family now, you don't judge your family. Everything was wonderful.

"You're such a great dancer."

"You should perform with us."

"Where are you going to stay tonight?"

"Tiene cansado?" my mother asked weakly, still not completely sure of the Spanish syntax.

At 4 A.M. we reluctantly said our last star-struck *adioses* and walked the two blocks to our hotel, filled with the dreams of our newfound family and the hope that maybe, just maybe, if we didn't think about it too much, our years of isolation, fear, and aloneness might be over.

The next day I began to explore Guadalajara on my own, having determined that I must learn Spanish so that we could live there forever. I snuck out into the morning of fresh-cut *guayabas*, *piñas*, warm corn pounded into breakfast, dust and diesel fuel with just a hint of jasmine. The morning in a semi-tropical climate is always the best time because all the smells travel on a small breeze attached to a delicate coolness, while the sky ponders its cloud formations for the day.

I stood on the corner waiting for almost an hour as one after another tilted, coughing bus, bulbous with the overload of human cargo, passed the bus-stop without stopping. Actually, they did stop, but it took me a while to catch on to the odd boarding method, which included holding onto the bumper, climbing in one of the windows, or running behind the bus while it was moving and jumping on.

After six unsuccessful tries, I finally boarded by jumping onto the door and holding on to the rubber window seams with splayed arms. As my fingers clutched at the edges, coursing with the adrenaline of extreme joy and danger, I looked up; the sky had settled on a river of blue-tinted clouds parting the bright azure background. A portable radio blasted the sweet sounds of Los Tres Aces in perfect harmony with the cacophony of humans and small animals as the sputtering engine tentatively accelerated and inched away from the curb.

Having been well-indoctrinated into Americanness, my first destination was Gigante, the local *supermercado*, a tribute to all that is western, large and facile—although I was confused by just how super that super was. They had everything from pigs' feet to underwear, with bright fluorescent-colored labels. I was determined to purchase something, I just wasn't sure what. Eventually I settled on a banana. At the checkout counter I nervously employed my "fake Spanish," that is, very limited vocabulary spoken with a determined Spanish feeling. All the clerks humored me—I guess because I was a kid. I paid 5 pesos for my banana and trotted out feeling very proud and capable.

After my success in the *supermercado*, I felt I could take on all challenges. On subsequent mornings I visited the outdoor market, drug stores, taquerias and, my favorite place, the car dealership, piled high with ancient American cars reeking of *I Love Lucy* reruns and Elvis Presley songs. At 1 P.M. every day, no matter where I was, I started running. I had to get back to the hotel by 1:30, or else! My mother must never know about my morning activities—in her view I would have been taking way too many chances, putting our already precarious situation in danger of getting more dire. At 1:30 P.M. when I would casually re-enter the hotel, my mother would awaken and we would continue our quixotic attempt at "getting established" in Guadalajara.

We spoke almost every day about how much money we had left.

"Lisa, I'm not sure what we're going to do, we only have enough to last us one more week."

We had been living in the hotel for a month. My mother had been to at least six job interviews. I was so proud of her— she was freed-up emotionally and almost never yelled at me or got upset. A look of dazed relaxation had settled on her face, and even these normally terrified discussions were carried on in an atmosphere of odd weightlessness, softened by the intermittent clouds and light tropical rain.

One particularly warm night, Isaias picked us up in the Camaro. "Tonight we will go salsa dancing," he proclaimed. I didn't listen, not really, unclear what that even meant, but determined not to miss this adventure. We drove to a new club where the willow trees that surrounded the building swished and swayed to a light sound that emanated from within. Small white lights flickered in the blackness, paper fans clicked against the sky.

We entered a dark room lit only by the glittering stage; the rhythm moved the room as I stood in the elaborate doorway arch. A very short boy, probably twelve years old, inched his way over to me. *"Baile?"* he held his hand out to me, his wide face filled by a smile with tiny black eyes peering out. He was wearing a bright pink polyester suit and his head was crowned with a circle-puff of black hair, a combination that I remember thinking made him look like an overdressed squirrel, but he was a ticket to that sound and fury, so I quickly took his hand, entering that mythical space of movement and light.

That night, guided by the insistent thighs and hot breath of a wannabe man, I learned to dance to the music of Celia Cruz, Tito Puente, Benny Velarde and many more. I was forever changed by that sound, and to this day, when I hear salsa, afro-cuban, charanga, or merengue, I am calmed, a smile illuminates my mind and I am taken away.

CHAPTER 9

adios

One day as I was making my morning exodus, I discovered a small note that had been folded and slipped under our door. On the outside of it was written one word: *Oficina*. It was only one simple noun, and yet I knew it marked "The End." It was as if someone had delicately typed "murder" across the embossed hotel stationary. They had put it there while we slept—that's when most crimes are committed, while people are sleeping. I didn't know what to do. I felt a small pit beginning to form in the center of my gut; I knew this was serious and I was too terrified to leave the room. I wasn't a late sleeper—I was always up at 6 or 7 A.M.—so going back to sleep was out of the question, and because the room was always kept very dark until my mother was ready to get up, reading was not a possibility. The thought of just sitting in that room doing nothing for hours was dreadful, but I knew that, no matter what, I couldn't go anywhere until my mom woke up and we began to strategize our next move.

"What's this?" my mother yelled from the door.

I guess I had fallen asleep. My mother was up now, and had discovered the note. Her voice barely registered fear, and I knew she was only slightly aware of its possible contents.

"Have you been downstairs yet?"

"No. I was sort of afraid to."

"Well, I can't read it until I've been outside. Who knows what it might say?"

"Yeah, but Mom, we've got to read it, it might be—"

"Well, you read it then, but don't tell me what it says."

"Okay." I opened it slowly, unable to focus for a while on any of the words on the carefully typed page.

Please come downstairs, there is a problem with your credit card.

I didn't need to read the actual words; I felt them burning the page, singeing my hands, my trembling fingers. I stayed near the door as my mother took a shower, fixed her hair and make-up, and pretended that she didn't know what I knew.

An hour later we marched downstairs, our heads held as high as possible. It was a beautiful day, the light shining through the lobby's stained glass, a Muzak derivative of "Guadalajara" playing on the endless tape loop that streamed from the speakers. A small fountain babbled gently. We approached the front desk. They all had their best front-desk faces on, masks of discomfort and the result of customer-service training manuals.

"May I help you?" as though they didn't know that "we were the ones," and of course in these situations my mother employed her best "Do you have a problem?" voice and demeanor, which came off like an over-enunciated James Cagney: "You said there was a problem with my credit card? What's the problem?"

With barely a blink of his eyes, the man behind the desk proceeded to tell us that we had to leave the hotel that day if we could not give him another form of payment immediately. His mouth barely moved as he spoke, and he kept his small watery eyes from focusing on us as he spoke. He finished with the requisite, "I'm afraid there is nothing we can do."

"Well, I need to use a phone. We're going to call our bank manager, and he will extend our credit."

The man with no facial expression seemed startled, obviously thinking, "No bank managers are going to speak to bums like you."

"Did you hear me? Get me to a phone down here and I'll straighten this whole thing out!"

My mother was quickly led to a small glass-enclosed room, not as much to accommodate her request as to get her ever-increasing volume out of the lobby and its reign of sacrosanct "quiet-noise." I watched her as she curled into the phone and launched into a beg-and-plead-fest with our local "bank manager," actually, the customer service supervisor. She did this very carefully so as not to seem like she was begging and pleading, but in fact just asking for what she had a perfect right to ask for: access to a very small savings account that we were not supposed to touch for another six months, and a wire transfer to Mexico. Today.

After two hours she emerged, visibly worn down. Apparently she was able to get our $200 savings account balance wired to the hotel, which was just enough for us to pay our bill and leave the next morning. No, she was not able to get any credit extended, and in fact they were going to destroy our credit card, which the officious desk clerk then carried out with one vicious snip of his scissors.

My mother and I wandered around the lobby for hours discussing our current lack of options.

"What are we going to do?"

"We could stay with Miguel and his family."

"Yes, I'm sure we could, but we have absolutely no more money. We can't be here with no money."

"Well, we can go back home and sell our car and stereo and come right back. We found that cute little apartment for only $150.00 a month, and you said you almost got a job."

"Yes, but leaving means we have to get back; it was so hard to even get here."

"But what else do we have?"

We walked all around the city that night, pondering and re-pondering our impossible situation until we finally settled on a plan, and yet we both secretly knew there was no hope. Travel itself was too hard, everydayness was too hard.

The ride to the airport was quiet. We'd told no one of our departure, since it seemed that telling anyone would seal our fate completely. No addresses were exchanged, no promises made, no commitments adhered to. I watched the dramatic semi-tropical sky dance with the sun one last time, my eyes filled with the tears of punctured dreams and lost possibilities.

The return home was horrific. It was like we had been traveling in space—only six weeks had passed, and yet it felt as though years had gone by. We got to work as quickly as possible, proceeding as planned. We tried to sell our old car for what it was worth, $1500. Six weeks later we were happy to get $600. We hastily purchased our tickets and made a series of reservations once again. No notes were written, hardly a word was spoken between us. Our moments were filled with the tenuousness of everything.

It was September in Los Angeles and the smog and dusty heat were at their worst, propelled by the Santa Ana winds. The sky was a perpetual brown-yellow glare and the trees took on their sickest droop. My mother was having asthma attacks every day, and the countdown to our departure became more and more desperate. Three more days . . . we *had* to go . . . it was like we were both praying to avoid a crisis; we couldn't afford one wrong move. My mom paid the rent in L.A. for one more month out, giving us exactly thirty days to make it work in Mexico.

And then the departure day arrived. Our plane left at 4 P.M., at the height of rush hour traffic. The cab arrived, and my mother could barely get a breath. We drove silently to the airport.

"I feel really sick, Lisa."

The white zone is for immediate loading and unloading of passengers only.

Airport announcements filled the atmosphere. Exhaust spewed from a multitude of idling vehicles. People with tense faces ran to and fro, filled with the unbridled anxiety that pulls at travelers gathered at any point of departure. We were a part of that mini-terror, and the air was a custard of imminent doom.

The white zone is for immediate loading and unloading of passengers only. No parking.

"That'll be $32.00."

"Can you please move this cab now?"

"Lisa, I feel really sick."

"Sir, you have to move NOW!"

"Can't you see I have customers unloading?"

"I don't care if you have horses unloading—if you don't move now I'm going to cite you."

"Mom, we've got to get out of here—"

"Don't you think I know that?"

The cabdriver slammed the trunk defiantly as the airport police officer hovered over us with his citation pad.

"Thank you so much, I'm sorry there's not more of a tip—that's all I have."

"That's okay, miss."

"Goodbye."

"Get moving!"

"I heard you, man!"

"Then go, already!"

"Fuck you!"

"Okay, that's it . . ."

I tried to follow their voices as far as the moving sidewalk would let me. The flight gates were ahead of us, but we had at least forty minutes of requisite confusion before we would actually board. Excitement, joy, and sorrow filtered through the air: "I love you"; "I'm going to miss you"; "I'll call you"; "Write me, please don't forget"; "Say hello to Dad"; "I'm so glad he finally left."

"Lisa, give me the backpack. I'm really getting sick. This isn't good."

AeroMexico Flight Number 156 for Guadalajara is now boarding. Please line up at Gate 5.

"Okay Mom, it's time to board."

"Get the pack. Can you get my water bottle? I'm having trouble walking," her breathing was coming in short, clipped spasms.

"It's okay, take it slow, we'll make it."

The man directly behind us in the boarding line started to stare. At first it wasn't obvious or done with any intent to humiliate, just a focused, conspicuous look. He progressed to an unmoving, fixed gaze, hardly bothering to look away when we looked back, projecting an intentional hostility born of his disgust with our cheap duffel bags and non-Armani aesthetic, our poor-single-mother-and-child-on-welfare-ness and inevitable economy class tickets. We were everything he despised. Who knew? Perhaps at any moment we might try using food stamps instead of plane tickets or ask him for spare change.

"Your boarding passes, please . . . miss?" The stewardess was tall, with long legs. Her deep brown hair was set in large sweeping curls, and her bright white teeth were frozen in a smile of impatience.

"Here," I shoved the boarding passes into her hands. Her fingernails were long and shiny, like ten delicately polished daggers.

It all happened in a matter of seconds, the way most horrific events are meted out, swiftly and without a second to think. We were beginning the descent down the carpeted walkway, the temporary walls were shuddering with gusts of aeronautic wind, the floors registered a hollow echo with each step. My mother held onto my arm. Her hands were cold, and I couldn't hear her breathing. Suddenly, she clutched at me tightly, "I'm going to faint, Lisa, get me out of here." An ashen color filled my mother's face while her eyes registered a blank gaze. I screamed to the ticket lady, but she couldn't hear me, only the man who hated us heard, and he quickly passed our crumbling forms, pushing to get past us in the small jetway. And then everything stopped, all the ambient jet noise was shut out as the lady with the red fingernails shouted into her walkie talkie and ran to where we were. As she ran toward us, the light rose up behind her while the jet exhaust blew through her long silky hair. She looked like some kind of *Charlie's Angels* apparition, running in a wind machine in filmic slow motion. Our dreams had ended in 25 seconds, and it all seemed like a bad '70s movie.

CHAPTER 10

estados unidos

I can't describe the drive home that day because it's too dangerous to remember—dark black corners of sharp-edged buildings, clouds with vicious teeth descended, bludgeoning us in our confusion. Nights and days to come tore at my mind, and an unruly, treacherous, impossible sorrow cut large incisions in my heart. On that drive home my heart and mind plunged together off a cliff in a suicidal drag race. For the first time, I was truly without hope. We were never okay after that experience. Fallout characteristics began to occur from that day on in both of us—eruptions and cysts on our personalities that even if "things got better" would never really go away.

Not long after our return, my mother instituted a daily 3-hour walk to and from the Larchmont district, a bite-size enclave of old-money-meets-small-town simulacrum. My mother loved it because it "had everything" and it reminded her of the brief years she'd spent with my father, swathed in the privilege of being a doctor's wife. We embarked on our silent journeys in the dead center of each smog-filled day. We walked through those infinitely quiet streets that exist in the middle of every California city, even one as big as L.A., a silence which gave the odd impression that all humans had died suddenly or been captured by aliens.

Time stood still for us in those days—there was no morning or midday or afternoon, just the time between light and dark, the time when things were not as bad as the other times. The walk was always preceded by a lengthy process of getting ready, a scream-fest or some other desperate emotional struggle. We would argue in a mind-crunching, violent way that anyone hearing would probably assume would be the death of either one, or both of us. Somehow we lived through each horrible argument to survive until the next one. Somehow.

"You're a great therapist, and you *will* find work again. It's not going to be that hard get a job—think of all the great work you did for the girls at the convent—you were meant to be a therapist."

"I can't apply for a job when I'm feeling this way!"

"Well, that's why you need to get into counseling and go back to school."

In the spaces between our desperate tussles, I had begun to develop elaborate inspirational speeches and lawyer-style arguments about why my mother should go on, have hope and wake up the next day. On one hand, this gave me an oversized sense of myself as the hero and savior, and on the other, it scared the hell out of me because I could never seem to completely convince her that things would really be okay.

I had also developed an intense longing for school. It had become more and more clear to me that I would never go back, and I began to believe that everything important, sane or joyous was related to school. This obsession, as with all the best obsessions, started to destroy me. A laugh, a squeal, a giggle, a shout from any group of kids on a school playground would throw me into a quiet state of desperation and sorrow. That sorrow began to build to a level of depression and a sense of things being out of control that made me feel that ending my life would be the only way to feel better. It was at this time that I began dreaming of the ways I could kill myself; it would always end with a gunshot.

"We have to get out of this smog, and if we can't afford anything else, maybe we need to try Santa Monica."

"How can we afford Santa Monica?"

After several weeks of list-writing, phone-calling, and ponder-talking, with intermittent bouts of severe asthma, we tentatively embarked on the Santa Monica apartment search. But after three months of relentless looking, we'd found that every place was either too expensive, required perfect credit, or the impossible, "No kids allowed."

Finally, I devised what I thought was a foolproof plan: I would fabricate an identity, a person so completely perfect that they couldn't possibly reject her application, and thus, my first survival persona as "Rent-Starter" was formally launched.

My mother and I went to Bullock's in Westwood and began to scout for the perfect rent-starter outfit, the look that would convince a prospective landlord that I was "the one," the perfect tenant who would cause no problems, pay my rent on time, and not bother them with any annoying repair problems. To create this perfect cocktail one had to affect an odd admixture of sincerity, strength, and extreme sycophantism.

I was always a friendly person with a tendency to act silly whenever possible—my favorite thing was to laugh too loud over things that weren't that funny to anyone but me. I always attempted to get along with everyone and was devastated if people didn't like me more than anyone else. I was schooled in the scholarship of partying, a canon born of extended residence in L.A. and an endless attempt to be accepted by the "in" crowd. These attributes, along with some very creative character development, enabled me to secure housing for my mother and myself when we were essentially homeless, jobless, and without a reference to our name.

It was a sunny day, framed by an unusually blue and glistening sky. The day before, the Los Angeles basin had experienced the rare occurrence of a heavy rain that had washed the air and wrung out all the soot and old smog. I climbed onto the bus to Santa Monica wearing my recently purchased suit, feeling extremely proud even though I stumbled in my Payless mini-heels and accidentally scratched a hole in my cheap nylons. My mother and I had been unable to afford the suit at Bullock's, but it had given us big ideas which we'd happily translated to K-mart, and we felt quite satisfied with what we'd acquired. My mother always said, "Anybody can look good in expensive clothes, but it's something else entirely to look good in cheap clothes."

The suit was made of simulated-wool polyester the color of rusty nails, with a shiny nylon lining that crinkled and crunched when I walked. When I sat down on the bus, I wasn't sure how to hold my legs, continually crossing and uncrossing them until I became dizzy with the tension of possible protocol infractions.

"You have great legs."

"Huh?"

"You have great legs," his voice was low and strange, like every child molestor/rapist I'd been warned about, those scratchy yet whiny tones reserved for obscene phone calls and horror movies.

"Thanks," I looked up and down, unsure where to place my eyes for fear he would feel "encouraged," the worst thing to do when encountering a child molestor/rapist type.

"On your way to Santa Monica?"

"Yeah," I tried to mumble a non-answer while also answering nicely because I was trained to be polite.

"Oh really? Where are you heading?"

Now I started to get really nervous. I had a whole hour's ride ahead of me. What should I say?

Of course, part of the problem was that nobody in Los Angeles except really messed-up individuals and kids use the bus system. Anyone marginally sane or somewhat alive has a car, and it has nothing to do with poverty because in L.A., no matter how poor you are, you still manage to get some funky vehicle to pollute the air and call your own, and if you are any kind of self-respecting drug dealer, pimp, or underground-economy worker, you simply must drive in L.A.

This minimal demographic left me with my new buddy, pasty of skin, small of eyes, with sparse, shoe-black, greasy hair strands draped across an oily forehead. But did I get up? Did I move? Did I tell him that I didn't want to talk? No, I tried desperately to appease this person I didn't know, didn't like, and was increasingly afraid of.

"I'm Rick by the way. What's your name?"

"Legs, shmegs! You and your kind will be doomed till death. There's no hope for the rot that makes up your mind, or the life that you're part of. You are evil incarnate, and I DON'T GOT MILK!"

At first I only saw the wig—it was large and shiny and twisted on the top into a lopsided partial beehive. He was about 6'5", and while screaming a breathless rant he was standing in the aisle nudging my rapist buddy to move over.

Unbeknownst to me, he was sort of stalking "Rick," and while Rick was trying to make time with me, the wig-man had been organizing his assorted plastic bags so they'd be a little more portable, to make sure that I didn't interfere with his chances to get Rick.

"And I'm not a man, I'm not a transsexual, and I'm not a drag queen. I want you to love me for who I am."

"Fuck-off," Rick spat.

"How dare you talk to me like that! Don't try to impress this whore you insist on fraternizing with. I know you, and I love you for who you are, not who I want you to be. She doesn't care about you, and besides—"

"Oh for Christ sakes!" Rick lurched from his seat, yelled over his shoulder at me, "Nice talking to you," and ran to the exit door.

"See? You're trying to impress her again. I know your type, and I know where you live, and besides, I DON'T JUST DO IT," and here the wig-man broke into a sort of aria-like song that I assumed was in response to the Nike campaign, and he ran off the bus after Rick.

The rest of the trip was uneventful, peaceful even, with strip malls passing by the bus window. The majority of L.A. architecture consists of low-slung strip malls filled with taquerias, small dress shops, photo developers, KFC's, AM/PM's and 7-11's, with new ones being built every day. I looked with a quiet appreciation at the taupe, off-white, gray and light yellow structures fronted by the regulation six-to-ten asphalt car slots. I had never expected anything beautiful or dazzling, and it was comforting not to be shocked or shown otherwise; the ever-changing, never-changing order of ugliness made me feel safe.

"San-taaaa Mon-icaaaaaaa," the bus driver sang me out of a semi-trance.

I'd arrived. The light was different, brighter than Hollywood, the streets were wider and quieter. I thought I had experienced quiet in midday Hollywood, but this was a deafening silence, and it pinged against a crisp-cool sky, which, due to Santa Monica's proximity to the ocean, felt fresh and tight and in collaboration with the silence.

I wasn't sure where to go, but it only took a second to configure my location. Everything in Santa Monica is arranged at right angles, numbered streets and simple square blocks. I took one left turn from my bus stop and I was on the right street. I walked down a short block and I had reached my final destination. It was too easy somehow, and the simplicity of it all frightened me.

It was a small building, two stories at most, constructed in the best '60s/'70s style you could hope for, and it was the purest, ugliest color of mustard ever developed in an exterior paint tone. I was standing in front of a giant jar of Gulden's shaped into an apartment complex. I thought this was a bad sign.

One weak tree stood squarely in the middle of the manicured grass plot in front of the building. I stood for a moment in the silence, hoping to hear some form of life, a car, or a voice, or a clomp of footsteps. Then I heard a scream, not a bad scream or a scream of distress, but the scream of a child, a child playing, a squeal really, a beautiful, happy, amazing squeal. I knew that sound could be coming from only one place: a playground, a playground in a school. Oh my god . . . there was a school nearby. My heart rose and fell with the mythic possibilities of my attendance.

"Are you here to see the apartment?"

The man talking to me had the oddest hair. Light orange feathery strands barely clinging to their follicles were pulled clear across to the other side, attempting to cover a vast expanse of empty freckled head.

"I am Mr. Humphries," he paused, took a breath, and then said with increased volume, "And you can call me Mr. Humphries."

"Okay, oh, yes . . . yes. I'm here to see the apartment. Thank you for showing it to me, Mr. Humphries," honeyed tones dripped into my voice.

Without acknowledging my effusive greeting, Mr. Humphries marched abruptly into the mustard palace.

"It's on the first floor, and it has a beeeuu-tee-ful balcony."

I only realized mid-sentence that he'd already embarked on a litany of apartment features, spoken in a quiet Scottish-accented mumblespeak. I was nodding in complete agreement to everything he said.

"There are two *large* closets in every room."

As he spoke, he led me down a dark cement hallway lined with a greenish-yellow stucco variation on the external mustard tone, with matching gold mailboxes. He stopped at a wide green door that had a large gold A on it.

"Here it is!" he sprung open the door. "We just shampooed the carpet. See how nicely it matches the walls?"

I blinked my eyes twice, hardly able to make out any carpet color in the dim light emanating from the sliding glass door's northern exposure, and then I saw it: the carpet was a thin acrylic ply of avocado-green with mustard threads. I followed him into a small, dark bedroom.

"This is the master bedroom; the cars don't come by hardly at all. It's really very quiet."

On the back wall of the "master bedroom" there was a sliver

of window that faced a parking lot and an adjoining alley. And next we saw the box-sized bathroom.

"And here's the most elegant kitchen you'll ever see," he jutted his right arm nervously in the direction of a tiny rectangle of a room containing a mini-sink, a tiny oven, and a pint-sized refrigerator.

"Look at these nice new cabinets. I spent so much time installing these cabinets. Aren't they beautiful? At $600 a month, this place is a deal. This apartment is very clean, and it has to stay that way. I run a nice building, no bums or wise guys, there's a nice lady upstairs, she can tell you. Well, I can't say anymore, the place speaks for itself," and he turned abruptly towards me and stared, his mouth sealed completely shut in a ziplock vertical line.

I sucked in a nervous gulp of excess saliva, and with barely a breath of consideration at the horribleness of it all, proclaimed in my best I-am-so-nice-and-responsible-and-I-won't-cause-you-a-second-of-trouble voice, "I love the place. Can I fill out an application?"

"How old are you?" Mr. Humphries' point-size, watery yellow eyes were looking straight at me, and I realized too late that he was actually focusing his gaze.

I mustn't show anything. I must not gulp, or blink, or even think about being twelve years old . . .

"I'm twenty-six. I can't believe how beautiful those cabinets are! Where did you get them? I know exactly how you feel; it's so hard to get cabinets in exactly the right shade."

His eyes looked like baked pinenuts that had been implanted in his sharp, bony face. He refused to blink or look away and was not deterred by my gratuitous compliments, but I could tell he was actually weighing something about me.

After a full three-minute pause, he finally broke his gaze and asked, "Do you work?"

"Of course. I work full-time, actually, I'm always working. I never have any time to do anything else."

"You know, there are no parties allowed here. I run a quiet

building, with quiet people, and no one complains. That's how I want to keep it."

"I never have parties. I never go to parties. All I do is work." Toward the end of my sentence, Mr. Humphries gave a little snort.

"The applications are in the kitchen. I thoroughly check *all* references on that application," he said as he turned away from me and marched out of the room.

Two days later we got the place—a terse Scottish-accented phone call announced my acceptance, and we moved one foggy-smoggy day into a deadly abyss of nothingness that almost completely destroyed us.

The torture began on the first day—the complete utter torture of nothingness setting in on day one as I ventured out into the alley framed by other equally ugly mid-'70s constructions. Each building was titled with names like *The Californian, The Surf, The Ocean Breeze,* and yet there was nothing inherently nice or breeze-like about any of those hideous buildings; on the contrary, they resembled cheaply constructed stucco motels, with absolutely no concept of how to capture the beauty and light of a California day or moonlit night.

The regimen of daily walks was transferred to Santa Monica. And somehow they increased in length. My mom was still writing to-do lists for me each day, but we were cruising so quickly into complete poverty that the stress level was severely increased for both of us. Our sole source of income was my father's child support, and now the rent was taking the whole amount. Every day was a futile search for money. Every day included a screaming fight. Every day my mother was extremely depressed and hopeless.

On morning after dreary morning I walked down the alley, unsure of where I was going, what I was going toward or what I was going to do, feeling a pit of confusion and disorientation growing in my gut. As I started to panic, I passed the occasional human washing his car or getting home from work—they had soft expressions of melancholy and never said anything, and I have always marveled at the way we humans can live side by side and do nothing about each other. How could they not know that we were suffering so; how could they not help us; how could they not know that it was only a matter of moments before we were down to our last hundred dollars? I usually ended up in the nearby supermarket, the only problem being that I had no money to buy anything.

I walked through the huge glass mouth leading to the glistening innards of the nearby Safeway grocery store. It was the 20th of the month, and my mother and I didn't have any food stamps left. From the corner of my eye I caught the squinted gaze of a store official. I escaped his view by turning into the dairy section. My hand was swift as I darted for the glimmering blue vessel of cottage cheese at $1.59. It tumbled gracefully into my backpack. Now for the bread. I had a list: bread, cheese, milk, chicken, jam. I arrived at the jam section to find nothing priced at less than $4.29 a jar. I knew intuitively that my plan was about to fail.

Approximately three times a month, my feet would caress the liquid floors of Safeway. My illicit food gathering always increased in size depending on our shortage of money or food stamps. I would usually purchase one or two things so as not to cause suspicion, and the rest would end up in my backpack. Today I had only $2.00, and in an intoxicating mix of 12-year-old omnipotence and severe hunger, I took a chance: I stole everything. As I walked out, those squints became furtive glances and signals to action leading to the advancement of unknown troops and suddenly, as my feet barely tasted the asphalt parking lot, I felt the arms and smelled the sweet-sick aftershave of a 19-year-old box boy turned security guard.

They dragged me into the security office, a very hot, closet-sized room with three video cameras and a two-way window facing the produce section. This was my first run-in for crimes of poverty and yes, I was scared of being taken to jail as they were threatening, but I was more afraid of them calling a truancy officer. I had not been to any kind of school for almost a year, and if they took me now it would all come out.

I relied on a defense mechanism that began to set in for life in those years, one that would get me through a variety of difficult situations: I lied. And in retrospect, it was really too easy. I told them I was thirty years old, and they believed me. I didn't really look thirty but they were short-staffed and really had no time to deal with my obviously lying 12-year-old self. Rather than continue to question me about my obvious lie they let me go, and I was free to spend my time in more walks of confusion and hungry afternoons.

Days from that time in Santa Monica only come to me in excerpts, alternately filled with or completely devoid of sound:
"Ha ha! I told you I was going to get you, Sandy! Now *you're* it! You like her, oooohh, I'm telling!" Children my age were laughing, playing, teasing each other, running, skipping down that dreary alley directly under my window everyday at 3:15 P.M., pouring out of the school down the street. Each shrill, excited thread of their voices shattered the blank stillness with a momentary drop of life in a sea of empty air. Oh how I longed to be them for even a second, to have friends, to worry about my clothes, homework, boys. Maybe mine was the ultimate in covetousness—the desire for the other, the other me I was beginning to realize I would never be again and yet still I thought I somehow was. The desperate, bone-aching desire to be normal, to go back to school, to have friends, and to not worry about money ever again. Finally, I just desired something, anything, that was alive, that wasn't part of the dreadful silence of Santa Monica, the disdain of the omnipresent Mr. Humphries asking for his rent and, worst of all, the alley, filled with the sounds of happy children, or filled more often, and more oppressively, with nothing at all.

The ticket out of the silence was leaning against a wall in Venice Beach, smoking a cigarette, James Dean-meets-cholo-

79

style. Brown-orange rays from the setting sun stretched across the flat asphalt that lined the boardwalk when my mother and I went there the first time. We were dazzled by everything, the least of which was Miguel.

What happened next was a blur of Dinah Washington records, fresh fish dinners prepared by Miguel and astrological predictions foretold by Miguel's "gyspy" friend, the amazing Lila. Before I knew it, I had a new stepfather—he and my mother sealed their relationship with a strange marriage ceremony at a local office of the Salvation Army in Venice Beach.

In many ways, Lila and Miguel were old-school grifters, living off the kindness of strangers, duping anyone dumb or needy enough to let them. But we had nothing to give, and needed even more. To this day I am still unsure what Miguel got out of the whole deal, but I'm grateful to him nonetheless. Because of him we moved out of impending homelessness in Santa Monica into the wondrous buzz of barely clothed men and women, old hippies, gentrifying neighborhoods, street artists and miles of off-white sand that was Venice Beach.

CHAPTER 11

venice beach

The morning fog reaches up out of the gray-green Pacific Ocean and tastes the burning sun at around 7:00 A.M. on any morning in the infamous semi-town of Venice Beach. It's still quiet then, barely humming, but the salty cool air will soon heat up and be filled with the multilayered sound of a day on the boardwalk. It was here that I launched an enterprise that would become the bane of my existence, which would sustain my mother and me for many years, just barely. It would eventually become so loathsome that it would almost drive me insane.

"Whaddaya think you're doin' here, kid?" I was introduced to the third-world-in-the-first-world reality of street vending—or what should be called micro-business—by an extremely rude Cockney-accented man in a tiny ruby-red Speedo. "Get the fuck out of here," his large yellow teeth were less than an inch away from my face with this last sentence.

"NO!" The desperation of wanting to buy luxuries like fresh blueberries (and no longer able to safely shoplift) gave my 12-year-old self the wild courage to stand up to this intimidating, six-foot-tall old hippie with hardly any clothes on.

"What makes you think you can sell here? This is *my* spot!" a droplet of pot-stained spit fell from his loose lips.

"Because I need to and I have to," I really didn't know what

I was saying; a whole lot of free-floating fake bravado just poured from my hungry mouth.

After I convinced my mother to move in with Miguel to get us out of the poverty and isolation of Santa Monica, we all moved to a tiny house in the "Dogtown" section of Venice; it was the pre-gentrification Venice ghetto, filled with African-American, Latino and Laotian families living in cheap houses with tiny yards full of low-rider, souped-up cars, pit bulls and young brown and black gangstas fighting the undeclared war against displacement. We moved into this battleground, filled with the hopes and dreams of new love and endless possibilities, a sense of anything-can-happen.

In the first year of our residence in that little house my mother got to work, giving me focused lists of calls and making many herself, aiming to put her MSW degree to use again. After an extensive process of paperwork, interviews and fingerprint checks, we were approved to run a daycare center for babies from very low-income families referred to us by the County. My mom did well for a while, but eventually we had to close it down because we didn't make enough money to pay the exorbitant increases of the quickly gentrifying Venice Beach rents.

Things began to fall apart between my mother and Miguel. As is often the case with poor folks suffering from the multi-trauma fallouts of race and class oppression, there tend to be skeletons living quietly in closets that, given a little time, will jump out and bite. And bite they did. The fights became more severe as our collective poverty worsened. Eventually, they had no relationship at all, just breaks between fights. And then there were no breaks.

One particularly bad night Miguel came home from his restaurant job still wearing his cook's hat, his requisite "salmon-cutting" machete dangling at his side. He sat on the front step of our little house and smoked his cigarette with a particular emphasis on the ex-con stylizations of the puff and drag.

"So Debra, what are we gonna do about the rent?" he asked my mom, his black-brown eyes turning into small shiny pellets of fury. His question was meant as little more than a provocation, since he was the only one with any money in our trio, and he already knew there was really nothing to be done about the rent. Miguel's favorite thing to do was fight: squabbles, small fights, big dangerous fights and all-out domestic violence battles. Whenever he and my mom were in the same room it was only a matter of time before a battle of some scale was waged.

It was this new era of violent poverty that launched the vending weekends in Venice Beach. In between all the fights and police calls and screams and weird manifestations of a broken relationship holding onto itself for dear life, my mother convinced Miguel to put his art talent "to some use," and in a matter of weeks I was on the boardwalk, selling hand-printed t-shirts with horrendously cute little brown bears on them.

One morning on his way out to surf (and then to work), Miguel pronounced, as he had done many times before, that as soon as his new surf board was in he was "outta here-Boom." He had said the same thing many times before, but this time it resonated with a new kind of certainty that both my mom and I heard, sending chills up both our spines. After many hours of discussion it was decided that I would have to meet Miguel at work when he got off and convince (read: beg) him to change his mind. I was to tell him how much we really did care about him, find out if he was leaving for another woman and, finally, ask him to at least postpone his plans until we had more time to prepare.

At 1 A.M. I was there as planned, waiting outside the restaurant, elaborate stories of why he should stay ready to drop from my lips like water. He saw me and began walking quickly in the other direction.

Lincoln Boulevard at the edge of Venice Beach at 1 A.M. was empty. Empty and oddly quiet, as almost all of California, urban and suburban alike, becomes after 1:00 A.M. Even this, one of the longest, ugliest and most developed streets in Los

Angeles that traveled from one end of the city to the other, was completely empty and so quiet that the occasional car seemed like an intrusion.

"Miguel . . . Miguel . . . Miguellllll!" I screamed in vain into the silent air.

He kept walking, his checkerboard cook pants billowing out from his thin legs with each stride, the puff of one cigarette after another wafting up from his head. We passed block after block, and then at the corner of Santa Monica Boulevard I caught up with him. He continued to walk, and the beginning of several hours of begging and pleading began.

At four o'clock in the morning he agreed to stay a little longer. I will never forget that night. Something very disturbing and different happened. At some point I no longer felt like I was fighting for my mother *and* me, but in fact only for me. I no longer could differentiate between who was in the relationship with Miguel, and a vague feeling of love-desperation-attraction-incest set in, never to truly go away.

The threat of covert incest/abuse experiences between a fatherless child and the mother's boyfriend are the bane of all single mothers, causing many a mother to never seek a partner, or worse, to "look the other way" when the abuse does occur if it helps the mother's chances of being fed and housed and a little less lonely. My mother worked very hard at not letting that ever happen to me, dropping men if they so much as looked at me or spoke in an inappropriate way. But in the end it was a testimony to our level of desperation, our intimacy with the vicious jaws of poverty, that she only weakly considered that possibility with Miguel, and then went on to devise "our next move" to get Miguel to stay.

They continued to fight and finally, after the last really bad incident, which included the machete, a visit from the police and a lot of expletives out of my mom's hella ghetto mouth, my mother decided we needed to live separately from Miguel. The only trouble was that between the three of us we really didn't have the money to support one apartment, much less two. Still, we tried, and this is when our serial evictions began. It would always begin innocently. We would have a particularly good weekend selling a lot of bear shirts, clearing at least $500. My mom would direct me to put on "the suit" and I would go and get us an apartment. Venice was a transient community at that time and the landlords were traditionally laid back, so they never checked on my credit, my age or even my references, which was good, since everything I wrote on the applications were lies.

One to six months would pass of on-time rent paying, and then we would have a bad weekend. The 30-day Notice to Pay Rent or Quit would be taped to the door, followed by the Unlawful Detainer notice to evict, and then the marshal's notice, and then we would ask Miguel for money and I would put on the suit, acquire a new apartment and then it would start all over again.

Meanwhile, my mother and Miguel barely saw each other but they would still fight, if only by proxy. I was my mother's cowboy, roping in Miguel wherever he would roam—I would check on him while he surfed at Malibu, check on him at his cooking jobs to make sure he wasn't cheating with the waitresses, check on him at the apartment where he was living. When necessary, I would be the stand-in for her in their fights, but the bulk of my role was to beg Miguel not to leave us.

The time that terrified me more than all the rest was the night it seemed like it was really over. My mother had me deliver a note to Miguel, to let him know that once again we didn't have any rent money and needed him to help us get another apartment. Somehow, on this night it was the straw that broke Miguel's back.

It was late, the electricity at the Brooks Street apartment had long ago been turned off due to non-payment, and the long, almost empty room was awash in an eerie darkness. My mother and I had left this apartment to live in a tiny one-room studio, and only Miguel remained here now.

85

"Miguel, are you here?" I walked gingerly into the room, calling his name half-heartedly, hoping not to find him. I called his name again, softer this time. He didn't answer, and so I thought the coast was clear. I would leave the note containing the "news" that once again we had ran out of money and this place would be served with a notice to vacate the premises on Monday morning at 5 A.M. I left it on the one piece of furniture that remained in the place, a small, chipped wooden table that we'd gotten from the Goodwill that sat in the middle of the room.

After dropping the note I ran out, but I realized I'd forgotten my keys, so I turned around and tiptoed back in. The note wasn't there.

"I got the note," Miguel snarled through gritted teeth in an almost inaudible voice, thick with fury.

Those four words, which hung in the air for seconds that seemed like hours, froze the moment in a capsule of dread, the most frightening moment I have ever had. "Well, I'm just gonna go," I inched for the door.

"D'you think this is okay?" Suddenly Miguel was a millimeter away from my face, the snarl had turned into a whisper. He was holding the note in a clenched fist trembling at his side.

"No, but there was no way ar—" before I could finish my weak explanation, I felt Miguel's hands grip my shoulders and then I felt the wall in my back. Miguel had thrown me against the wall of the apartment and was now pushing a plywood slat that doubled as a door to the kitchen into my face.

The fear of impending death is like no other, and as I stood there, my head rushing with adrenaline and pain, it was harder than one would imagine to think about escape. But suddenly, without even thinking, my body writhed and twisted in an odd maneuver and I was out from under the door. I ran like I had never run before for the back door, which luckily was still ajar.

I never looked back, and continued to run down the alleys and walkways of Venice Beach until I reached the boardwalk, the sand and then the shore, where I still ran and didn't stop for what seemed like miles. It was times like these, of complete fear and confusion, that I always thanked the sea for being there, crashing, breaking and re-inventing itself with every wave, every gust of wind.

No one ever mentioned that encounter with Miguel. Not me. Not Miguel. And certainly not my mother, since it would be many years before I would tell her the details of that terrifying night.

Miguel found some sort of peace after that, I think out of guilt for what he had done to me. He lived quietly and without incident in a little '50s trailer that we bought for $50 from a guy on the boardwalk and parked in an abandoned parking lot in Dogtown. Whenever we drove by to give him one of my mother's notes he would be sitting on the little steps leading up to the trailer casually smoking a cigarette, with only a little bit of James Dean, Marlon Brando or "Wilmos" cholo attitude thrown in.

Six months later, Miguel made the final declaration of his intention to leave. The odd thing was that this time no one really fought it. It wasn't that we were any more stabilized or less likely to be homeless, and we were still bereft of options, but after Brooks Street things were just too bad for me to hang on to any longer. As for my mom, I think she was just tired.

Dee and Tiny in Venice Beach, doing a site-specific, performance/ conceptual art piece: "The Depressed Box—give us a dollar and we'll tell you how depressed we are."

CHAPTER 12

the art of survival

My mother was an artist, a conceptual artist to be exact. She was also crazy. But then again, one can always question what is "artistic" behavior and what is craziness. Perhaps she was really just artistic, given that her whole take on life was somewhat skewed and alternative and that she, like many other artistically inclined people, never did anything normally, consistently or regularly.

One day, after several months of endless bear shirt production, my mother's tendencies toward fiber art were born; without warning, she began cutting patterns into the form of a kind of postmodern Zoot Suit. It turned out well, and she was inspired to continue, coming up with a number of innovative wearable art ensembles, which we entitled the "La Bamba" line.

With that, we began to be a part of the very diverse, yet oddly tight-knit community that was "the boardwalk." There was Bird, an ageless "designer-artist" who had a proclivity for gay men, art openings and redecorating; Peter, the hippie street musician extraordinaire who sang multiple renditions of "Brown-Eyed Girl" all day as the boardwalk went from the afternoon's sun-glare yellow to the gray-brown-gold blanket of warm dusk; and countless others. Venice at that time was a community of houseless hippies, colonized Native people pacified into drunken submission with the white man's brew, confused, yet beautiful young men and women bent on some vague form of stardom, with no plans but several party invitations, extremely rich, extremely successful Hollywood art and industry folk who were slowly but surely gentrifying Venice with each addition of their multimillion-dollar mansions, and everyone else, all galvanized by some sort of shared '70s nostalgia that never let up.

The La Bamba line of shirts, pants and skirts was named first for the song, one of my mom's favorites, and second for a dance I choreographed for one of our first performance art presentations that doubled as the opening for the clothing line. And my wordsmithing began with the business name of the "company" that produced the clothes: Street Clothes, so-named because in many moments of our design process we were actually on the street.

Street Clothes was our first adventure in what would become an ongoing series of life-meeting-art-meeting-tragedy-meeting-innovation, leading us to a sort of serendipitous underground fame that always seemed to be our odd reality after that.

With no experience in clothing design or knowledge of the fashion industry, my mother and I used our usual tactics to begin: there was a series of intensely focused phone calls to find out what we needed to know. We discovered that in order to get your clothing line into department stores you had to get a sales rep who worked out of the Design Center in downtown Los Angeles. So, in another moment of do-it-yourself fabulousness, we sewed, cut and painted a truly beautiful assortment of all of our Street Clothes and carried them to each and every rep we could manage to get an appointment with until we got a bite. That bite led to a mini-season of Street Clothes being sold in Macy's and a few other select California boutiques.

The sales rep launched a media buzz for the line that started with a full-color spread in *Playgirl*, the magazine ostensibly created for women who wanted to see naked men but probably "read" by plenty of gay men as well. Suffice to say it wasn't a mainstream readership. I'm not sure we ever made any sales from that spread, but we were thrilled.

The store accounts actually produced hardly any money once the sales rep had taken his cut and we'd paid for the expensive fabric that my perfectionist mom insisted on using. The fact that we'd spent everything we had and made almost nothing was standard for most start-up businesses, but it was a big disappointment to my mother, who had thought we really had a chance to finally make it.

We decided to focus on opening our own store, thinking in vain that we would have more control of our product, our process and our clientele that way. We launched Street Clothes: The Store at the end of that wild summer in a tiny (2' by 1') corner of a building on the Venice boardwalk. My mother would create weekly art installations in front of our store, and each one would include some aspect of live performance. Sometimes I performed solo, often an androgynous song-and-dance routine, inspired by my mom's urgent desire to vicariously realize her dream of being a singer/dancer. We also performed some duo pieces, inaugurating what would become a long and somewhat infamous line of conceptual art personas. Sometimes it was interactive, for example, the "Depressed Box," where we dressed in head-to-toe black and sat next to a large "donation" box with a sign that read, "Give us a dollar and we'll tell you why we're depressed." Other times it might be a wild mix of dance, sound, found objects and clothing under the vague title of "The Mother-Daughter Fashion Twins: Dee and Tiny."

Thus we birthed the characters of Dee and Tiny, and we would go on to mythologize that duo, living out their created story, blurring the lines between art and life for years. My moniker, Tiny, was chosen for its androgyny and its sound effect next to "Dee," but in later years it would become a necessary pseudonym in my poverty criminal and poverty resistor reality.

Our work got so much attention that we were written up in the alternative newspaper, the *LA Weekly* and then in other local papers as the next "big thing." Of course, it's not that hard to be the next big thing in L.A.—that's why L.A. is so cool: If you do, create, or instigate something, anything that's new, different or exciting, you'll become the next big thing.

During that wonderful summer I captured a mini-moment of teen-ness, the first and last brush with it that I would ever have. Without a formal entrance or acquaintance, just working on the access of a young female, I hung out with three crowds: mini-wannabe-gangstas, white, black and brown, who did graffiti art on any and every wall that they could get away with; surfer/skater dudes who rode skateboards endlessly and dangerously late into the night; and finally, "kids of stars." I never actually went to middle school or high school, but via these three crowds I gained access to the highways and byways of nearby Santa Monica High School, including a semi-crush from the wayward and slightly disturbed son of a prominent actor who loved me from afar.

CHAPTER 13

1984

1984. The year began with tropical clouds filled with dense piles of rain. Mists of rare, cleansing moisture slid across the sky all day and into the night, and as if to meet the cool wet from above, the ocean climbed up the flat, broad beach and filled it with gray and white breakwater.

"It never rains in (Southern) California. . ." That old '70s song doesn't lie. It really doesn't. So when it does rain in Los Angeles for more than an hour or two, people literally coil up into confused balls and rarely leave their houses. Most of the time you can count on the fact that it will only rain for a minute and then be over, so no one actually makes plans around the possibility of rain; when it really does occur, the entire city enters into a strange state of mutually understood paralysis.

Suffice to say that in 1984 everything that had almost looked like hope for my mom and me ended. We had started Street Clothes with absolutely nothing, no money, no bank loan, no business plan. Just hope, extremely hard work and a lot of raw creativity. Every sale, every customer kept us alive from week to week. It paid the rent, paid our expenses, and had started, after that first summer, to really begin to grow into a viable profit-making venture.

And then it rained . . . and rained and rained. Day after day, week after week it just kept coming down, cleansing the dry earth, purging the air of its thick layers of dust and smog, and paralyzing the city. Sunday after Sunday the boardwalk remained empty and frighteningly quiet. The occasional lone skateboarder passed every so often, breaking the deafening silence with their "whoosh swish" and inevitable "slap clap" as they crashed on the cement to then start all over again. I rarely even ventured out on my own "board," too scared to have fun. Wet day after wet day ended in the same dread.

The old adage that it takes money to make money is undeniably true. Whether it's actual cash or just good connections to some folks who have your back financially, without either of those you really can't make it in your own business, notwithstanding the mythic American Dream or "Just pull up your bootstraps and work hard and you'll succeed" lie. We worked harder than two people could have ever worked, we pursued our dreams, and if there were any bootstraps left to pull up we had worn them to a tether.

Almost thirty consecutive days of rain had destroyed our outdoor sales-dependent business. Realizing that we were about to fail completely, my mom convinced me to call my wealthy dad and ask for some help to get us through this period, since if we didn't get some help we truly would lose everything and end up on the street. It would have taken less than a thousand dollars to save our little business till the rains were over, but "I don't believe in the entrepreneurial spirit" was his reply.

As he spoke those devastating words, my heart imploded and I lost all the breath in my body. Of course, he had never helped us out before, so why I had agreed to call him and be made to feel even smaller and less important than I already felt, I don't know. It wouldn't be the last time either, just one of the worst. He ended with a patronizing mini-cure, "I can send you $100 hon, maybe that'll help."

"I have to get a job. I could work anywhere, I could do anything," I pleaded with my mother.

"What are you talking about, you're only fourteen."

"So what, I drive, I rent apartments, I run the business, I can lie about my age to get a job, what's the big deal?"

"You *know* why you can't," with those words, almost always spoken menacingly through gritted teeth by my exasperated mom, all talking about jobs would cease.

After the unsuccessful call to my dad, my mother and I had one of our endless fights about me getting a job. The original reason for the sidewalk vending had been that it meant we could control our own time—in other words, it meant that she could come with me or have me come back home if she had a panic attack. But when the business failed and there was clearly no way for us to survive, I began endlessly, mercilessly begging to go out and get a job, knowing every time I brought it up that it had no chance of going over, but hoping against hope that this time she might be convinced. Getting, having or at least just trying for a job became an obsession for me, and it seemed to offer a panacea to all of our impossible problems. Since my mom couldn't really get out of the house without my help, I understood the inherent impossibility of seeking work away from her, but that didn't stop me from bringing it up again and again, until much later, when I finally gave up completely.

We held on in the store for another three weeks until the landlord nicely nudged us for the third month in a row, saying that they really couldn't wait any longer for the rent. They were some of the nicest landlords we ever encountered, even giving us extra time to pay the rent and trying to extend us some credit; when we finally left owing them money, they agreed to "let it go."

The departure from Venice Beach was when our official homelessness began. Of course we'd been homeless before that, but we'd always had some hustle, plan or roof under which to crawl. The last few days at the Street Clothes office/apartment were spent filling our old '70s-model station wagon with everything we owned, wondering where we were going to go, and how. We were down to our last little bit of money and had no way to get any more.

The bulk of the car packing job was left up to me, which was kind of a travesty because I knew nothing about packing and was then, as I am now, "organizationally challenged." Worst of all, I knew nothing about tying knots, so everything was hilariously precarious. A mattress was piled upon clothing, couches made quick friends with lamps, sheets, pillows, silverware, TV, stereo, records, boxes, cat toys, and on and on. An end table sort of rested on the corner rack on the top of the car, a box of papers leaned against another box. By the end of our journey the state of California would be littered with our personal belongings.

With the car completely filled and only a little bit of denial money left to our name, my mom decided we would go out in style and stay at the Shangri-La Hotel in Santa Monica. (I called it denial money because my mom was going to act like it was a lot more than it actually was and deny our impending vehicular housing as long as possible.) The Shangri-La was an odd place, belying its lofty name. The tiny box-like rooms looked as if they'd previously been used as an old-school mental hospital, and there was an eerie background sound like a perpetual scream whistling through the long empty halls.

I experienced my first bitter taste of class discrimination at the Shangri-La.

"Miss, how long are you planning to stay here?" the undertaker-like front desk man would ask us each day. Theoretically, that was none of his business since we were paying him every day before check-out time, but still he would ask, and then suddenly, one week after our arrival he shook his head from side to side in a defiant "no" when I tried to pay him for that night's stay.

"I'm sorry miss, but I can't extend your stay."

"But why?" my breath began to leave my chest.

"We're booked," he wouldn't look at me.

"But you told us the room was available all winter when we checked in."

"Well, I'm sorry," and that was by far the most stiff, hateful "sorry" I had ever heard. Nails on a thousand blackboards would have sounded sweeter than that "sorry."

Later that day as were dragging out our burgeoning Hefty bags containing everything we could carry (we didn't have money for luggage and would try to make the white and black plastic bags look less like trash bags by tying them in elaborate knots at the top) the bellman told us quietly, sadly, and in solidarity that the hotel management had gotten a lot of "comments" about us. "Comments" is code for "trash," "homeless," "bums," et al, and as I thought about it I couldn't understand what would elicit those comments—we didn't smell, our clothes were clean and relatively new, our hair was clean, we were showered. What had condemned us, then?

But it didn't matter, we were homeless, we were two women alone. Our car was old, filled with everything we owned, topped off by a weary, blue king-size mattress perched on its side like a cloth wave in mid-break. We didn't belong to anyone or anything. We paid with cash, we had no credit cards, we owned nothing of value.

That night we drove around, terrified and unsure of where to go and what to do. The traffic lights seemed to change and blend into one long beam of blood red. It was still raining so the streets were wet and glowing, there were almost no other cars on the road so that even the comforting whir of traffic was absent.

"Should we go to San Francisco?"

We drove from strip mall to strip mall, gas station to mini-mart and then back again. From Westwood to Crenshaw, the Valley to Long Beach, San Pedro to Hollywood, never stopping, because if we stopped we would have to turn off the heater and freeze in the cold, wet car with a bed frame sticking in our ears. My mom was talking obsessively about whether to go to the Bay Area or to stay in Los Angeles, "We have friends here, but no money and no hope of any money. I can't get a job here because I can't breathe. On the other hand, we might have money-making options up there, but no friends and no place to live . . . Well, I guess we can always get a place . . . I just don't know what to do . . ."

And then we saw it. The first in a series of signs leading the way to our escape. When all else fails, there are always signs. Or perhaps, there were always signs and that's why everything else failed. My mother had just asked her question for the 60th time, and for some unknown reason we both looked up at the same time, and as we did a giant truck almost sideswiped us into certain death. On its 20'-long side was pasted a giant billboard with the words in large black type: KEEP TRYIN'. And then suddenly, coming right at us from the front, again almost sideswiping us was a Greyhound bus, and in the destination marquis was: SAN FRANCISCO.

We looked at each other, and for a moment nothing, not the undertaker front-deskman, not the cold wet, not even the bed frame in our necks could stop the thick laugh of ridiculousness, art-imitating-tragedy, pure unadulterated silliness that overtook both our souls and enveloped our entire weary beings, and we laughed and laughed for some healing, joyous minutes that felt like hours. Yes, we both said, it could not be denied, we were given the signs, we must go, we must KEEP TRYIN' to go to SAN FRANCISCO. And off we went into the slick moist streets, raising our arms out to clutch the sides of the wavering mattress we began the long journey that would spirit us into new lands, new tragedies and most of all, new possibilities.

CHAPTER 14

seven days and seven nights

I once heard that it took seven days and seven nights to create the world. So maybe my mom and I were really re-creating the world instead of just driving to the Bay Area from Los Angeles, because it did, in fact, take us seven days and seven nights.

It was on this trip that the myth of Dee and Tiny was born in what seemed to be a journey of life-imitating-art-imitating-life, tragedy-becoming-reality-becoming some kind of strange performance art piece. Dee and Tiny, our performance personas had already debuted in Venice Beach, but that trip somehow let us begin to see ourselves as tragic heroines, indomitable superfriends locked in a drama of struggle and triumph. Or maybe it was just a really long and miserable drive.

My mother hated driving, even if she wasn't the actual driver, she just hated being in the car for more than two hours at a stretch. And then, because we really weren't sure of our destination, she would stop to consider each dumb, strip-mall-infested California town along the way as a possible place to reside.

"I wonder what life here would be like," she ventured one day, her spoon wading through a bowl of green mush.

"Where?" I asked, shocked that she could be considering a motel known for its pea soup and pea soup accoutrements as an actual home.

"Here," she answered with a sly smile, pointing up to the giant green spoon and neon portrait of a plump little Dutch man in lederhösen who was ostensibly the proprietor/founder of Pea Soup Anderson, a little pea soup community located in Buellton, a barren freeway off-ramp town in the middle of California.

"I wonder if I could get a job here, or how much the apartments would run," and she went on talking about our possible residence in Pea Soup Anderson Town throughout the night until I fell into a strange, dream-riddled sleep on the dusty shag carpet of a Pea Soup Anderson motel room; we'd rented the cheapest room in the motel, which had only one twin bed, a fake-wood end table, dark brown curtains with double plastic lining, and which happened to be located right under the belly of Mr. Anderson himself.

The next day I awoke to the view of "Mr. P's" midriff peeking out of his lederhosen—I guessed the signmaker wanted to indicate how his tummy was filled with delicious pea soup. As my mother sardonically considered all the benefits of life in Pea Soup, I was noticing that, in fact, there was no actual town surrounding the restaurant, the gift shop and the motel. Where did the people who worked there live? In trailers buried under the ground? Thirty miles away, someplace in the vast stretch of nowhereness that made up the surrounding environment? This kind of extreme small-town weirdness frightened me. I just couldn't get used to the miles and miles of undefined, blank country that made up the middle of California. It seemed unsafe, these unprotected zones where large white men wearing cowboy hats and driving huge trucks could drive up at any moment and decide to do away with you, and worst of all, in towns this quiet, this barren and this small, no one would know it had happened.

Later that day after breakfast, lunch and midday coffee, all in preparation for the "long drive," we finally got back in the car and sped away from all those green legumes.

Two hours later, we were in another town and another

cheap motel, and another mini-mart and then another, and on and on. The odd thing about the entire trip was the fact that the "culture" was so synchronized, each town having the exact same Chevron, Shell or 76 gas station mini-marts, Starbucks, McDonalds, Wendy's, Burger King and so on, with only one or two exceptions. And that kind of capitalist comfort can be addictive, since no matter how sleepy you become on the road, you know there will always be a nearby Coke, some beef jerky or hot tamales around the corner to jar you, if only for a few more minutes, from your road exhaustion. But then it becomes eerie, like a bad horror movie, and you expect some Sissy Spacek look-alike to emerge from the "spotless" Chevron toilets, her blood-soaked prom dress sparkling in the endlessly bright fluorescent gas station light.

We drove on like this for seven days, and then one day we were finally in Berkeley. It was about 5 P.M. and my mom had begun to complain that we'd been driving for too long, and there it was, a green freeway exit sign with a plain, non-descript freeway font, and the re-creation of the world was finally finished. We had arrived.

In the beginning.... Dee and tiny drive from LA to San Francisco taking 7 days and 7 nights because Dee "didn't like to drive" and the dee and tiny station wagon/hooptie "broke down alot"

Ford station wagon weighed down with all of Dee and Tiny's Household and life belongings

No ropes holding things down cause neither Dee nor Tiny could figure out the "knots"

Really ugly green striped cheap 80's couch, stuffed bear picked up along the way, for its performance value

Next >>

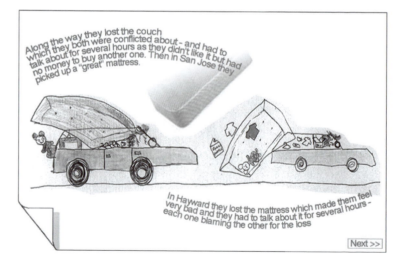

Along the way they lost the couch which they both were conflicted about- and had to talk about for several hours as they didn't like it but had no money to buy another one. Then in San Jose they picked up a "great" mattress.

In Hayward they lost the mattress which made them feel very bad and they had to talk about it for several hours - each one blaming the other for the loss

Next >>

Cartoons by Tiny. Layout by Marissa Kunz

CHAPTER 15

berkeley

Our first year in Berkeley was sheer chaos. We had come to the Bay Area based on my mother's vague memory of those years when she'd posed as a hippie and breathed in the beautiful foggy nights, escaping her foster home reality and believing in another incarnation of herself.

A few decades of cuts to social services and housing had done much to transform the entire Bay Area, and specifically the East Bay. Hippies lounging in public places had been replaced by houseless youth and homeless adults, many of whom were suffering with untreated mental illnesses and/or substance abuse problems. And then there were the cops, so many cops: UC Police, Berkeley police, BART police, AC Transit police, federal police, Vista College police, Housing Authority police—just name the quasi-institution and they would probably boast their own police force, giving parking tickets, issuing Driving While Poor tickets (no registration, broken tail light, sleeping in a vehicle, nuisance, etc.) and generally giving people a hard time whenever they could.

"Hah! *Nobody* can get an apartment in Berkeley."

Soon after our arrival, we were checking out the vending tables on the sidewalks of Telegraph Avenue and talking with a particularly smug old hippie. Scratching his dusty beard after a long, disdainful chuckle, he told us there was a serious housing shortage in Berkeley. It would take us six months or longer to actually find a place, and if we did manage to find a place it would not be, as my mom had idealistically hoped, close to Telegraph Avenue where she wanted to sell her art— not the half-dozen Miguel bear shirts we had squirreled away in the trunk in case of dire emergency, but some truly amazing wearable art that she was producing with found fabrics and medals. It seemed that our only housing option was going to be a room in one of Berkeley's overpriced Single Room Occupancy hotels which, even though run down and filled with old men with soiled beards and semen-stained hands, would still cost us $45-60 a night.

After resigning ourselves to that option, we were told that we couldn't stay in any of those hotels for more than three weeks at a time, since the landlords would kick you out to insure that you wouldn't acquire the dreaded "tenants' rights," which in Berkeley translated into a powerful form of rent control, the hard-won gain of an activist housing rights struggle.

After a week of part-time car dwelling and ongoing cop harassment, we decided to stay in one of the motels that led up to the campus. We ended up in Maylene and Earl's Motel 6.

Maylene and Earl were true-blue, Klan-leaning southern white trash with a bad case of self-loathing, which meant that anyone who looked poor, acted poor or was in fact poor, like me and my mom, were hated on sight. It didn't help that my mom was obviously non-white and also somewhat strange in dress (she was in her punk rock, pink-and-yellow-haired stage at the time), and so she was even more hated, as was I, her mohawk-headed daughter. But notwithstanding all that hate, the room had a refrigerator, and that was something.

Within a few weeks we had used all of our savings, which had been meant for the first and last month's rent and security deposit on the elusive Berkeley apartment, and within a few more weeks we were completely out of *all* cash, and still the

$55 for the room had to be paid, in cash, by noon every day, no matter what.

"The bank has put a hold on our funds, because of a problem with the Swedish account," I cried in the tiny office Maylene shared with the motel's ice machine. I had begun making up a series of excuses to deliver to Maylene each day before I left the motel about why I couldn't pay that day's rent until later in the day, none of which she ever believed.

"Reaaallllly," her tongue rolled out the word to signify her utter disgust for me and my ilk.

"Yeah, ever since we got the Swiss account, it's been nothing but trouble," her disgust made me compound the original lie with more lies, all to acquire the desired one-hour extension to 1 P.M.

At this point Maylene would promise, in her best Alabama drawl, to make good on her threats, "I will change the locks and kick you people out on yer ear." In my grab bag of complex lies and omissions, I always failed to mention that my mom was still in the room.

So at 7 A.M. each morning I would begin the terrifying race to make that day's rent by selling enough shirts on Telegraph Avenue. This was always hard because we had no vendor's license, and without a license the other vendors could turn you in to the vendor police. The notion of unregulated micro-business (the Telegraph Ave. vending model of the '70s, for example) had fallen prey to an extreme level of regulation; there was now a series of bureaucratic hoops that one had to jump through, replete with a one-year (or longer) waiting list to even qualify for a license, not to mention a lengthy screening process to make sure you actually made your product by hand (rather than imported it), a hefty license fee (over $300) and the requisite six-page application.

I would begin setting up the series of galvanized steel and pipe fittings that comprised our clothing display racks at 9 A.M. I chose the not-so-popular part of the avenue, where I hoped the licensed vendors wouldn't want to set up. I'd start early, in the hopes of catching the morning crowd and not being seen while the daily lottery for licensed spaces was conducted.

Sad hour after sad and hungry hour would pass, with nary an inquiry into all of our very avant garde products, such as elaborately hand-dyed, hand-painted dress shirts and jackets. Suffice to say, we finally didn't get Maylene her money one day, and after a few short weeks we were back in our car again.

"Knock, knock, knock!" A flashlight banging on your car window always sounds the same, hollow and dense at the same time, and just shy of causing your window to shatter. "Miss, you need to move or you will be towed."

There is absolutely nothing romantic about sleeping in your car. The whole experience, in perhaps anywhere but the tropics, can be summed up in three single-syllable words: cold, cold and cold. In fact, the whole experience of outsideness, whether it be on the sidewalk, in your car, on a bench or in an alcove, is always about struggling with an unending, powerfully insidious form of cold.

Blankets on top of Goodwill-purchased blankets were piled on our already overdressed bodies, crunched behind a protruding steering wheel, gear stick and dashboard, and still, minute corners of inexplicably exposed skin would catch the icy drifts of air from the black California nights. And even if you did get a moment of mock warmth, on any given night the police were sure to show up and threaten you with a citation, towing or arrest.

In retrospect, the cops that "tapped" on our window and asked us to move were nicer than the parking and traffic officers who roamed the streets at all hours of the day and night in the Bay Area, slapping our windshield with those foreboding pieces of paper that foretold a future of court dates, fines and stress.

And so the first wave of tickets began to hit. Coming from L.A. where the police harassment is more focused on out-of-car experiences, it wasn't clear to us at the time that we must do something about the pile-up of citations, so they kept coming and we kept driving.

Week after week of homelessness and postmodern art-making passed. Our refusal to change our product had nothing to do with pride, just ignorance of, as a business person would call it, "the market." Unfortunately, the average allowance-driven student would not spend $50 for a hand-dyed pair of jeans that my mother had painstakingly created, no matter how cool they were.

In the end, just to get some money for food, we began to drastically reduce our prices and scale down the "artifice" in our products. In other words, within a month we were making and selling what any true artist could only describe as schlock. I, being a truly starving artist, described it as survival by any art necessary. From our desperate hands came jackets and dress shirts strewn with paint à la Jackson Pollock, t-shirts and sweat-shirts, hand-painted and silkscreened with any number of popular cartoon icons from Warner Brothers to Disney: you name it, we painted it on any wearable surface I was able to get my ink-stained hands on.

In the first few days of this hunger-inspired "artmaking," all of which was being painted, dyed and silkscreened surreptitiously in the early morning or late at night on the streets, in alleys, in abandoned lots and on the sidewalks in different neighborhoods in Berkeley and Oakland, we actually took in at least $50 a day or more, landing us back in another motel.

Once in a motel, any motel, the best days of our vending would ensue, and the "production workshop" moved indoors, at least most of the time. A minute motel closet would become a mini-art studio, and our move from motel to motel had to be done at night, since no one could know that we had turned their off-white, needle-strewn closets into a Jackson Pollock masterpiece.

Cartoon by Tiny. Layout by Marissa Kunz

CHAPTER 16

the hustle

"Wow, that looks so great on you! I think it's because of the shade of white, it's sooo . . . ice-like in contrast with your dark hair."

"That is such an amazing fit! Just in terms of the 'butt-fit' alone, it's a keeper!"

"Every shirt is hand-painted and hand-dyed. Each one is truly a work of art!"

The übersaleswoman/street hustler in me was born out of desperation for food and shelter. I found I could convince almost anyone to buy anything, well, at least a $15 t-shirt, and I would say so much bullshit just to make that happen that I would surprise even myself. As the money flowed in where there was absolutely none before, I began to feel that anything was possible and that all my dreams of food, shelter and new underwear were realities just waiting to happen.

The process of making money all on your own when you're very poor and very young is a heady one. Success, no matter how small, feeds directly into your ego, not to mention your pocket, and once you make that $20, $50 or $100 you feel large, if only for that night. You buy blueberries at a whopping $4.99 a pint, you eat out and blow $20 without thinking twice, you even fill your gas tank or buy a whole week's worth of groceries. But the next day you wake up like an alcoholic after a binge, left with the almost-emptied pocket, with barely enough to pay that day's room rent, or worse, not even enough to buy that morning's coffee, and I would scramble back to the scene of the hustle to nervously re-create my pseudosuccess of the previous day.

And so on it went, day after day, month after month, with me and my hustle in full-time residence on Telegraph Avenue, trying in vain to become homeful, to get out of the motels, to buy lunch.

The students would pour from the mouth of the University in rushes of 50-100 at a time, filled with thoughts of critical theory, political analysis, science, language, art. My hungry eyes would scope out the possible targets and my mouth would begin the onslaught of words, sure to convince the overwhelmed student with a few surplus dollars to part with their tens and twenties. At first the rush of some money, any money, filled my mind, helping me to forget my own desire to learn, to read, to think about something other than food and shelter. But after what seemed like an eternity of standing on a corner selling a product I couldn't stand to people that I wanted so badly to be, it began to tear me up.

I was sixteen years old. We had been in Berkeley for two years, and as I hawked my wares seven days a week, twelve hours a day, with no end in sight, pandering to the masses of what seemed like carefree college students, a feeling of powerlessness and hopelessness was growing inside me. And along with the hopelessness came another feeling: a covetousness of the seemingly uncomplicated lives of the students who passed me daily increased to the point that I began to imagine perpetrating large-scale violence against the entire student body. My role in the massacre was never completely fleshed out in my mind, but the shadowy deaths of many students were accomplished without any blood, just a lot of screams and mayhem. Fortunately for the UC Berkeley students, those kind of tableaus take a lot of energy and the privilege of time, money and/or organization to plan and carry out, and since I could barely get enough t-shirts bought, painted and sold, not to mention washing my own clothes and my mother's, as well as every other chore and life hassle that had to be completed just to get through each day, they were safe.

In lieu of sniper scenarios, I manifested a smaller form of terror: love. Or better yet, a particular form of love, unrequited and with intentional pain meted out to the other party. I guess I thought that if I could control the mind and body of at least one privileged student with an otherwise uncomplicated life, maybe I could get some kind of revenge.

He was tall, very tall, with a paintbrush of chocolate brown hair that perpetually fell in his eyes. He walked fast, not intentionally so, but because his legs were so long he couldn't help but cover a lot of distance quickly. He smiled like someone or something I'd been charmed by before, and it would transform his face, which otherwise seemed stuck in a paralyzing smirk.

"How much are these stupid coats?" he would ask with a chuckle. "You don't really like these, do you?" another chuckle, and then the smirk would settle in.

He was the perfect target for my nonviolent takeover. He was a womanizer of the L.A. variety. Like me, he was the child of a wealthy doctor from Palos Verdes, the expensive town my father had started his private practice in, but unlike me, he had been raised there his whole life.

Within a few short weeks I began an illicit relationship with him. I snuck out of my house and visited him at 6 A.M., before my mom would find out I was gone. Months passed and we would only share furtive glances in public. My rules were simple: no sex, no kissing, no dates, no calls. And yet, despite my cool exterior, I fell in love. A deep, strange, painful love that was really just a direly needed escape from all of the hassle of my complex life.

On our last night together, a yellow-orange sun quietly colored the sky. It was a rare moment of late afternoon freedom, baked in a thick August heat—I had snuck away from work w minutes to visit with him. He was leaving the next ı "trip to Europe, and possibly India, I've always wanted ɔ India, it's so beautiful." His trip was to be the kind of exploration into third world and fourth world poverty that wealthy white kids like him were prone to do when they reached a certain age. He was twenty-two years old and done with school. I knew as I stood there, my head buried deep in his wool prep-gone-bad sweater, that he and I were over.

At that hour his house was full of roommates, cigarette smoke and dirty clothes, so in search of a moment of privacy I pulled him out of the house to the closest bit of nature, the median strip lodged awkwardly in the middle of the tiny street in front of his rented house. When we reached the slice of grass, my mind transported us to a vast meadow in the High Sierra: I couldn't see the BART parking lot to our immediate left, spewing out rush-hour cars by the hundreds; I couldn't hear the trains honking and spitting their arrival directly underground; I could only see his dark hair as it fell into my hot face, feel his long fingers as they caressed my tear-stained cheeks. All I heard was the sound of his pounding heart against mine, as he whispered a too slow goodbye.

My mother, meanwhile, was alternately waging the battle to create unappreciated textile art while also trying in vain to find the elusive free psychotherapy to fight the ongoing battle against hopelessness and depression. After all that time, there we still were, unable to save the money needed to get into an apartment, which we continued to search for anyway in the random available moments stolen from our incredibly long workdays, which included silkscreening and hand painting 20-50 shirts a night after the day's vending was through. Even with our nonstop labor we couldn't ever seem to earn much beyond each day's room rent, and on bad (no sale) days not even that, which meant we were in and out of our car, the police harassment increasing.

The beginning of most days spent "outside" were marked with fluttering citations tucked under our broken windshield wiper, scribbled with the badge numbers of various police officers and parking and traffic agents. These tickets, filled with assignments of court dates, fines and section numbers that coincided with multiple violations, bench warrants and unconsidered consequences joined a dashboard already stuffed with bills and classified ads, and at some unknown point they would land on the soiled floor of our over-filled station wagon, to be looked at when time permitted and crises ebbed.

One morning I awoke to a note from my mother, still prone to making her daily lists: TAKE CARE OF THE TICKETS!! with an extra-bold line under the words TAKE CARE and TICKETS. At this point I had several thousand dollars worth of tickets in my name—six months earlier we had registered the car in my name because my mom had tickets in her name, and you can't get a car registered unless you pay any out-standing tickets.

So off I went to Alameda County Courthouse. After waiting in a line winding out the front door and then sitting in court for several more hours, I finally stood in front of a rather bored-looking judge. I explained that I had no money to pay the tickets and requested community service or very small pay-ments, but the judge replied that he wasn't giving out commu-nity service except in special cases because they had closed the Alameda County volunteer center due to funding cuts. I pleaded for small payments of $20 per month, but the judge said at that rate it would take far too long to pay off the debt. Finally, he reduced the fine from $2,800 to $2,700 and gave me six months to pay.

Dee and Tiny's first storefront (and living space) in Oakland.

Dee directs Tiny and Model X in the "Art of Homelessness," a fashion performance with wearable art by Dee and choreography by Dee and Tiny.

CHAPTER 17

the "apartment"

In the midst of chaos and overwhelming poverty, the art-making continued. My mother begged, cajoled, made promises and eventually wrote bad checks in order to attend classes for a single semester at a small, private art school in Berkeley that specialized in fiber art. In her short tenure there she developed a large body of works of wearable and non-wearable clothing that were really kinetic sculptures. Every piece was a collaborative production between the two of us: she would create the physical manifestation of the art, and I would develop the story or myth that would accompany it in the form of audio, video or live performance.

One day as we were scouring the neighborhoods of Berkeley and Oakland in our daily search for apartments, my mother noticed a FOR RENT sign on a narrow storefront lodged under a carport attached to a five-story apartment building in Oakland. The window looked as if it had just been installed, and the structure behind the window appeared as if someone had simply added on walls to part of the carport. The whole combination was so small and so makeshift that we guessed it would be very cheap. We were right. A hastily printed sign in a barely readable red felt pen stated the price: $350 per month.

"Hello, I am Billy Jaffe," his black moustache glistened in

the morning sunlight. "You are interested in the store. What is it that you do, exactly?"

"Oh, well, we manufacture clothing, I mean, we actually design and manufacture," there went my mouth again, moving autonomously from my brain. "Oh yes, we have many clothing lines and we sell them to individuals, but they also sell in stores all over the country."

"Oh really. Are you able to make a profit?"

"Oh yes, a large profit!"

"You understand there is no living allowed in this unit, it's really just a storage space."

"Yes of course; we're only interested in the storefront."

"Well, I need you to fill out this application, and if your credit passes, then it's yours."

"Okay," I grabbed the paper and began writing. Inventing lives, identities, names and numbers as fast as I could write. If I didn't think about it too long, I could come up with plenty of creative and believable combinations of real and fake, misspellings with mis-statements. I had given up a long time ago actually telling the truth on rental applications, my real identity having been lost in the eviction wars of Venice Beach.

"Here," I handed it back to him.

"Okay, we'll run it tonight and I'll call you tomorrow," with that, he clicked his briefcase closed with an especially sharp snap.

I knew the drill, after all, I was Rent Starter, but for some reason this felt different. I was so afraid. He couldn't say no: this was literally the only affordable place we had found after two years of searching; it would bring all our dreams to truth; we could create installations in the window; it wasn't so far from Berkeley, in fact, it was *on* Telegraph (just the Oakland version). But more than anything else, I felt that I couldn't live through another night in our car.

I had been dreaming of suicide every night as I tried to capture some sliver of warmth that might exist somewhere under the car seat. I would imagine the kind of gun I would use, how it would feel in my hands and the relief it would give me. The horror of our impossible situation was like Santa Monica all over again, and each ticket, each secret shower, the endless night shivers and non-stop parking struggles, were silently killing my spirit.

The next morning I was on a pay phone first thing, calling in to my $10-a-month voice mail, one of several numbers I had acquired in order to appear as though my mother and I had a home, and I a full-time job at a reputable business.

"Ms. Graham, you can have the place if you want it."

I heard those words as if they were the announcement of an Academy Award nomination or the winning numbers of a Lotto jackpot.

"Yeeeeeeaaaassssssss!" I screamed. My head filled with the vision of a heater and a mattress and a refrigerator filled with unspoiled milk and meat.

I ran to my mom to tell her the news, and we both raced to the bank to turn our crumpled 5, 10 and 20 dollar bills into a clean, organized cashier's check for a whopping $700.00, this being the total cost of move-in fees to our new dream house—or rather, our dream carport-turned-storefront-turned illegal living space.

Within weeks of moving in we had installed the first Northern California Street Clothes store in the tiny front room. The whole place was less than a 100 square feet, and the rest of the space acted as our post-homeless, haphazard living area. My mother immediately claimed the largest floor space for her queen-size mattress. No matter how poor we were, my mother always managed to acquire a brand new, firm mattress; creditors acting on behalf of mattress stores still plague me to this day.

It was in the Jaffes' place, the first after such a long stretch in the depths of homelessness, that I began my permanent residence in the closet—from then on, no matter the size of any of our apartments, I was always assured the closet. It was an adaptation of necessity, since most of the places we got were too small to afford me the luxury of a separate room, but in the end, it was the safest and most secure container for my severe disorganization. As I later put it, "I was organizationally challenged."

I never developed deep attachments to any of my belongings; I was just unable to arrange or contain the things I was able to hold on to. Between the serial evictions and constant moves, nary a stuffed animal or childhood picture remained in my possession. Throughout the life of a homeless child, you lose everything; it's like going through a fire or a hurricane every day, and the little things that really matter like baby pictures, school yearbooks and letters from important people all drift away like water from a shore.

I don't know how much of my crazy life created my organizational disorder, but contrary to popular belief, homelessness and poverty have no inherent connection with disorganization. One of the many myths associated with poor folk is the idea that they are "messy," "dirty" or "lazy," but the truth is that some of the most organized people I know are living and working on the street. Imagine fitting the entire contents of your apartment, car, and/or office into a shopping cart, a cardboard box or a Hefty bag.

As it turned out, the Jaffes' warning about not living in the unit was meaningless. For the first few weeks we snuck in and out of the place late at night and early in the morning, fearing that our "living in" status would be cause for eviction, but eventually we realized that the only thing that the Jaffe family cared about was money, how to get it, and how not to spend it.

"When are you going to fix this sink?!!!" my mother began screaming at the Jaffes almost from day one about a running list of serious problems. "This is our thirteenth call about the broken window. Why aren't you answering us?"

"No one else ever had a problem with the sink."

Despite my mother's onslaught of letters, followed by very contentious calls, the Jaffes were from the landlord school that believed the tenant was always wrong, answering every complaint with a vague accusation of our own wrongdoing. They refused to deal with any of our calls or letters about faulty plumbing, broken appliances or bug infestation, and as it turned out the entire unit was so hastily thrown together that within weeks of our tenancy it began to fall apart. The tile in the bathroom curled into a perfect vinyl wave, the windows cracked and shattered when we opened them, and the ants and roaches didn't stop marching in once they caught a whiff of us.

Our Northern California eviction wars were unwittingly launched with the Jaffes. They continued to refuse to make any of the increasingly serious repairs, but they still expected their rent on time, which we paid by any means necessary. The final blow came when they decided that they wanted even more rent for that tiny, messed-up place, and as our un-luck would have it, the rent increase coincided with yet another impossible poverty crisis.

Crisis has a way of hitting you right when you most can't handle it, which with poor folks is all the time. It wasn't the rain this time, it was the car. After our third month in the Jaffes' the transmission on our old car completely stopped shifting into drive, and on a gray, wind-filled day in January we coasted it gingerly to a mechanic down the street and left for a few hours, hoping for the best.

Later that day when we went to pick it up, a man wearing a blackened uniform with a name-tag on his chest that said "John" looked up from the underbelly of a shiny gray Toyota and said wearily, "It's not worth it."

My heart and stomach filled with acid and dread at the same time. "What's not worth it?" I asked.

"Fixing your car wouldn't be worth it. You should buy a new one."

"But we don't have the money for a new car."

"Well, I don't know what to tell you, because you probably don't have the money to fix this one then, either."

"Can you please just tell me how much it's gonna be to fix our car?"

For dramatic effect, John didn't answer me, instead he gave me a disgusted smirk and loped over to an oil-stained desk in the corner of the auto shop. He shuffled around in one of the piles and pulled out my estimate, handed it to me and continued to shuffle through the pile in search of something else.

Scribbled breakdowns of multiple numbers filled the page. On the bottom in the right hand corner was the most terrifying combination of numbers: $900.00 This was everything we didn't have and then some—a month's worth of food, rent and utilities combined.

The poor people's dilemma discourse ensued. My mother and I went around and around, desperate to find a solution where there was none.

"We could get another car," I would plead.

"With what? A semi-decent car would cost at least $1000, and then it would still be a used car, meaning you're inheriting someone else's problems, and who knows how much it would cost to fix those problems?"

"Maybe we could get rid of the car."

"Then how would we transport the shirts?"

"But if we pay for the car to be fixed, then we won't have any money to pay rent . . . or anything else . . ."

And so it went, the end of all of our money and barely tasted stability, and the specter of no shelter, not even a car, looming.

We did fix the car with what little money we made that month, but the vicious cycle was now in full swing. After the car broke down I got sick and missed an entire week of vending, so we lost that income. We had to spend almost $100 on antibiotics, and that $100 was supposed to go toward our very overdue utilities bill, and so on it went, crisis building upon crisis.

CHAPTER 18

pacific gas & electric

I was so cold. The February wind whipped up and circled through what felt like invisible holes in my pants. It was dark and I could barely see the phone I was holding. The chill was starting to get to me. I was standing in my closet.

It had been twenty-four days since the PG&E worker had lumbered into the communal mailbox room of our building carrying a large Orwellian time-clock device, asking everyone in a very loud voice "Where is Unit #1? I'm here to turn off the utilities for nonpayment."

I considered pretending not to be there. Perhaps that would delay the inevitable. But instead I chose a direct plea. I ran out of the storefront and into the mail room, motioning to him furtively, trying not to look at the crowd of tenants that had gathered.

Before I could say anything, he called across the room to me in an over-loud baritone, "So, Miss Garcia, are you prepared to pay your bill or should I proceed with the shut-off?"

"But we asked for a five-day extension. I've been very sick. And we have to use all of our money for the rent. We can't be without heat—aren't you a public utility?"

His eyes stared down at me, then closed once before coming to rest at half-mast. His face settled into a fixed gaze befitting his Master of Heat and Lord of Electricity status and he stated loudly, "We are a business, Miss Garcia, not a social service."

Twenty-four days of no service passed, and now the suffocating odor of rotting dairy products from our fridge permeated the air of our dark, cold mini apartment as I stood there with the phone on hold. Thirteen calls to service agencies had elicited only a constant refrain, "We have no more funding for utilities."

"But we have no heat," I would yell.

"I'm sorry."

"Name?" a voice sliced through my dark silence, resonant, disgusted.

"Oh, ah, Lisa Garcia," I answered.

"Age?" barked at me. I had taken too long with the first answer.

"Amount of last bill?" any traces of human kindness had long ago been erased from her voice.

"Income?" I scrambled to answer in the five seconds this woman was giving for replies.

If you didn't answer everything correctly, based on the county needs sheet, you were not helped—no PG&E, no nothing. But I was getting really tired. I was still not well and I didn't have the energy to think of all the right answers.

"We'll call you in two or three days." Click. It was over.

Had I made an information misstep? The fear lingered. I fumbled in the dark to hang up the phone.

Five days later a call came in. "Be at 1238 San Pablo, Golden Gate Rec Center, 10 A.M. *sharp.* Be on time."

"But I have to take my mother to the doctor. Is there another time?" I asked. A long pause—too long.

"That's your only option." Click.

I arrived at 9:55 A.M. to a tiny, abandoned school building located on a cul-de-sac in Oakland. There were dark, resolute shadows lurking in all the corners and an icy wind whipping around the concrete walls. At the front was a large gate where several people stood, trying to stay warm. I listened as they talked.

"The water's leaking all over the floor. I kept it going with several extension cords out to the hall, but then the landlord didn't pay the electric for the building, so now no more fridge," the woman closest to me said. She punched out each sentence in a thick Hawaiian pidgin. Her face was a study in pleats, each brown fold waiting for the smile that would break them free.

"Oh, we haven't had it on for about thirty days," another woman said. "But then my babies started to get sick, ya know, the cold and all." She had slanted, honey-colored eyes and tight, fine curls. She spoke between asthmatic breaths as she looked down at two very small children. The boy's face had an ashen film that clouded his light brown skin—his left eye was red and didn't stop dripping, and he held his head with his small hand. The little girl by his side said nothing. She seemed unable to get a deep breath, and her soiled pink parka was zipped all the way up.

"It really gets cold at night," the woman whispered. Then there was a silence. "But I didn't have money for the rent *and* the utilities," she continued. We all nodded violent yesses. "I'd figured I'd let them be off for a while—until I caught up. I worked ten days at the market as a relief worker last month, that's how I get my food for my babies, but then the Salvation Army disqualified me for making an income, so I have to lie or not work at all 'cause what I make isn't enough to pay the utilities." Everyone fell silent again.

Minutes inched by, and then it was 11:30 A.M., and fewer and fewer jokes could be manufactured about the good ol' days when you had your PG&E and could have parties, entertaining your guests with the wonder of dinners and refrigerated beer. After twenty minutes I took my shivering body to a patch of sun out in the yard. I was followed by a man who was screaming to himself, "You just missed me asshole Gemini—

two days ago—your fault they put the cream on lemon pies—your fault—I'm alive—you Aries asshole—I know how many miles to the sun—right, asshole, they're all Aries in Oakland."

At 12:40 P.M., a small Oakland city government car pulled up, and rather like a bite-sized Mafia they got out all at once: four women of basically the same size, wearing a similar amount of make-up, and all with variations on the same hairstyle.

They came with the power to take us out of our collective misery by bringing us one small step closer to attaining normal human needs. Our hearts started to beat, our stomachs to churn—would we have heat? We were all collectively afraid, weakened by the struggle to tell the overlords of aid exactly the right answers. We stumbled inside, carefully selecting small, wooden chairs.

"That woman in the gray dress—she's the bitch," my Hawaiian friend was mumbling loudly. "With that dress—a real bitch."

The women were motioning for us to be silent. "You're here today to apply for help from the energy program of Alameda County," one of them announced. "We want you to understand that you only get help from us once a year. It doesn't matter if your lights get turned off—don't call us. We get funding once a year, and we have received an order to give special help to those of you who haven't received help from us before."

As she talked, I thought about what I'd learned in the course of my phone calls to various agencies: Over 5,000 people per year in Oakland seek aid to pay utilities; the program, however, helps only 1,500 clients. The majority are families with children, and senior citizens.

Meanwhile, the woman was still talking. "We can't promise you'll receive help, but the fact that you've been called here today is a good sign. You should know that PG&E is tracing social security numbers, so if you've had any unpaid bills in the last ten years they can find you and will shut off your current service until you've paid the unpaid balance. Also, if you call us and only get a busy signal, that's because we don't have staff to answer the phones. Alameda County has cut 50 percent of our funding."

With that last statement, she stopped speaking. We all waited. Somehow, the clock crawled toward 3:00 P.M. I decided it was a good sign that the worker who called on me had the best hairdo—a crest of gray flowing into billowing waves of varying shades. She checked all my information and granted me preliminary aid that would cover our past-due bill at the Jaffes and at least the next thirty days of utilities.

I went back to my seat to await my final evaluation. A new woman had joined our group. Her face was pulled tightly across oversized, dark yellow teeth that she showed often. "I used to weigh 240 pounds," she said with a laugh. Her jeans were draped over skinny thighs. "But it's sorta funny 'cause when I met my boyfriend he weighed 100 pounds and now he weighs 240, and I weigh 90." She pulled at her nails as she spoke, revealing with a series of innuendoes the extent of her crack addiction.

At this point the Hawaiian woman cut in, "Yah, I know that crack pipe is smooth. I tried once, but no more. But my man, he's on it, girl. If I didn't hide all the money he'd have us on the street. But I make sure the rent is paid. Any extra, I spend on food. He can get off himself—no help from me."

Right then, as I was sitting in that rec room with all these women, thinking about all the depressing things we had to do to as poor people just to get a meal, to secure housing, get a shelter bed or pay for utilities, I began to understand the lure of substance abuse, no matter how destructive, as the ultimate numbing distraction to a horrific reality.

I was eventually granted the compensation, dispensed along with a warning not to come back. My Hawaiian friend was not given aid—she had received help one other time in the last twelve months. She walked out mumbling, "I had to get that bitch." The woman with two children got only partial aid because she admitted to the crime of working ten days that month, which put her income above the allowable level. The lady with the crack addiction gave up in the application process because she had to have proof of income, which she was afraid to retrieve because it was in the apartment of her abusive ex-husband. Those of us who had "won" smiled conspiratorially at each other and caressed our yellow aid receipts. As I walked out the oversized doors into the windy shadows that filled the long hallways, I was a little lighter in my step. A problem was actually solved.

Outside the steel gates of the building, the little boy and girl stood with their mother—the boy was wheezing, his eyes a hollow stare. The mother looked up at me, almost embarrassed, as she attempted to find a hidden button on his coat. "I haven't been able to afford his asthma inhaler," she whispered to me. "Now it's the PG&E or his medicine. I have to pay the past-due before they'll help me out here."

CHAPTER 19

three-day notice

My victory was short-lived. Our utilities were covered but we had no money left at all, not even for soap or toilet paper, much less food, so we began writing bad checks to Walgreens, Safeway and Longs Drugs just to get the basics. We promised ourselves that as soon as we started selling stuff again we would make good on all the checks.

And then one short week after the PG&E struggle I woke up to a gentle flapping noise coming from the front glass window of the store. THREE DAYS TO PAY RENT OR QUIT. The letters were large and black and ran in a straight line across the top of the fluttering paper attached with extra-wide masking tape.

I leaned my upper body out of the door only long enough to snatch the paper. As I read the words, small painful tremors ran through my body. I should have been used to it, but you never stop being terrified of homelessness. Never. No matter how many times you live through the receipt of those words, the feeling of overwhelming fear of the instability that ensues hits you as new, fresh and more insurmountable each time.

In the Jaffes' place we'd mistakenly thought we had a chance for stability, but the final blow to our homefulness was dealt to us by their unjustified rent increase. On the first day of that last month the Jaffes returned the rent payment that we'd barely scraped together and gave us the notice for a $100 rent increase, effective immediately. They had threatened us with that increase the month before, and we had responded with a certified letter and made several phone calls asking for a reconsideration, or at the very least that they only assess the increase after they'd dealt with the flagrant habitability issues.

But we got no reply. The Jaffes were the type of landlord who believed that the fact that they owned the property and you did not meant that you had no rights. Issues of legality, habitability, accountability, ethics and/or professionalism ceased when it came to tenants. So, after they had the three-day notice posted on our front window, our car and in the communal mail box room, they counted down the three days and on the third day they were waiting for us outside our front door with their arms crossed.

"Where are your moving boxes?"

When I tried to leave that morning to go to work they were all there waiting for me: Billy Jaffe, the adult son, property manager and all-purpose henchman, Mr. Jaffe, father and owner, and Mrs. Jaffe, the mother and real money behind the whole operation. I tried to push past them, but they stopped me with more questions. Finally, I managed to get by them and as I strode away with whatever front of pride and defiance I could muster, they yelled after me, "You're supposed to be out of here today, so I hope you're packing."

That day passed, and then another, and then another, and they were completely baffled about what we were doing. We simply refused to go. They tried to call the police several times, but the police kept telling them that it wasn't a criminal matter; it was a civil matter and they needed to get a lawyer. I guess they finally heeded that advice and did the unthinkable, spending money to hire an attorney. I'm sure that the cost for the attorney's retainer was what caused them to wait as long as they did, and it bought my mother and me just a little more time.

CHAPTER 20

one court date away from homelessness

10:00 A.M. Municipal Court, Department C, Eviction Day. I was one court date away from homelessness.

The oddly bright fluorescent bulbs clashed with the deep cherry wood paneling. It was a Perry Mason courtroom with Safeway lighting.

Suits in various shades of muted gray and brown paced in and out of my courtroom, walking briskly through the swinging doors with the Keep Out sign that separated tenants and other civil criminals from the officers of the court. These were the attorneys—almost exclusively landlords' attorneys—and periodically they would call out a name. Finally, a man in a gray, slightly wrinkled suit barked out my name. The hand that clutched his bulging briefcase shook lightly. I got up slowly, turning to follow him outside.

"Miss Garcia, we have a settlement offer for you," he started in right away. He didn't look at me, focusing instead on a spot somewhere behind me. I paused for a second, naively hopeful that maybe he really was offering me an actual settlement, but then I remembered what this well-known "eviction specialist" (as his business card read) had "offered" to the other 22 cases in the files held in his swollen briefcase. This "settlement offer" was just a part of the eviction process masquerading in court-speak that really meant: save my client some money and move out.

I tried to explain my situation to this man: how we had deposits on file that weren't mentioned in their court papers, and how none of our documented inhabitability claims were included, along with the fact that there was still no working heater or refrigerator.

"What!?" he shouted. His eyes began to dart wildly. "Do you have the rent?" he glared down at me. I proffered another shortened explanation and a counteroffer, such as a retroactive rent reduction for the months with no repairs.

He cut in loudly, "I'll ask you once more: Do you have the rent?" He spit slightly with this last demand/command.

"I do, but I don't want to pay an increase until the apartment is habitable," I pleaded.

"Well, I just don't have time for this anymore," he got up from our bench and marched back into the courtroom.

I should not be scared, I chanted, this man cannot hurt me. But I knew that indeed he could, as he whisked back to the judge's chambers in a conspiratorial conference. He would brand me as a defrauder, a liar, a cheat, and worst of all, a tenant — the most disempowered, unimportant member of this court system, usually unrepresented or at best under-represented for lack of funds. This man held my homefulness in the balance, and he had just checked the box on his form, "Won't Settle."

"All rise." The judge entered. We recited the oath and then he began, "Marcus vs. Malone. Please approach the bench."

Marcus was an older African American woman who had been sitting next to me. She had looked straight ahead while the same attorney presented a signed "Settlement Offer" to the judge. Apparently it was a habitability case, and this woman had been shuttled outside the courtroom before me by that same lawyer. After a couple of officious shuffles of his papers, and with the utmost legal brevity, he'd "convinced" her of the advantages of leaving the home she had lived in for the last twenty years, rather than proceeding with a court trial and facing the danger of losing the case. If she had protested, it would have cost his client, the landlord, another $375 in court appearances, but he did not mention that to her. She acquiesced, since she had no counsel and no money for an attorney, and therefore not much choice. She quietly approached the bench, her head slightly bowed.

"Do you understand what you signed, Ms. Marcus?" the judge proffered.

Her eyes darted up, "Well, not really. I'm not sure if the leaking water in my apartment, that ruined all of my furniture is a solid case to take to trial."

"Ms. Marcus, that sounds like a legal question, and I cannot answer a legal question. You need to consult with an attorney for that information."

"But I don't have an attorney."

"Well, then what do you want to do?"

"Maybe I could get a continuance."

"I don't think so. I don't grant those on eviction cases. Counsel, is this for possession?"

"Yes, yes, your honor, and there really are no more possible disclosures in this case. A continuance would be a waste of the court's time," the lawyer said in a carefully modulated tone.

With each of the overly enunciated words, Ms. Marcus's head dropped a little bit lower. Shortly, the gavel was down. The settlement had been reached. She was out.

"Lincoln vs. Housing Authority," the judge called the next case. A family of three, headed by one very young woman, approached the bench. It was a housing authority issue. This young mother had been late on rent three months in a row, and for the last two had only made partial payments. After some lengthy paper shuffling by a very disinterested housing authority official, the judge requested a recess for deliberation. Some of us walked outside.

"Do you have any matches?" a short, pre-owned cigarette wavered in her small fingers.

"Uh, no, sorry." It was her, the young mother. What could I say? I focused on the fuchsia sheen from her nylon running pants.

"Rent's a bitch," she murmured. "They gonna put me and my babies on the street. Why? 'Cause of rent. I won't be able to get another place. This whole thing really messed us up." Her eyes began to shine with an anxious glaze, "Sometimes it's jus' too hard to be dealin' with all these problems . . ."

"I know how it is . . ."

"I already called all my family. No one's got any room," she continued. "I even called about the shelters—they're all filled."

"It all comes down to energy, honey," a bright pink, pencil-like finger clutched at a new cigarette addition to our group. She wheezed out the rest of her monologue, "After you deal with all of life's regular problems, there's no energy left to deal with these kinds of problems—so you end up on the street."

I thought about energy, about how if I'd had just a little bit more, maybe I could have researched just one more option. Court noises drifted past my ears as I recalled the process I'd gone through to get advocacy in the thirty days leading up to this court date.

Third appointment, 14th phone call: Legal Aid

It was a gray stone building with a walkway that edged you around its corner with a small, oft-replaced paper arrow: "Legal Aid," it said. I walked through doors made of beveled glass, the kind a detective would have had in *The Maltese Falcon*. The elevator was paneled in aging pine, the buttons for each floor worn down with years of use. The fourth floor was awash in dusty sunlight.

After a short wait I was directed to room 404. As I inched down the hall, droplets of sweat crept down my spine, invading the soft, dry cotton of my new underwear. There were no obvious signs of the law; one might have mistaken this for an accountant's office. A man who appeared not much older than me sat at a very big desk in the middle of the room. As I entered he didn't look all the way up, just a partial upswing of his eyes and head. After gulp-coughing I started right in, having rehearsed my brief introduction nine or ten times in the waiting room so as not to waste any of my allotted six-minute appointment.

"Well, my problem is complex, but I'll try to give you a brief intro—"

"Do you have your papers?" he sliced through my tense wheeze of words.

"Huh?"

"Can I see your papers?"

"Yes, but they make no sense without the—"

"I need to see your papers," a weary edge entered his voice with this last command, again without looking up.

After a minute or two of humiliating paper shuffling, I handed him the skewed, one-sided paperwork, mostly documents prepared and constructed by the attorneys for the plaintiff, the landlord.

He hummed and sighed as he read, accompanied by a side-to-side shaking of his head, and then I saw it: a click of the eyes, a particularly long open and shut of the lids, and I knew I had lost him forever. He had discovered a definitive legal reason why he couldn't help me. He let me go on with my superfluous explanations, but we both knew the "I can't help you" was just a matter of a few more seconds.

"Why didn't you come here sooner? Not that I could have helped you, but you would have had a few more options."

"Because I didn't know about your program. I was told by all the referral agencies that I could only go to the clinics, not receive actual representation."

"Well, I'm sorry," his eyes had flicked briefly in my direction, but were now comfortably locked into an intense study of his doorknob. "But there's really nothing we can do. For whatever reason, you waited too long before you came to us, and essentially they are asking for possession to be granted, which, in an eviction process, the landlord always gets."

"But I have the rent money, and this would be an extreme hardship for us."

"Unfortunately, that's not enough. I really can't represent you because there's no chance you could win; therefore, it's not a justifiable expenditure of our time."

I climbed out of my chair, unable to say an even pseudo-pleasant goodbye, and tumbled outside. I watched the masses pass me, certain that each of their twinkling laughs was unfettered by the imminent danger of homelessness. I had never felt so desperately sad. My bones ached with the overwhelming impossibility of it all. Dry tears welled in the corners of my eyes, large gulps of unused air stalled in my chest. I could not explain this sadness to the apartment dwellers who surrounded me. They had no idea of the precious comforts they took for granted: to be able to know your kitchen sink, to look at it comfortably and know it will always be yours; to sit on your back step and contemplate your yard; to look calmly upon your front door with no danger of not seeing it again; to lavish in insideness, your walls, your light fixtures, your toilet paper holder.

Fourth appointment, 25th call: A pro bono attorney visit

Glass, so much glass. Tinted, solarized, sparkling expanses begging a light caress from the clouds. My referral slip said 450 Jackson #1300. My first real attorney. I entered through walnut doors onto thick, blood-red carpet, took the smooth elevator ride with a silky-voiced operator.

"Thirteenth floor," he murmured.

Suite 1300. There were ten hand-engraved gold surnames on the redwood door.

"Can I help you?" I was greeted by a well-dressed secretary shifting delicately in her Macy's ensemble, ever so slightly hip.

"Uh, yes. I'm here to see John Sandal."

"One second please. Take a seat," she directed me to a series of small chairs lining the office.

And then He came out. Round-faced, tall, small bright eyes hidden behind rimless glasses.

"Please come in," he beckoned me with a soft nasal tone —

a worked-on accent, probably originating from a central California town like Modesto or Fresno. "So, what's the problem?"

As he spoke these words and settled his gaze on me, I noticed his hand glide across the desk and flip a switch on a tiny box to his right. A red light began flashing at intervals. He noticed my eyes following his discreet action.

"Oh, this? Well, since we only have thirty minutes at this cut-rate price, I find I must keep track of every minute or before you know it, I'm giving away a whole $100 phone call for nothing. Hey, it's hard times. Just the other day a client called up screaming after he got his statement because his entire $1500 retainer had been used up in five long-distance question calls. He argued that he hardly ever reached me, and most of the time, indeed, we hadn't actually spoken, but what he didn't understand is that I have to charge for the time I'm on hold, as well as messages left on his machine, any extensive dialing time, all in addition to our actual phone conversations. Anyway, enough of that, please go on."

"Uh . . . okay," and I embarked uncertainly into the recitation of my "facts." Somehow, I couldn't get it straight where our fall had originated. We had the rent money like we'd always had. As messed up as the Jaffes were, we never wanted to move; we just didn't want to pay a rent increase for a place that had no working refrigerator or heater.

The timer whirred softly in the corner. He blinked twice, then licked his line-thin lips.

"Oh-h-h yes, you have options. There's a thing called Relief from Forfeiture . . . there are also negotiations . . . and subsequent out-of-court settlements . . . I could even get you some cash . . . there are many options for you." He proceeded to list an array of procedural manipulations that he could wield with his legal knowledge. I stopped listening at a certain point, unable to follow anymore legalese, my eyes resting on the whirring timer, which sounded a muffled bell.

"Miss Garcia, I guess that's it. I'll make a proposal retainer statement for you, and you can decide what you want to do." With that, he got up with a college athlete's thrust, "I'll be right back."

I watched the city move below his thirteenth-floor vista. Silver-lined clouds shifted. A gold-framed, milky-colored wife holding a very pale baby stared at me from his desk. A grandparent group in another frame smiled at the pencil sharpener.

A few minutes passed, and then a swoosh of Ivory soap and a touch of just-ingested pastry rushed back in the room.

"Here's your estimate. Take a few seconds to read through it," he dropped his papers into my trembling hands. There were many careful equations, numerical rivers and deltas streaming down the page. I touched it ever so gently, forcing my futile hope to lodge in my neck muscles as I ran my fingers tentatively over the bottom figure of $1,496. I gulped softly and lowered my gaze.

"I don't know if I'll be able to afford this. I really only have my rent money. If I use any of it I won't have enough for the rent that's owed. Is there any way you could help me to do this myself?"

"Oh, no, there are so many documents to file, this is a complex court procedure," he looked at me flatly through his translucent blue pupils, blinking exactly twice. "I understand . . . times are hard . . . you'll do whatever you have to do," and then the vocal pace quickened, "Just remember, you do have options!"

We stood up together.

"Thanks for coming."

I nodded stiffly to the secretary, pushing through the heavy wooden doors. I rode down the thirteen floors with the elevator operator in silence. Once outside, I noticed the sky's delicate transitions. A cold breeze bit at my legs.

"Order. All rise. Judge Derk presiding. Housing Authority vs. Lincoln."

"Yes, your honor. John Magaw, attorney for the plaintiffs,"

he stated in loud, clipped tones. "She has no case, your honor, it's been three months. We have served her timely notice. She already requested one stay. These requests for stays are just delaying tactics. We gave her plenty of time to pay or vacate."

"Do you have anything to add, Ms. Lincoln?"

"I offered payments for the rent owed after I lost my job. They refused unless I had the whole rent. I was just asking for reduced payments until I was employed again. I was laid off."

"Your honor, she's three months behind. That's almost $1,800."

"How much money can you give toward the rent today?"

"I only get $980 a month for myself and my two babies."

"Please answer the question directly, Ms. Lincoln. How much can you deposit with the court today toward the rent?"

"I brought $580," she replied, almost in a whisper.

"That's not enough for my client, your honor."

"I'm afraid I can't extend any more stays on this case, Ms. Lincoln."

"Thank you, your honor," the attorney's mouth was small, almost invisible as he formed his closing remarks. He turned to the waiting audience, his black eyes finally resting on me. I was next.

The brown floor began to churn and I could hear the whispering of the other plaintiffs seated around me.

"He usually doesn't show up in person."

"He's the eviction king—it's all he does."

"He only works for landlords," muffled voices surrounded me.

A thick starch smell suddenly filled the air. I looked up to see a cardboard-like shirt standing above us. In a fury-filled whisper the courtroom sheriff screamed, "Do I need to eject you from the courtroom? There is NO TALKING!"

We all nodded in unison, "I'm sorry," and "Excuse me," immediately on our collective lips.

"Call the next case," a voice rang out from the bench.

"Garcia vs. Jaffe."

"John Magaw, attorney for the plaintiff here."

"Who is here for the defendant?"

I stood up. This was it. I stepped carefully through the brown waves beneath my feet. I would not fall. My legs would not buckle under me. My eyes would focus on a place just to the left of the judge, and no one would see the red terror passing before them.

"Lisa Gray Garcia, in pro per," I stood up and stated my non-attorney status.

"We're asking for possession, and that you deny the request for relief from forfeiture she is asking for, your honor."

"Proceed, Mr. Magaw."

"Well, first I'll present to the court a copy of the original notice served in a timely manner." A paper was passed to the judge. "We've already been granted possession, your honor. It's a simple case. Her request is just a delaying tactic."

"Miss Garcia, what would you like to say?"

"Your honor, I'm here to request a relief from forfeiture. We have the rent money that's owed. It would be an extreme hardship for us to be forced to move."

"But possession was granted to the plaintiff, Miss Garcia."

"I had no money for legal representation, so I didn't know how to present the issues of the unfair rent increase and flagrant inhabitability that brought this into court." At this point I looked up from my paperwork, finally prepared to see my failure reflected in his glassy eyes. Moments dripped by, a paper shuffling and rattling sound rose into the voiceless air in an orchestrated cacophony. Then he looked at me, his face filled with resigned disinterest. A slight smile seemed to play at the sides of his lips.

"Miss Garcia, I'm sorry you went to all this trouble, and I have to ask, why did you bother? I rarely, if ever, grant a relief from forfeiture on an eviction case. As you know, the possession is granted, and I am going to deny this request for relief. I hope you have found another place. You'll have about five days before the marshal comes with the writ."

"Is there any chance of getting an appeal?"

"Not unless you can deposit five or six months' rent in advance with the court at the time of filing. Counsel, please approach the bench."

There was a momentary hush.

"Call the next case."

CHAPTER 21

incarceration—poverty criminal

"You are trash!"

Our relationship with the Jaffes ended six days after that court date with that one sentence spit through Billy Jaffe's gritted teeth and manicured moustache. I could have yelled back about the broken plumbing, the ants and roaches and the forever-cracked window, I could have added the broken heater and the peeling paint. But I just cringed, agreeing with his assessment as most beaten down people do, loathing myself and my mother for our poverty even more than he did.

We drove away that morning with all of our things in and on the car, our rear view completely obstructed. We drove off fast, desperado-style, and even made an illegal U-turn on Telegraph Avenue, attempting to incorporate a mini-screech as much as our old station wagon's tires could muster.

But we had nowhere to go, no family waiting, no planes to catch, no apartment to furnish, no people to talk to. So, in a suffocating layer of sadness, we drove around Oakland fighting about what to do, picking desperately over our meager choices like birds fighting over a crumb of stale bread, and within seconds we were screaming at each other, throwing blame as fast as we could manufacture the words.

"I tried, but I was working on the PG&E thing!"

"That was a waste of time."

"I did it 'cause *you* said to."

"I didn't *say* to . . . We had no heat, no lights and no hot water, whaddaya mean I said to?"

"None of this matters anyway. The point is what are we gonna do now?"

And that was the end of the fight, at least momentarily, as it crushed out any air that either of us had in our lungs, and we both felt how terrified and hopeless we were all over again.

That horrible day ushered in another endless series of horrible nights of outsideness. The deadening cold was my bed partner again. In the six months we'd been at the Jaffes' place the car had gotten another dent and a new hole in the floorboard, so new currents of night wind reached up and bit into my flesh like small daggers.

The tickets started up again, and the pile of belongings and paper on the floor and dashboard got higher, swaying to and fro with every breeze.

One very dark and cold night after a successful day of vending, we stayed up on Telegraph Avenue to eat, take a walk and hang out. At approximately 10:25 P.M. we returned to the car, which was in a University of California parking lot. As I jiggled the key into the stiff ignition, an ominous white light hit the hood, illuminating the dust that lay in its deep crevices.

"UC Police, don't move," a loudspeaker voice filled the air around us. And then we saw them, two oversized vehicles circled us and then stopped. Within seconds there was a heavy click-click of door handles, the crunch of heels hitting asphalt, the deep *whumph* of doors slamming, faint police-band radio yelps that grew louder until a pair of thighs appeared at my window, swathed in too-tight tan polyester. Bits of arrests came through a shoulder radio as he slowly squatted to reveal a white-mustached face, his pores glistening in the parking lot lights.

"Why are you parked in a University of California parking lot at 10:30 P.M.? And what is all this stuff in the back?" his high-powered flashlight traveled the wagon portion of our car, and then he added, "And the registration on this vehicle has expired."

I quickly tried to explain that my mother and I were art vendors and that we were transporting stock—unusual, perhaps, but not a crime. I didn't add that currently we were homeless, but that detail didn't seem to matter to him. He wanted to see my driver's license. I fumbled—where had I put it? Oh shit! It was in my other jacket.

"Sorry, officer, I didn't bring it, but I remember the number," I recited it slowly, tremulously.

"Just a minute," he said, retreating from my car, caressing his shoulder radio as he murmured into it softly.

Meanwhile, the officer from the other squad car had been staring into the back of the station wagon at the clothing, boxes and small appliances lumped into an ever-growing pile. A brush of cold, wet air flowed around the tape I'd pasted over the broken vent window. I was hoping that they wouldn't research further and find out about the lapsed insurance, but considering this was clearly a DWP stop (Driving While Poor), they were probably compiling a complete dossier of my crimes of poverty while we waited.

Suddenly, the second officer's pace began to quicken, and the first one's thighs again appeared at my window. This time he didn't bother squatting, but stated in an oddly mechanized tone, "You're going to have to come with me, Miss Garcia."

Inwardly I screamed in despair, but I said quietly, slowly, "What are you talking about?"

"There's a warrant out for your arrest, so we're going to have to take you to jail."

"For what?"

"A warrant for $2,800 in unpaid tickets."

"What about my car?"

"We're going to be towing your car."

"But my mother can't get home without me. Can't she at least stay in the car and wait for a friend?"

"I'm sorry, but we're required to tow unregistered vehicles parked in University lots."

"But it's only been expired for two days."

"Please step out of the car, Miss Garcia."

His hands seemed oversized as he clanked the steel shackles on my wrists. He didn't look me in the eye anymore; he spoke to some place in the air that I happened to inhabit. I stood numbly as a female officer they had called in frisked me. As we were driving away, I looked back; men had descended on the car. It was being fed via a giant fishhook onto an immense yellow truck, while my mother stood off to one side in the dark garage, clutching her backpack with both hands.

As we drove off, I sat back on the hard plastic shell that masqueraded as a seat. Every bump in the road cut into my vertebrae. They could kill me, I thought. Moments became hours and then we were there.

Big grates of steel with prison-movie peepholes were opened by immense steel keys. Code words were barked through more peepholes, and then we were allowed final entry. Since it was a Saturday night, I was told I would be booked by the UC Police and then transferred to the City of Berkeley's jail, and from there, depending on the severity of my crime, I might be transferred to the county jail at Santa Rita.

I was led into a small cubicle and ordered to remove all of my "personal effects." What did that mean?, I wondered. I started to pull off all my large jewelry, extracting each expression of myself, putting it all in the brown paper vomit bag they gave me. I was done, I thought, until a female cop called out, "Your belt and shoes as well."

"But my pants are only kept up with this belt. It's a style," I explained.

"I'm sorry," and then she left me alone again.

I realized I had lost the right to rock a "look." Style wasn't for criminals like me. I took off my belt and held my pants up, crumpled into a ball in my right fist. With that belt went my last trace of power.

Eventually, another cop pulled me out of the cubicle to ask me some questions, to take my fingerprints and my mug shot. The men talked about me while I was waiting, making jokes about whether I was single, how they had missed their coffee break all for me. Finally, I was brought to a cell to await transfer.

Through the tiny air holes in the windowless room I heard the man from the next cell scream, "Bloody showers—people take bloody showers." Then he started whispering directly into the screen connecting our cells, "They'll make you take showers. Insist that you see their kidneys before you give up your dirt. They'll take the oxygen right out of your pores." Then silence.

After almost six hours of "procedure" and paperwork, the arresting officer determined that I needed to be incarcerated for the weekend, with a possible transfer to Santa Rita. He was quick to inform me that I could have taken care of the tickets and not have landed in this mess. I didn't have the energy left to explain to him all that I had done to try to prevent this.

When the policeman implied that I was "lazy," and that's the reason why I was in jail, a new feeling began to take hold—I started to feel relaxed about my fate. Life, problems, landlords, phones, cars, it was all just too difficult; I would stop trying to fight. I would just let myself be eaten up by this jail—it would be like suicide, but without the mess. There would be a kind of withdrawal, a relaxed death of self. Two of my teeth were aching badly—I hadn't taken care of them because I had no money for a dentist, but hey, I won't need my teeth in jail, I thought. I'll learn to like cigarettes and sip black coffee and never worry about anything again.

The arresting officer came in again, this time saying nothing, bypassing me with his disgusted eyes as he unshackled me and led me down narrow corridors, back to his vehicle for our short ride to Berkeley's city jail—more peepholes, a dirty, cage-like elevator, more codes, locks and whispers. I was left in a yellowish room where two new police officers took my bag of possessions. After a few disdainful chuckles about the incompetence of the UC police, I was led into a too-bright cell filled with women and shown to an upper steel bunk with a gray/yellow quilted mattress that looked like a futon from hell.

I moved it gingerly aside and attempted to lie on the ribs of the bright steel bed, but I couldn't seem to close my eyes tight enough to shut out the white intensity of the light. A headache began that would not depart for the duration of my stay.

Voices—quiet, resolved, yet lightly shaking—started to fill the air: bits of disconnected fear, fragmented concerns, expressions of collective desperation and shared terror. One voice finally cut through, "I was only getting a cigarette, one fucking cigarette. The Berkeley PD has a quota. My son always says the police are too eager. I never believed him, thought he was just making excuses for getting arrested all the time. But it didn't matter what I said, it just seemed to get me further into it. At the end of my explaining this cop would ask the same questions all over again: What were you doing on the corner at 4 A.M.? Who were you supposed to meet? Why were you talking to those boys? I tried to tell him I only knew them because of my son, but he wouldn't listen. My son always said it didn't matter what you said—they'd only believe what they wanted to. Why did I need that cigarette?"

Suddenly, from below, a small voice broke in, "Oh, shit, did you get your sandwich yet? Excuse me, did you get your sandwich yet? I'm so cold." The breathy plea was coming from the bunk under mine.

"No," I called down, "but when I get it, I'll give it to you."

"Oh, thank you," the thin voice replied, and then she coughed and sneezed and got up to pee in the little toilet at the foot of our bunk bed. My headache was a knife lodged in the back of my neck, the ambient voices reduced to an occasional murmur. I began to wonder what time it was, and then if time was passing at all. There were no clocks, watches, radios, variations from dark to light. At first this filled me with terror, but then I started to feel a comfort in the timelessness because it was a further separation from all that was reality. An extremely loud bell signaled us; now it was time for sleep.

Several hours later—or maybe fifteen minutes—it was mealtime; we were informed by the bell. The warden's compassion was gauged by her food-serving technique. How she brought us our food became extremely important to us—whether she would actually say our names, or take the food all the way into our common area and put it on the table, or just shove it through the hole in the door. This first warden was nice, so we were happy. We all sat together as we ate, and I began to attach names to voices.

Alice, a 56-year-old retired teacher in the Oakland schools, had had an unfortunate relapse in her attempt to quit smoking. At 4 A.M. she had ventured out of her apartment and walked to her friend's house a block away. A cop patrolling the neighborhood saw an African American woman and figured she must be a suspect. After extensive questioning and a subsequent search he couldn't find any evidence, but he called in her driver's license number anyway and found she had a $3,000 warrant for failures to appear on a moving violation. He took her to jail.

Penny, a white homeless woman, had been picked up from her parked car in Berkeley. She'd become homeless after leaving her abusive husband. Her car's registration had just expired, and while she was parked on Saturday night she was arrested for the expiration and one moving violation that had mounted to $3,200 in fines. None of us had drug or alcohol violations, or had been driving under the influence.

The strange psychology of "cool" comes into play in jail—the gaze, how long it lingers, what is said about little things, how much complaining is okay, and about what. "She's so nice," Penny proclaimed about one warden. "Be careful of that other one; she won't even look at you, but this one, I asked her for a toothbrush. She looked right at me and said she'd try."

I thought about how I hated that same warden—how she

had taken my Vaseline away even though I had begged her, explaining that I used it for my lips, to keep them from cracking and bleeding. She had looked right at me and said, "Too bad." I didn't mention any of this because she was Penny's favorite warden and she needed to believe that there was some humanity left around us. Privately, I resolved to continue my quixotic struggle over the Vaseline—to fight all wardens nice or mean until I imposed my miniscule will to keep my lip salve.

Suddenly—clank, clank—the outer door sounded and then the inner locks opened. The newcomer was beautiful: charcoal brown, thick woven plaits, olive-shaped eyes, still in the shock state, brimming equally with fear and hope. First time, I thought. Our gaze was careful.

"Sit down," Alice offered her a seat at the table. Penny had been carefully positioning her bed mat on the floor under the suspended television, readying herself for when and if it came on. She got up immediately to offer her mat space. We observed such delicate etiquette, strangely happy to be able to give, to hold on to our gallantry. We had been completely forgotten; our respect was reserved only for each other. Even our friends outside had become distant, suddenly out of our league.

Gently, we questioned the new woman, "Why are you in?"

Her eyes were excited, dilated. "Warrants. I couldn't keep up with my community service assignment and pay for childcare, so I got a job, but there wasn't enough money to pay the tickets and survive. So I went back to court to ask for an extension or lower payments, or even a smaller community service assignment, but the judge said there was no more community service and $50 a month is the least you can pay. So I just gave up. Three months later they caught me—wrong place, wrong time."

We all looked at one another; all of us locked in the same vicious cycle. Alice began to repeat her cigarette story, punctuating each sentence with an "uh-huh." My head was starting to pulse with pain, but somehow it didn't matter. For the first time in my life I felt at ease, no longer a wannabe fraternizing with people outside my reality. These women wouldn't think I was scum because I couldn't pay my rent and got evicted, because my car was rickety and filled with junk, because my jeans weren't the perfect brand and my shoes were wrong. They might even appreciate my struggle to care for my family in a society that encourages you to abandon anything that interferes with your independence. I didn't have to hide my pain; in fact, I was soothed that a society that will drop you in a heartbeat had finally just let me go. I no longer cared that I could never overcome these problems.

"Gotta get some candy, just somethin'. What about your man, would he bring you some?" Penny was pleading with the new woman in hushed tones.

Loud clanks, keys jangling. We all turned toward the door as it swung open dramatically. It was my favorite Vaseline warden. She was motioning to me, "Garcia, you're going to court. Get moving. NOW!"

I looked quickly at everyone. We cheered together, promising foreverness. I was overcome by guilt and terror. The system wanted another look at me.

I was taken to court in an orange suit and shackles. I was led into a tiny cell with a blurry glass wall and a phone with no dial tone. I was told to expect a visit from my newly appointed public defender, with whom I would negotiate the conditions of my freedom. A tall man in a nondescript suit flew in and out in a matter of seconds.

Part of the craziness of the system is that it's almost impossible to get free legal help over traffic matters, i.e., sleeping in a vehicle, moving violations and other supposed "civil" matters, and the only way you can get a court-appointed attorney — which most poor folks call a "public pretender" due to their disinterest and/or lack of job experience — is if you've been incarcerated. It wouldn't be until the next time I was incarcerated that I would meet up with an innovative attorney who would help me in ways that would change my life forever. This time I was led to court in ankle shackles like the poverty criminal that I was, accompanied by a flagrantly inexperienced law appointee, a.k.a. public pretender.

When we got into court, they unshackled me before the tense-looking audience of co-defendants. I read desperation in everyone's face that Wednesday morning. It was our one chance to redeem ourselves, to clear our record, whatever that meant. So when the rather ashen, yawning man wearing a sheriff's uniform gruffly said, "Paperwork," we shook in our collective boots and showed him what we had. If it was sufficient, he would check our name off on the list that he submitted to the judge and direct us to a seat with a detached snarl.

Without warning, a whir came from the upper right corner of the room where a TV screen was mounted. A face appeared, to inform us in an extremely nasal voice, "I am Judge Rasmussen. I am here through video to tell you the laws of the court."

As he read us our rights, I found myself fading in and out. After his droning video introduction, Judge Rasmussen appeared in person. Sheer terror shone from the eyes of the Middle Eastern man sitting on my left. Finally, a translator was acquired, but somehow I thought the man might have fared better without one, as his fix-it ticket progressed to a license suspension and a $300 fine.

The man sitting in the front row had been charged with not making a complete stop. He had a large diagram, which he'd mapped out on newsprint. After some muffled questions, the judge looked up once and dismissed the case.

When my name was called, I explained that I'd served time in jail and had no money except what I made selling art on the street, and that I was the sole caregiver for my mom who was disabled. The judge reviewed my papers and decided he would convert my huge fine to a huge community service assignment. I nodded in agreement, even though I knew that 2700 hours of community service would be virtually impossible for me to complete. Still shaking with jailhouse residue, I backed away from the bench without a word. Our car, riddled with unpaid tickets, was a distant memory.

After the bailiff unshackled me, I was directed to turn in my papers at the building across the street. I waited in line behind a small woman who barely reached the window. An adamant employee was telling her, "No, we can't make a court date for you unless you pay the bail on these parking tickets."

"But I can't afford the bail, that's why I need to go to court," she said.

"I'm sorry. These tickets are over three months old; you'll have to pay the bail before you go to court."

The woman gave up and withdrew from the window. She seemed to get smaller as she left the jail building, free for now. I turned in my papers and ran after her, hoping to give her some advice, nervously clutching the tube of Vaseline in my pocket.

Fear of the Marketplace," a conceptual art installation in one of Dee and Tiny's squatted storefronts in Oakland—"Throw in your money and we will throw out the product."

Tiny and Dee in another squatted storefront, writing the "Myth of Dee & Tiny" on the wall.

CHAPTER 22

the storefront

The headache from jail clung to my head like stale gum on hot cement for over six months, but it really wasn't the headache—it was the memory of the headache, the fear, the powerlessness, and in some ways the beginning of consciousness. The realization that we poor women, poor people in America, were so vulnerable, so powerless, so connected, was the beginning of my enlightenment. The seeds had been planted for a redefinition of my life: the ability to see our impossible situation in a new light.

Meanwhile, the artmaking and the poverty crimes got more serious, more complex and more dangerous. After I got out of jail my mother was determined that we absolutely could not be without a roof, and that we would get one by any means necessary. Yet, we had even less resources than we'd had before.

Getting our car back was a time-consuming, money-eating project. We had to travel to four different locations, appear in court several times, go to the DMV, pay upfront the hundreds of sleeping-in-vehicle citations and the ridiculous costs incurred just to "house" the vehicle at the shady towing company. All of this ended up totaling much more than the car was worth, of course, and the ironic thing was that the car's rent was paid in lieu of ours.

I was then directed to put on the rent-starter suit and get us a place, and if possible, a storefront—our growing life-as-art project, our fictional/real/art/life needed a "frame."

While we were still at the Jaffes my mother had nurtured the belief that somehow we would be able to pay for the over-priced tuition at the boutique art school she was attending, that if we just worked long enough, hard enough, we would amass the small fortune that was needed. There was really never any possibility of that, but my mom had endless determination, which I wholeheartedly encouraged when she was focused on something. And she was so happy there. She absolutely loved learning, being around all kinds of artmaking and design. I benefited from it too, and before the last of a series of bounced checks to the school spelled the end, my mom and I had gained an extensive knowledge of textile art, postmodern art theory, and had planted the roots of all the wild performance work we would embark on shortly after she was kicked out.

This was when our tenure at San Francisco State University began, where we sat in on a variety of performance, installation and art theory classes. We had the honor to meet conceptual and sound artists like Ellen Zweig, Doug Kahn and Pamela Z, not to mention teachers like Leonard Hunter and Lise Swenson who encouraged us, critiqued us, showcased our work and learned themselves from our radical notions of melding life and art, reality and fiction. We created a series of street-based tableaus, performances, installations and a video, *Dee and Tiny's Mom and Dad's Birthplace*, a fictional life story based on generations of nuclear American families and their lives of pathology and ease that both terrified and enticed my mother and me.

One night when we were driving through the Berkeley streets searching for that night's parking place, pondering our pennies to see if we could afford a motel room, we stumbled upon a sign: STORE WITH LIVING SPACE FOR RENT.

154

"Hello, I'm calling about the store for rent," I started calling about it the next morning at 8:30 A.M.

"Oh yes dear, it's a beautiful place, although it needs a little work. Well, come and pick up the keys and you can see for yourself," a sing-song old lady voice shouted into the phone. Within minutes we had the keys; within hours we had moved in.

"Did you like the place, dear?" Mrs. Lyon was a tiny woman who wore her shiny white hair in a swirling bun like silver cotton candy, and whose dress and demeanor epitomized the notion of "old money." I met her only once, when I went to get the keys at her palatial Berkeley hills home. We worked out the rest by phone, and due to her diminished hearing she would always shout into the phone as though I was very far away.

"Oh yes, but there's no working bathroom. Can we get a toilet put in, and maybe a sink?" I tried to sound nonchalant as I listed the problems with the place. "And there's no tile in the kitchen, or carpet, or any drapes or anything. I mean, we can do a lot of the repairs, but we don't really have a lot of money."

"Well dear, if you can do the repairs, then we can give you something off the rent."

"How much is the rent?"

"Well dear, I can give it to you for $1 per square foot."

"How many square feet is it?"

"Well, its 1800 dear."

"Oh," I gulped audibly, knowing that one month's rent at that rate would take six months of nonstop t-shirt sales. Maybe.

Without any papers signed, credit checks run or calls made, but rather just a very long sycophantic conversation and a verbal agreement to "fix up the place in return for rent," Mrs. Lyon believed my elaborate lie about being a college student with a job and a car and money in the bank.

Within a month we had "installed" the storefront windows with a series of tableaus, including: "The Phobia Support Group," a group of cut-out cartoon characters who all suffered from severe phobias and other assorted pathologies and "met" as a group on a 24/7 basis under a table; "Count the Heads," an interactive contest where passersby could guess which mannequin head had the number under it and throw their "guesses" through the mail slot; and "The Myth of Dee and Tiny," a story that was painstakingly written out on the wall of the store, from one end to the other.

And there were clothes, so many clothes—on racks, on the walls, on the floor. My mother continued to create complex pieces of wearable art, including the "night of a thousand faces coat" that integrated sound and light, with the thousand stories available as sound chips attached to every "face" handprinted on the coat.

Inspired by the work of some of the conceptual performance artists we were being exposed to in school, my mother had created a series of hilarious personas for me to act out. Her favorite was Frank, based on a fleeting relationship she'd had with a man who claimed to be the proud owner of a thousand women's phone numbers. With me posing as Frank, my mom and I would go to clubs and bars and other venues, and solicit phone numbers. It was a time of so much instability and wrongness in our lives, but we had so much fun with our art wildness. My mom was one of the silliest, coolest cats you'd ever want to meet, and she loved to laugh, and I with her.

As our "appropriated" education at SF State continued, our art got more and more complex, incorporating elements of sound, theory, video and dance. Our own versions of Linda Montano meets Hugo Ball with a smidgeon of Chris Burden thrown in began gaining media attention. Suddenly we were riding on this incredible high of performance and installation art infamy; we had articles written about us and we appeared on local radio shows. We were doing extremely innovative "life-art." Our mythos was building, our poverty compounding.

One morning I awoke to a cold wetness lapping at my feet. As usual, I'd taken the closet as my room, but this one was so small that it didn't fit my entire body, leaving my calves and feet sticking out into the main room. On this day, I opened my eyes and found my feet submerged in water. One of the pipes that led from the makeshift toilet we'd installed had broken, and water was gushing over the entire floor.

"Mrs. Lyon, please send a plumber. A pipe has broken and this place is flooded."

"You aren't supposed to be living in there. Who are you?"

"You told us to move in if we could fix the place."

"I said no such thing. You need to get out of my house. You are trespassing on my land."

After our original discussion Mrs. Lyon had never come by, called us or inquired after her keys. So now, after living there for six months and investing our time, money and sweat to improve a place that hadn't been fit to live in previously, we were suddenly trespassers. The police arrived within minutes.

BOOM, BOOM, BOOM! "Police! OPEN THE DOOR!!!" Their black-gloved hands pounded on the long bay windows of the storefront, causing them to shake and tremble.

When we opened the door, they marched in as though they expected to find a crack lab in the corner of the room. They looked around and began to question us as to what we were doing there. Five minutes passed during which we produced every document we had in order to prove we'd been there for the last six months doing repairs, and then, without explaining anything to us, they walked out. We found out later that they had determined that it was a tenant/landlord dispute, and not an incident of trespassing. Mrs. Lyon would have to get an attorney and file papers to get us evicted.

Within 24 hours we received a Notice To Vacate, and within 72 more hours we received an illegal Unlawful Detainer notice. It was illegal because they didn't properly "notice" us, but in the end it didn't matter; we couldn't stay there anymore with the entire contents of our life floating in rusty water like lost ships at sea.

The eviction was swift and illegal. Mrs. Lyon retained one of the slimiest real estate attorneys around: he lied to the judge about the illegal notice; he didn't inform us about the court date; and then he falsified dates so we were forced to move almost immediately. In the fifteen days that the whole process took, they never once tried to fix the plumbing and they refused all of our calls.

The attorney's smarmy lack of ethics was matched only by my mother's determination not to be roofless again. Mrs. Lyon's place became a template for a new Dee & Tiny model: move in without paying any money at all. I later found out this was called "squatting," and it had been done successfully by other very low-income families and later transformed through several forms of resistance into something called "homesteading."

CHAPTER 23

art as life as art

The last storefront in our "Berkeley-Oakland series" was the most uninhabitable of them all. The building was an old theater. Built at the turn of the century, it had long ago been turned into a series of unsuccessful businesses, then abandoned, and now it stood empty, dark and perpetually lost in the shadows on the dark side of San Pablo Avenue in West Berkeley. It had 2000 square feet of stone flooring and absolutely no heat.

Our acquisition of this place was perhaps the most dangerous of all, since we got the keys from the realtor and then just moved in, without an agreement, any conversation, or even a nod. The police were called several times, but every time they came we weren't there. Eventually, the magical 30 days of habitation passed and now it would take a court process to evict us. The same residency law that had sleazy hotel and motel managers kicking us out after 27 days was working in our favor this time.

We installed the storefront with a highly conceptual piece: "Fear of the Marketplace," a literal and metaphorical translation of my mother's disability. In the 20' x 30' storefront window was a collection of haphazardly placed "items for sale": broken chairs and couches, upended tables, clothing draped over pieces of mannequins, and plastic garbage bags, the real and metaphoric "arti-FACTS," as we called them, of past evictions and personal strife. In the middle of it all was a carefully printed sign that read: *If you want an item in the window, throw your money through the mail slot in the door, and we will throw the product out to you.* There were no price tags or actual "products", just a crafted mayhem that spoke of hundreds of evictions, years of homelessness and ongoing chaos.

In a side window I installed my first foray into public literary art: my "books" were a series of painted furniture, with my poems painted in large black letters all over the end tables, stools and broken lamps piled in a corner of the window.

Our art and life merged in this place to launch "The Art of Homelessness," replete with docent tours through our life as we were living it. And it was there that the conceptual seeds were planted for our video "documentary" on the myth of Dee and Tiny.

Although we weren't financially supported by our art, nor even really considered artists, people were intrigued by us, I suppose in the way they're now drawn to reality TV shows. At the time, and even more so in retrospect, I believed, along with some of the instructors and artists who had become our friends, that our personal-as-political, persona-as-metaphor work was pure genius, but without a context, without a network, our art and we, a homeless mother-daughter artist duo, only seemed weird.

People did come through for docent tours, which included a cassette of my mom and I telling several differing mythical stories about ourselves, and then an elaborate conversation/ argument between us about how we were going to solve some impending financial crisis. Every installation was laced with humor and irony, sarcasm and violence, and things were implied, never explained. My mother believed that true art was always subtle. No hitting people over the head, no ranting, no overt politics, she demanded, as we began a disagreement that would continue throughout our lives together about the power/necessity of the overt versus the covert message.

160

My mom subscribed, as I did, to the notion that art didn't mean anything unless it was causing change or serving a function, which is why she liked textile and wearable art—you could wear it, it would keep you warm. And we both felt that every performance or conceptual piece we created together must come from something real, a truth, an experience, a struggle. But she was adamant about her belief that it was okay to make art about homelessness, isolation, racism and poverty that only implied a social justice message. I didn't agree, and eventually we would have no choice; the time was coming when all art would stop as it collided head-on with our real life.

The "Dee & Tiny" series of work was, for both of us, a very serious representation of the trauma of otherness and outsiderness experienced by poor, disenfranchised families who are never able to attain the so-called American Dream. Informed by media, propaganda, corporations and government bodies that everyone has/should have a home, a family, a car and new clothes, we're told that we have to consume, get a job to be productive, leave our families to go to college, get married and start another consuming unit with more cars, more homes, more clothes. We're saturated with this "reality" every day in every way, and the desire for all that poor families could not be, could not attain, was to us as hilarious, as ironic, as it was tragic. Her own, my own, desire for all the Cosby Kids and Brady Bunch moments we would/could/should never be included in, was as ridiculous as it was desperately sad.

I realize in retrospect that my mother's refusal to take anything too seriously was one of her most creative survival mechanisms. My mom had an amazing sense of humor, and for her almost nothing was sacred, nothing was too serious not to laugh at and laugh with. This was her practice within her own tragic life, and it was why, in the middle of some of our worst crises, she and I would be laughing uproariously about some weird, illogical aspect of it all. It was also how I knew when things had gotten really bad, because then even my mom couldn't laugh about things anymore.

Due to the severe chill pervasive in the new space, I began an intimate relationship with a tiny space heater, acquired on our last illicit Walgreens run. One night when the temperature had dropped to a low of 36 degrees, I cuddled up to the soothing orange lines of electrical warmth emanating from the tiny metal box. At 5 or 6 A.M. I awoke to the thick smell of something cooking. As I tried to identify the odor, I became aware of a deep, searing pain and looked down to find my leg melting into the black grid of the heater cover. The process of extracting one's own skin off of burning metal is one of the most disgusting things a human being can do.

That was only one of a series of tragicomic experiences we had in that place. There was no toilet, sink, bathtub or shower, and with the exception of the storefront itself there were no windows in the entire 2000-square-foot room, which meant we had no light or air circulation. The problem was, at this point we barely had money for food, much less major capital improvements.

"My boyfriend can do anything. He can plumb the place, he can put in a window, he can fix a car, whatever you need done, he can do it," a woman we were friendly with from Telegraph Avenue told us about her boyfriend when we told her about our dilemma.

"When can I talk to him?"

"Never. He doesn't speak to people—he has a lot of phobias. But his assistant does, and I can set it all up if you tell me what needs to be done."

"Oh, well . . . uh . . . when can he start?"

The next day a '60s van that had been painted over so many times that its green paint seemed like the bumpy hide of some prehistoric reptile rolled up San Pablo Avenue and stopped in front of our store. The windows were dark, almost black and the license plates were barely visible, blanketed by the fluttering remnants of three generations of political bumper stickers. As it grumbled to a stop, a man emerged whose face was almost entirely covered in hair, sideburns melding into beard melding into a thick moustache melding into wayward eyebrows with two tiny bright eyes peeking out. Next to him was a wisp of a man with a starter beard and a hint of a moustache capped off by thick, rimless glasses that looked like acrylic shields for his large round eyes, which were in perpetual, nervous movement.

"Hi, I'm Steve and this is Plumber," the little man spoke first, his skinny thighs dangling inside of his supposed-to-be-tight bell bottoms. "We're here to do an estimate for the job."

"Oh yes, please come on in." I wasn't sure I'd heard him correctly, and I was afraid to ask again in case it might seem like an insult, but yes, it turned out that the hairy man's name was, in fact, "Plumber."

We were given a mumbled estimate of $250 to install a toilet, sink and stall shower, and an extra "$25 thrown in for a window install," all delivered in a barely audible voice, spoken through the gritted yellow teeth and surrounding hair of Plumber. Wow, I thought, he must trust us; he sort of spoke!

And then the work began. Day after day the green van would lumber up the street, puttering and whirring for several minutes until it would finally stop. Both men would dismount, swagger meaningfully to the front door and pound on the glass, work belts a-janglin' and work boots a-stompin', and in they would march.

"We're eatin' it, Plumber."

"Yeah, I know man, we're eatin' it," Plumber would mumble back. His reputation for not speaking was, I found out, just a front to make him seem less insane, more dramatic. In reality, you couldn't shut him up about anything and everything; he spent the entire day listing what he couldn't stand about life and why he wanted to kill everyone, himself included. He would only break from this diatribe to start or respond to the

"We're eatin' it" comment, which always ended with, "This is two thousand dollar job, man!"

It was Plumber who proposed the installation of a sliding glass door, a quixotic and uninformed attempt to bring light into the space. We later discovered that where he'd decided to install it was, in fact, a retaining wall for the entire building, something that would have been clear to them if either Steve or Plumber were trained contractors. Of course, my mom was all for it regardless, which put our already precarious lives even more at-risk, since for the duration of our tenure there we slept under the sliding glass door area, which ultimately could have collapsed the whole building with us inside.

Six months after Steve and Plumber first coined their "We're eatin' it" anthem they were finished, and with the end of the sliding glass door project they determined that the $25 window job was in fact worth several hundred dollars more. It was only after we showed them the eviction papers asking for $25,000 in damages for destroying the building's retaining wall that they stopped bugging us for "their damn money," as Plumber would always phrase it when he drove by in the green van, slowing down just long enough to yell at me whenever he would see me vending.

During the thirteen months of our contentious, stress-filled and irony-laden stay in that storefront my mother became simultaneously more creative and more insane. She began a habit that continued for the rest of her life, needing to talk to me at least once, if not twice or ten times each hour, every day. With the advent of cell phones, that habit became easier to facilitate in later years, but back in the day people thought I was dealing drugs, since dealers were the only other people hanging around pay phones on random street corners throughout the Bay Area.

My mother and I would spend hours at a time, figuring and re-figuring how we could survive on so little money, where we could go next, how we would fight the eviction, who we could turn to for help and what, if any, resources we might have, what could we sell, how could we afford any blank t-shirts or clothes to paint, supplies like ink, paint, screens, brushes and dye, and how, if possible, could we pay for food, utilities, gas and/or the always at-risk phone bills. At the same time, we also spent hours plotting our next performance piece, writing the scenes and conceptualizing the ideas.

In addition to the Art of Homelessness installation, it was during this time in the Dee and Tiny mythistory that we conceptualized, choreographed and performed the multimedia "Car Piece," which put those who interacted with the installation into a position of enforced empathy: the "audience member" sat in the back seat of a car, facing two video monitors attached to the back of the front seat that played images of the backs of our heads, deep in conversation about where we could park that night to sleep. Before they could sit down, each participant was confronted with a bag of trash, and they had to either sit on trash or become perpetrators of a poverty crime (littering).

With the collaboration of friends and contacts we'd made at San Francisco State, we created a final act of performance art in tandem with the graduating class of 1988/89 (but of course we received no credit and no diploma, since we didn't have money for a luxury like tuition). We had decided to try vending at street fairs (a risky and extremely labor-intensive venture, but we'd heard you could make $1000 in a weekend if you could pull it off), and through juggle and struggle we'd managed to clear enough to rent the perfect location for our first full video production.

For one month we inhabited an empty apartment in the Park Merced apartment complex, an oddly Fred MacMurray-ish "community" that reeked of white middle-class dreams and unseen pathologies. We installed the place with the carefully demarcated "artifacts" of our lives, making it all appear like an archeological dig. Steve Jensen, a friend and fellow student in the arts program, shot the now infamous video, *Dee and Tiny's Mom and Dad's Birthplace*, a filmic version of the docent tours through our mythical history.

When we finished our SF State performance, a friend told us about a storefront his landlord was renting in San Francisco's Outer Mission district. The place was pretty cheap, and it was habitable, with big picture windows and hardwood floors. We moved in, and with the income from the street fairs we were able to afford it for a little over a year, an art-filled and joyous time lived in the hope that we could keep paying the rent. We were on a high of artmaking, creating ever more complex work in what would become our last storefront.

We created several interactive installations in that place, culminating in a performance art show featuring a complicated kinetic dance and sound piece that addressed the idea of advertising and its complex web of lies and deceptions entitled "The Art of Sales." I added an installation called "Becoming Rod Stewart's Leopardskin Outfit," and we also created a hilarious piece entitled "Things People Said About Us," filling an entire wall with letter-sized papers printed with sentences like *"You are trash"; "You should be locked up"; "You never pay your bills on time"; "You people are bums"* etc.

And then my mom broke her foot and had to be in a wheelchair for months. We missed a street fair due to a rain-filled weekend, and the reserve we had started to build was immediately used up. We didn't want to make trouble for our friend with his landlord, and so for the first time ever we didn't get evicted; we just moved out, depressed and discouraged, with just enough money for a single room in the same filthy SRO hotel in downtown Oakland we'd left behind a couple of years back.

CHAPTER 24

bleak

Things became increasingly bleak. After losing our public "frame" we tried for many weeks and months to produce our work in a gallery setting or even an outdoor location. But it soon became obvious that this was a futile effort, since we didn't have the basic resources of time or money to put on shows and lacked the knowledge, connections and built-in network one can derive from an art school education. We got nowhere, and eventually lost hope, falling further and further into the depths of poverty and homelessness. The reality was overcoming the mythology.

For the next three years we bounced from apartment to car to motel to apartment. We worked for hours on end trying to raise money, trying to do some kind of art, trying to survive. Our artmaking was almost solely limited to silkscreened and hand-painted t-shirts featuring popular cartoon characters. We tried to create our own original cartoons, but sales of those never even came close. We were bored out of our minds making the same cutesy images over and over, since although they were all hand-painted and hand-screened, they were basically formulaic. But in the end, to survive on the street, to eat, art was elitist and we did what we had to do.

After so many evictions, we had to amp up the housing

crimes. Newer and better manipulations of the court system were employed, tactics I won't reveal here as they might place current and future poverty criminals in danger, but suffice to say, the evictions became increasingly dangerous. We were in constant motion, either moving in, moving out or trying to find a place to move to. Sometimes I didn't even make enough money to eat lunch, much less pay into the rent fund or motel stay. And after two years our product was getting old, and even the pop-art images were less likely to sell. We didn't understand it yet but we'd basically saturated the Berkeley market.

It was during these horrible times that my relationship with my mom got more and more violent and difficult. We were fighting every day. No day would start without some kind of screaming about one of our impossible situations, followed up by hour-long pay phone calls to "work out" the problem.

Even if we didn't start out with a fight, we would still talk for hours. My mother's need to talk, to get counsel, to find some kind of hope, was equal to, or maybe worse than mine — I still had a little of the hope of youth left in me, and I dished it out to her in daily ad-hoc therapy sessions. The funny thing was, there really was never an answer to our problems, since both of our lives were caught in the same vicious cycle of poverty. There were just more problems added and skewed manipulations created that would compound the existing problems as we endlessly discussed them. Thoughts of suicide again became one of my few escapes, and I dreamed daily of the kind of gun I would use.

I began to transfer all my hope, all my escape needs, all my dreams of a saner life onto my current boyfriend, another solidly middle-class white boy with only a vague awareness of the life I was living. He was an artist in search of a muse, and I was a daughter in search of a father-alike. I had another sexless love affair with a cold, somewhat bland simulation of a male, a slightly skewed Greg Brady. Another recreation of the hazy memory I had managed to retain of my Dad.

We met in secret places, at secret times. I never completely revealed the reality of my situation with my mom or the desperation of our life; I played out a mythos that we created each day. Every meeting with him was like a tableau of text and image, and we spent all of our time in the middle of my stories.

We made plans and promises, we planned trips and created art, all in a dream sequence of secret meetings so my mom would never find out. And we must never be found out or it would be over, since even the mere mention of a boyfriend would be met with a terrified shriek by my increasingly phobic mother.

I was twenty-three years old and had never been on a real date. My mother's fear of losing me was coupled with her very old-school methods of "protecting" me, and she openly stated her belief in arranged marriages. She wanted to find me a "nice" man of color, preferably not from this country, one who respected his elders. I actually agreed with her on this, though we were too caught up in our web of poverty and survival to do much about it.

My boyfriend told me that I should just leave, that I could go to school, get a career and be something, that I needed my independence. I only felt the cold chill of those words — of course I was strong, I wanted to say, strong *because* of my mom. So yes, I could leave and only concern myself with my own survival. But in the process of my self-centered pursuit of so-called success, my mother would have gone into a mental hospital or roamed the streets, sleeping in the Sidewalk Motel.

CHAPTER 25

go directly to jail

We were quickly approaching the middle of the boom boom 90s, and the taste of redevelopment was already on the lips of Oakland's landlords. Our most recent apartment, one room in the heart of downtown Oakland, had been smaller, darker and more depressing than all the others. Six months after we moved in we received a completely unexpected and very large rent increase, and then a subsequent notice of termination. This was our first experience with eviction-for-profit.

At this, the 19th eviction, the 375th motel room and the 2,345th overnight parking space, my dreams of suicide increased. I was fantasizing about death almost hourly; it felt like a relief from our impossible situation. It was at this point that my secret boyfriend offered to take me to New York for a trip. It was absolutely the worst thing I could do as far as my relationship with my mom went, and yet I couldn't stand the prospect of one more day of our life. And after all, I reasoned, it was only five days. I would be right back.

Throughout the entire five days of urban blur, my blood coursed with guilt. I was back within minutes, it seemed. Only a few dreamy pictures shot by my photographer boyfriend lingered in my pocket, and within seconds of my return I was on the pay phone at the Oakland BART station apologizing profusely to my mom and dealing with her impenetrable wall of fear, anger, pain and sense of betrayal.

After the trip my mother's lingering fear, my guilt, and our collective hopelessness forged a permanent crack in our mythos/reality artmaking. We were no longer able to look at our life with the humor and irony necessary to make art. In fact, we were barely able to laugh.

It was in this general state of depression that I was driving down Bancroft Avenue in the heart of Berkeley one cold morning in December. Bancroft was one of the worst DWP traps in Berkeley. There was a pale glare in the sky that day, with an occasional breeze dragging through the blue-brown haze. I turned left off of Telegraph after a meager day of sales. This was one of those days when I hadn't even made enough for lunch. As I turned the wheel, a non-specific shudder shook my sad heart. I have since learned that that particular shudder is as close as I get to my psychic grandmother's magic; I always feel it before anything really devastating is about to happen.

Seconds later I caught the blink-flash of impending police arrest in my mirror. My hands clutched the steering wheel. This is it, I thought. I had never come close to completing the community service assignment. I did go in and get assigned to a county work program, but the worker had signed me up for 2700 hours of weekly street cleaning and other volunteer jobs that would span several months. I barely completed 100 hours. I could not help my mom, buy and paint enough shirts to get enough money to eat and/or pay for a room or rent, sell them on the street, move in and out of hotel rooms, cars and apartments *and* do all of those hours. I gave up, deciding instead to "not deal with it right now." In fact, not really deciding anything. Decisions born from overwhelming situations just happen to folks.

"STOP THE CAR AND PULL TO THE RIGHT," the mechanical shout rang through the air. My car chugged to the right. The catalytic converter had not passed the smog test, so we didn't have current registration; this along with the appearance of our old, poor people's car with too much stuff in it (read: homeless) was in and of itself enough for a Driving While Poor stop. For this reason, we only used the car to transport our stock as early in the morning as possible, so as to avoid the beat cops.

"License and registration, please."

"Officer, why are you stopping me?"

"License and registration," he repeated without a blink.

"I don't have my license with me."

"Do you remember the number?"

"Oh yes, its C0771169."

"Hold on, I'll be right back."

As I lied to the police officer about my license number, I told myself it would be okay, that I would actually get away with it, that he wouldn't find my name and my delinquent hours in the system, that he would trot back to my broken-down car and my broken-down life and tell me to move on.

"STEP OUTSIDE OF THE VEHICLE," this came through the megaphone. I grabbed my backpack and opened the car door.

"You need to come with us," he was towering above me, hands resting ever so slightly on the one snap in the holster covering his gun.

I was led into the back of the squad car, onto the hard plastic seats with grooves in precisely the wrong places, ensuring that no matter which way you sat, you'd be very uncomfortable.

At the station I was searched and relieved of all my accoutrements. I was placed in a tiny cell with ancient urine stains competing with new urine puddles.

I was kept in the holding cell for the first several hours; it seemed that lying to an officer was, in police culture, analogous to punching an officer, and my crime was considered so serious that I was not even able to join the regular jail population.

Every few minutes, shadows of sound and movement would seep under the tiny cell's door and darken the steel-threaded windows from the adjoining men's holding cell. The shadows belonged to feet pacing out unsaid fury, pounding out unscreamed expletives and unpunched blows. Begging forgiveness, justice and revenge.

The headache started again. This time it reached into the depths of my nerve endings, connecting thick surges of pain from my fingers up to my vertebrae, down to my toes and back up through the entire circumference of my skull. This headache, I was sure, would never leave.

"Why did you leave?"

"Who do you think you are bitch, I haven't been on a horse since last year!"

"Shao-La . . . Shao-La . . ."

As the hours, minutes and seconds dripped by in the holding cell I was joined by three severely mentally ill elders. All three were self-medicated with alcohol and some admixture of street-acquired psychotropic drugs. As each of them tumbled into the tiny room they alternately wept, screamed, rocked back and forth and repeated phrases meant for the ears of relatives and lovers long ago lost or rejected.

In addition to these three, there were momentary groups of other poor women on their way to the television-having luxury of an actual jail cell, in for homeless citations, Walking, Driving or Hanging Out While Black or Brown violations, and the minor drug violations of poor people, i.e., crack and alcohol use outside of a residence in the "wrong" neighborhood.

Seventy-two hours or 720 hours, I wasn't sure which, eventually crawled by, the fluorescent morning being identical to the fluorescent afternoon, evening and midnight.

"Garcia, you need to get ready, you're going to county (jail) on the 6 A.M. bus." Suddenly everything was accelerated. The warden yelled in warnings of my impending fate every few minutes.

"Girl, you don't want to go to Santa Rita (county jail). I almost got killed there . . . twice," the African American elder stopped rocking and repeating to whisper this dire warning into my ear. With her warning, the Asian elder and two weary sex workers who had just been thrown into the cell with us nodded their heads in agreement. She continued, "What did do you?"

"I got too many citations for being homeless and then I lied to a cop." With that, the whole room let out a collective nod.

"God bless you," and then she resumed rocking and looked away from me.

"Garcia, you're outta here."

On the day I was arrested, my mother had made many desperate phone calls, one of which was to the now "ex" boyfriend who had agreed to put up bail.

We'd broken up after the trip to New York because he was tired of my difficult situation, which I really couldn't blame him for; after all, how can you empathize with problems you've never had? My mother had contacted him right after I'd been arrested, but he'd apparently wanted to torture me with two nights in jail before he bailed me out with his VISA power

When I was released I was escorted to the exit, which was an oddly small door with no sign proclaiming that this was, in fact, an Exit and with no obvious path to the street. After several minutes of post-institutionalized befuddlement, I finally located an ivy-covered sidewalk and I walked around to the front of the jail where my ex was waiting. He looked at me square-jawed and said, "Did you learn your lesson?"

I screamed internally, watching him disengage the car alarm on his late-model Jeep Cherokee.

CHAPTER 26

the first intervention

My arraignment was later that day. I walked through the ice-cold Berkeley morning, running my fingers along the sides of buildings, cars and the trunks of trees. It wasn't that I had forgotten how they felt; it was just to know that they, things, were still there. It helped to ease the shudder, the ache and the tension that now felt permanently lodged in my head

"I will call all the cases in custody first." When I arrived, the judge was already seated, thumbing through that day's cases. He was thin-faced, with small dark eyes that showed little emotion, "First case: Garcia versus the City of Berkeley."

My first intervention. When my name was called, the man who would prove to be my savior slumped through the swinging doors in a Goodwill polyester suit with matching yellow nylon tie. He had a white-ish beard and a scruffy mop of grey-white hair that rose in tufts. The only clue that he was an attorney was the leather briefcase slung mightily over one shoulder and the legal look of omniscience that he wore when speaking to the judge. "Osha Neuman, counsel for the defendant, Lisa Garcia, present."

"Your honor we are requesting thirty days of jail time, in County, or at the very least a fine and a supervised probation," the City Attorney spat out the City's desired revenge for my crimes of poverty.

"Your honor, my client will submit to supervised probation and she is willing to accept a reassignment of the original 2700 hours of community service to a nonprofit organization, which I will personally supervise."

As they tossed about my fate in a series of rejoinders I stayed numb. I could not fight anymore, I would accept whatever was to be my fate, death at Santa Rita, more fines that I could never pay, more community service assignments I could never complete. They were only words after all, only words and agreements and promises. My ears stopped listening, my heart stopped hoping and then, a few minutes later, the white-haired man was talking to me in hushed tones, "Come to my office tomorrow morning and we'll work this all out."

I climbed up to the beginning of my life on rickety wooden stairs that led to a clapboard house with peeling yellow paint and white shutters. A tiny paper label taped precariously over the doorbell confirmed my location, "Community Defense, Inc., Law offices of Osha Neuman." I rang the bell, and within a few seconds the door was flung open.

"Just a minute," a distracted voice called from a room down the hall, "Wait in the room to the left, I'll be right there." I almost went into a small, dark office to the right, filled with piles of papers, yellow legal pads, law books, telephones, faxes and assorted post-its attached to everything, waving in the air like a mini tickertape parade. Not quite sure, I chose the other direction, a room that looked almost austere in a comfortable way, with rows and rows of law books lining the walls and a large, white couch positioned under the huge bay window flooding the room with morning sun.

The sun's rays alighted on a lone watercolor portrait of an older woman being thrown a coin. This was the first painting I had ever seen of a homeless person, and it was also one of the most beautiful paintings I had ever seen.

"Sorry you had to wait, our copy machine is acting up again. So, first of all, do you understand what the ruling was?" He proceeded to explain that the court had ruled that I must complete 2700 hours of supervised community service in a nonprofit agency. As my mind began to sink into the quicksand of those impossible words, I heard, "So, what can you do?"

"Huh?"

"I said, our agency is supervising those hours and I need to know what it is that you can do."

"Well, my mom is disabled, and vending is the job that I do, 12-20 hours a day, seven days a week. I paint in the morning and at night and sell during the day, just for basic expenses, and now we have no car and so I don't know how I'm going to sell at all, and we have to move 'cause we're being evicted again, and we probably won't have enough money to get another place so we'll end up homeless—"

"I understand that you have a very complicated life; that's why I said, what can *you* do."

This was odd, I thought, he was actually asking me a real question, so in response I felt it was safe to answer with a real answer. "I can write," I said this quietly, almost embarrassed. No one had told me I was a writer. I was homeless. I was a vendor, a salesperson perhaps, but a writer? I didn't look at him as I murmured those three little words.

Osha looked at me blankly. He didn't laugh or shake his head in disbelief; he just continued calmly without pause, "Well then, that's what you will do for the hours, write."

Well then, that's what you will do for the hours, write.

Well then, that's what you will do for the hours, write.

Write . . . write . . . write . . .

A zipper suddenly appeared in the small slice of morning sky above Osha's head. As it opened, letters, words and sentences sailed out on a tongue of light. They danced to salsa, merengue and hip hop. They dangled their feet over the fluffy wall of a cloud.

Well then, that's what you will dooooooooo . . .

I looked at him and said, "Okay."

Osha explained that he ran a nonprofit organization that practiced advocacy and civil rights law for homeless youth and adults, and as he spoke he crafted a scenario in which my court-mandated community service would be to write an essay on some issue related to poverty under his supervision; it would be an act of advocacy journalism. He went on to arrange a weekly check-in/critique appointment and created a timeline for me to follow. I listened and agreed and left his office. The heavy door closed with a thud behind me.

"Eeeaowwww!!! I Feeeeel Good!" They were there waiting for me, suspended just above Osha's rickety steps, the words, the sentences, moving in sync to the sounds of James Brown. The W from Write reached its hand down to pull me up. *"Da da da da da da dum. I feel good now . . ."*

The words and I sailed over the Bay Area for the remainder of the morning. We played James Brown, Billy Idol, Run-DMC and Celia Cruz on our cloud boombox at the highest volume. And then they delivered me back to the vendor space lottery at 10 A.M. sharp. But Osha had given me hope. For the first time in so long I actually wanted to be alive!

After that day's vending I ran back to our tiny Oakland apartment and dragged an ancient typewriter into the water-heater room that acted as my micro-painting studio and the bedroom for our nine cats. I piled two cat-fur-coated boxes on top of each other for a desk and unearthed a wobbly step stool to sit on. I dug furiously in all of our perpetually unpacked Hefty bags until I found a somewhat clean notebook, only semi-used by my mom for last month's call lists. I tore out ten pieces of only-written-on-one-side paper, carefully cut off the jagged edges, gingerly inserted one into the typewriter and began to write.

"Writing, reading, thinking, imagining, speculating. These are luxury activities, so I am reminded, permitted to a privileged few

180

whose idle hours of the day can be viewed otherwise than as a bowl of rice or a loaf of bread less to share with the family."
—from "Women, Native, Other" by Trin T. Minh-ha

A few years later I would be exposed to the revolutionary writings of Trin Minh-ha where she talks about the privilege of writing itself. This was my truth, my struggle; I did not have the time away from earning a loaf of bread. I did not have the paper, I did not have a computer and further, like all low-income and homeless folks, I did not even have the privilege of an organized life, knowing what I would be doing from one moment to the next. I couldn't count on the fact that my wobbly desk made of boxes would even be here after this week. Without Osha Neuman's innovative advocacy, I would *never* have had the privilege to write, to think, my vocation as a writer would never have occurred to me; and this is why I always refer to his help as the first intervention, or in some circles, the first miracle.

After much haphazard poking away at the broken keys on that old machine, I tentatively began a mini-schedule. Tucked in between painting, silkscreening and selling, running errands for my mom and talking through her increasingly long list of fears and anxieties, looking for a new apartment and acquiring, fixing and following towed vehicles, I actually managed to write for a whole 30 minutes each morning, as long as I woke up at my desired 6:30 A.M.

I had written endless reams of poetry since I was 15, and several hundred pages of a sprawling romance novel when I was 10, 11 and 12, all the texts for our performance pieces and some narrative essays in a creative writing class that I sat in on with my mom, but I had never written anything that would resemble journalism. Imbued with the writer's edict, "Write what you know," with the blood, sweat and tears of our daily survival coursing through my overwhelmed mind, I embarked on a first-person narrative about one of our poverty struggles.

Most importantly I created a little corner of order in my

life. Twenty-three-and-a-half hours a day were all in preparation for those 30 minutes. Nothing, including hours upon hours of depressing sales, a landlord who decided that threats of physical violence were the way to get us out of his apartment so he could raise the rent to "market value," long untreated dental problems that were beginning to plague me, nothing could deter me from my designated appointment with the furry desk and the broken-down typewriter.

Several months, a dangerous eviction and two broken teeth later, I finished the story. I had my last appointment with Osha. "This is great," he said after reading the 1500-word essay about my struggle to get PG&E turned on. He continued, "You should try to get it published."

"Published?! Who would want to read about this?"

"A lot of people. This is an important story, you're an excellent writer, and this is good work."

I walked out of his office that day on a new mission. I was going to get published. No matter what.

CHAPTER 27

the second intervention

Two weeks after I sent out my first draft to the *East Bay Express,* my favorite local paper, which happened to be based in Berkeley and specialized in narrative essays about all kinds of issues, I received an envelope at our P.O. Box.

Ms. Garcia, we have decided to publish your essay, please contact us about necessary editing . . .

There was more on that page but I could barely see the words through the tears streaming down my face.

Two weeks later, through a blurry acrylic window on a dented *Express* news rack in downtown Oakland, I saw the issue my essay was published in. My hands trembled as I reached inside to grab a copy. The newsprint felt like velvet to my paint-stained hands. I turned each page slowly, stopping to read every ad, every entertainment listing. I must not get to page 34 too quickly. And then all of a sudden: *Criminal of Poverty by Lisa and Dee Garcia Gray;* there it was in print, my name, my struggle to survive, my solutions, and my words. I was alive; someone had heard my voice. I had hope.

Recognition is very important for most writers and artists, but for folks dealing with extreme poverty, recognition can be a life-line with life changing implications. So much about the experience of homelessness and abject poverty is humiliation. In the eyes of society, you are worthless, trash, a burden or pitiful at best. Your awareness and knowledge are not considered scholarship, your words are not valued as art or theory, you are talked about, not spoken with, written about, not read. For me, recognition meant that now I had the strength to go on living because now I had hope that there would be change, that people would hear my voice, that I could affect my own life and maybe, someday, the lives of others.

I had decided to give co-authorship credit to my mother, believing that even though it was me writing the essay, it was her life as well as mine, her struggle as well as mine and her tenacity even more than mine that informed the writing. She deserved to be recognized along with me. With that essay and countless more later on, I always gave her credit, along with the other poverty scholars to follow.

After my first essay was published I was on a roll. I wanted to write all the time, but of course, nothing had really changed. We were still very poor. Sales were very bad, and we had just gotten evicted, again. Hoping to increase sales, I began taking the subway into San Francisco, hauling a dolly, our racks and all of our clothes. This was a new experience with new risks. We had no permit to sell in San Francisco and no money or time to wait for one.

And my teeth had begun to hurt so badly that I knew I had to do something about it.

CHAPTER 28

a healthy mouth is a wealthy mouth

"You don't have the money to keep your teeth," his voice, like his face, was flat. His eyes darted from scalpel to drill, arranging and re-arranging his tools as though he was preparing to solve my dental emergency.

"Ms. Garcia, I can't help you," this time the words were a bit louder, a slight edge around *can't*. "I'm afraid that saving your teeth would require a root canal, and you stated on your intake form that you don't have the financial resources to afford that kind of a procedure."

"What can I do?"

"You have no choice but to have these teeth pulled, and I would suggest that if you're in pain, you have the extractions done immediately."

"But you said these teeth are restorable, and if they were missing it would be pretty obvious—"

"That's all you can do." Suddenly he stopped arranging the tools, snapped off his latex gloves and threw them into the trash with a pointed thump. "Well, our time's up." He made a complete military pivot and left. The whack of the door-slam vibrated the steel clamp that had seized my skull since those two teeth had become inflamed. He left me to contemplate my "choices" in the overly reclined dental chair.

For the working poor or unemployed, dental work is a luxury, ongoing dental insurance an impossibility. Now I was being encouraged to pull two teeth that were very near the front of my mouth. Okay, okay, sure. Take 'em all out. I'll spend the rest of my years gumming my food like my poor grandmother, drinking cheap coffee and smoking Lucky Strikes.

As I staggered out, the secretary suggested I try the UC Dental Clinic.

Several calls and voice mail matrixes later, I arrived at the entrance of the clinic, its massive mirrored-glass windows reflecting a lush stand of trees moving in the soft wind— California redwoods, pine and fir, whistling, flirting, daring a touch at their shiny reflections.

"Can I help you?"

"I have an appointment. Lily Smith," I added.

"Fine, just fill out this form and the doctor will call you," her voice light, in the upper registers.

I walked slowly to the chair, my eyes focused on an angry arm of a redwood tree flogging its glass counterpart.

I sat down with the metal clipboard. The intake form crackled under my pen. A steady pounding began in my ears. The sweat on my fingers began to lubricate the pen. I glanced over at the secretary—did she see me?—she was turning on a Walkman.

I began to fill in the application. Lily Smith. I glanced over again—I knew she knew—I could see her lips move as she answered a phone call, "Can I help you?" This was a code phrase; she was saying "There's someone in the waiting room committing fraud."

The pounding in my ears became a synthesized drum. I started to move across the page more quickly with the false information. Under my sweaty pen a new person was born. A healthy, problem-free, well-paid, responsible individual with no bad credit record that smoked any computer it made contact with. Past surgery? No. Any health problems? No. Just a little too busy with all her many high paying business ventures to retain a permanent dentist.

As Lily Smith, the perfect patient was being birthed, the deep throb centered somewhere in my upper left jaw had become more solid, more comfortable in its systematic attack. The throb stood alone, ate alone, and when its host was under any kind of pressure it launched a special assault of reds and purples, a dripping bloody knife in the depths of my gums.

I stood up, guided by the throb, passing the ominous security guard and on to the secretary, thrusting the completed form onto her desk without even a blink. I returned to my seat. If I were arrested, I would plead, "Not guilty," coerced to commit fraud, I would tell the judge, by "The Throb."

The throb and I sat and watched the trees, listening to the distant Muzak, *"When you're down, and troubled, and need a helping hand . . . You've got a friend."*

"Ms. Smith. Lily Smith?" a tentative voice called out my name.

"Lily Smith?"

"Oh yes, here I am."

"Lily, I'm Dr. Rogers. How are you today?"

"Just fine," the throb answered bluntly.

"Well, let's see what we can do for you."

"Uh, yeah," my tongue glided across the gutted contents of my mouth. How could I explain all these rotted, broken teeth with partial fillings? Lily Smith would have been able to afford the necessary crowns, root canals, bridges and replacements; financial problems would not have impeded her dental health.

Dr. Rogers led me to a cubicle, "Have a seat, Lily."

I climbed into the pre-reclined dental chair.

"Open up," an odd smile contorted his face as he peered into my mouth. "Whoa, you have a lot of problems, just a minute," he left the cubicle, leaving me there with my jaw agape. Should I close it? Or will he really be right back?

Suddenly three very large men in soft linen shirts, wool garbardine slacks and hastily donned white coats entered the room. They began a brief procession around my chair; when each one would look up from my mouth he would shake his head. At one point I think I saw them all shake their heads together, almost in unison.

Trisyllabic dental terms were exchanged among the three men and then they turned inward, looking at one another while one spoke to me, "Ms. Smith, you have a serious set of problems that require a series of complicated surgical procedures; there will be at least eight visits over the next three weeks."

"Okay," I tried to nod without losing the dental dam.

"And you will have to brush every single time you ingest any substance."

"Okay."

"You won't be able to chew solid food during this time, and if you eat at all you'll need to floss immediately."

"Okay."

"I notice on your application, that you carry no insurance. These procedures are going to run into several thousand dollars. Are you able to handle that?"

"Uh . . . okay . . . but will you be able to take me out of pain today?"

"Sure, we'll be performing a pulpotomy, which is just the beginning of addressing one of your problems, but it'll take you out of pain temporarily. I notice you have a lot of unfinished procedures in your mouth. Why didn't you complete the work?"

"I was too busy."

They shook their collective heads and filed out of the cubicle. As they left, the fear began to settle in my abdomen, a chilling, nail-scraping terror slamming against the walls of my stomach. The throb had transformed into a dangerous animal caged against its will in my body, determined to torture its captor.

Tools were readied, protective gear was donned by the various white-coated technicians who would attempt to control the beast. I tried to keep up with the fight, stay awake through the lengthy procedure . . .

"Ms. Smith. Ms. Smith, wake up, you're all done for today."

Lily Smith held up my shattered body that day as I crept out of the cubicle, into the waiting room and past the secretary, my eyes downcast, my breath in small shallow parcels.

"Ms. Smith?" I almost didn't turn around.

"Yes?"

"I've made your next eight appointments, the doctors say it's urgent that you keep all of them."

"Okay."

She handed me a small piece of paper with a list of days and times on it. "Oh, and Miss Smith, please bring at least $500 next time. This will be your first payment."

"Okay."

In the subsequent months, depending on the severity of my pain, new identities were created, new treatment plans started for new people who never seemed to come back for their follow-up appointments.

To avoid committing these new crimes of poverty I would spend frustrating hours on the phone researching options, even a possible incremental payment plan at UC Dental, but always ending where I'd begun, with nothing.

I began to simply deny the pain when I had it. I drank smaller and smaller sips through increasingly smaller canals in my mouth; french bread, fresh carrots, gum, candy, steak, steamed vegetables, anything cold or hot, they all became dangerous luxuries I dared not risk salivating over. This life of culinary asceticism with a heavy dose of denial sort of worked for a while, until one particularly sunny day.

My weary face warmed by a sharp April sun, I bit into a lukewarm, pre-cut bite of processed turkey. At first I only felt a crumbling sensation, like gravel beneath your feet, and then, before I could figure out the origin of the crumble, deep, fresh cleaves of pain shot from my jaw and out through my skull. I looked out of my parked car's window, certain an earthquake had ripped open the middle of the street, but instead of people running, screaming and ducking for cover the passersby walked, laughed and casually consumed all variations of the dangerous substance known as lunch, while I sat in my car trying to contain blood curdling screams.

I tried to compose myself and start the car; I must get home, at least I'll be in a safe place for the next attack. I reached for the ignition and then it came down like a hammer, a new double-strength force struck the side of my head. I slumped over the steering wheel, the sun beating down on my broken body.

UC Dental Clinic, next day:

This time it was easy, too easy. The wind was strong, whipping the trees. I walked up to the front desk; in my attempt at deception I wore glasses and a new sweater.

"Do you have an appointment?"

"No."

"Have you been here before?"

"No."

"Are you sure?"

"Yes."

She tilted her head to the side at my reply; I guess she was trying to picture me in my other sweater. "What's your name?"

"Lisa Graham."

"Fill this out and have a seat."

The false information flowed freely from my pen, my wits dulled by the severity of my pain. I looked longingly at the concrete walls, thinking I could ease the pounding in my jaw if only I could smash my head against a hard surface. "Here," I handed over the clipboard.

I watched her over the top of my battered waiting room magazine. After making a few phone calls, with pointed stares in my direction and an excessive amount of paper straightening punctuated by a punch to the stapler, she abruptly left the front desk.

I waited in a throbbing daze for hours, and then a new secretary led me back to the dentist's area. As I left the waiting room I noticed that the wind had died down, the smallest hints of afternoon were streaking across the beige linoleum. It was too quiet; even the Muzak had become more faint. I was not only the last patient, it seemed I was the only patient. In the universe.

"Miss Graham," a round-faced woman wearing a too-small uniform was directing me to the chair.

I watched the polyester cut into her back and arms as she readied the tool tray, and then I heard a voice behind me.

"Thanks, Gina," those two words raced up my spine, the tone overly clear, on the edge of a laugh.

"So I guess you are Miss Garcia—oh excuse me, Miss Graham." He was tall, very tall. His head was full of soft chestnut curls, the fluorescent rays in our cubicle shone upon his delicate gold highlights. "So I guess these all belong to you," he slapped his hand on a large stack of files, each one of them rife with notes, bills and charts. The stack teetered under his fingers, threatening to tip over and reveal the multiple personalities associated with my mouth.

He watched me for a second. "I know how it is," he paused to laugh, a large comfortable laugh. "I used to sneak my friends in to get free dental care when I was in my first year of dental school." Again he chuckled, a wayward curl falling forward onto his wide brow, and then suddenly, he focused his eyes onto mine. "So what brings you in here today?"

"I'm in severe pain."

"Let me take a look," he peered into my mouth, "Wow, you've got a lot of problems. Let me see your arms, I mean, so we can take your blood pressure."

"Why?"

"Just routine."

No, it's not, I screamed inside, this man thinks I'm a junkie.

He got up from his chair to make room for Gina and her blood pressure apparatus. Gina started rolling up the sleeve of my shirt; he stood by long enough to see my veins, then left the cube momentarily.

"Well, Miss Garcia," he was talking very loudly in a new, sharp tone, eyes wandering over the walls of the cubicle, "you know there is really nothing I can do for you. Apparently you owe quite a bit in back fees, so I can't even do an emergency procedure until you pay off the balance." He smiled, "Hey, I know how it is."

Potrero Hill Dental Clinic, three months later:

His eyes were round pools of warm water; they watched me as I spoke, only interjecting when he was sure I was finished.

"Where is the pain from, which tooth?"

"My whole mouth is in pain. I'm not sure which tooth is the problem."

"Well, let's just say the worst pain you've been having recently?" he asked very gently, with no punitive tones. As we spoke he prepared for the procedure—a delicate snap, the gloves were on; a cushioned click, the face mask was down.

I watched the motion of his over-washed white coat as it hugged his shoulders, the soft lines that ran through his carmel-colored face as he guided the exaggerated needle into the depths of my jaw. I listened, trying not to cringe. "This will be very fast, only a moment of discomfort, it should pinch just a little, only for a second, that's it, that's it, it's going to be okay," and as he continued his soothing murmur I caught a glimpse of the oversized needle withdrawing back from my mouth. In the same soft murmur, he said, "The anesthesia takes a few minutes to take effect. I'll be back."

I tried to not focus on the corners of my mouth, my lips that were becoming strangely large. I tried, instead, to be over-joyed that I was actually able to access this reduced cost procedure, partially funded by the county. As I began to become terrorized that this procedure was actually about to begin, the dentist came back in the room, followed closely by the nurse who was calling after him, "Dr. Taylor, what should we do? The medical examiner from Delancy Street said no matter what they won't approve anything but extraction."

Nervous whispers were exchanged above my head. My dentist stopped, changed his gloves and looked at the piece of paper she'd been waving in the air. He began to shake his head emphatically, "That's ridiculous. That would be bad medicine. That tooth can be restored."

"So how do you feel?" My eyes opened, sort of. I saw the bottom of my pants. They seemed calm. My hands lay beside my body quietly, as if they had nothing to say.

"We're all done," my dentist watched me, his countenance stern, calm and sad.

I remembered the subtle encouragement by the receptionist not to make more than two appointments within one month. I knew it wasn't a perfect system, but I had received the luxurious root canal. A crooked, post-anesthetized smile spread over my cottony mouth as I left the dentist's office.

CHAPTER 29

the third intervention

"Poor single mothers in this society are some of the hardest working, most under appreciated folks I know. And to be a homeless mother, a homeless child and survive, that is pure heroism," her wide brown eyes catching mine, pouring spirit with each word, "Pure heroism." She was tall and lean, her hair in tiny dreads crowning a delicate skull. Cheekbones wide and high like chiseled mountains, her smooth skin like walnut butter.

I was privileged to meet Erica Huggins, former Black Panther, artist and teacher, in a class on incarcerated women. My mother, always the seeker of knowledge, had been inching her way into a series of life-changing Women's Studies, African American Studies and La Raza Studies classes at San Francisco State.

I was like a sponge meeting water for the first time. Every class fed me with political awareness about women in poverty, first, third and fourth world contrasts and similarities, black psychology and revolutionary literature: Zora Neale Hurston, Dorothy Allison, bell hooks, Trin Minh-ha, Toni Morrison and so many more. New analysis, possible solutions and resistance.

The scholarship of Dr. Chinosole, Angela Davis, Jose Cuellar, Velia Garcia, Mina Caulfield and Dr. Wade Nobles flowed like rivers of liquid inspiration coursing through my thirsty mind. But the turning point, the moment I became truly engaged was with Erica Huggins's delicate recognition of our struggle. She went on to relate her own experience of serving two and half years in a maximum security prison; she had been framed by COINTELPRO and made to do to hard time for her activism in the Black Panther party. She connected the struggles of poor women, poor mothers and poor families, locally and globally.

Theories and histories came together to awaken a new, politically conscious Tiny and Dee. Our extreme poverty and unending crisis began to have a framework. It was in that moment with Erica and others like it in those classes that I began to re-evaluate *everything* — every media message, every implied judgment of what I should be and should have. Telling me to be ashamed that my car was towed and I that was houseless, that I had been in jail and survived by peddling on the street, that I lived with my mother as an adult and took care of her, that I lacked a formal education, that because I was a sixth-grade "drop-out" who had struggled through poverty I could not be considered an expert in anything. That my voice was irrelevant.

For the first time I began to recognize the larger context of my mother's and my impossible life, seeing us against the backdrop of a global poverty struggle. How the criminalizing effects of poverty reach across borders and oceans. How in many ways my family shares a struggle with poor families in Mexico, Africa and India. How our fears of day to day living, surviving in the underground economy, our micro-business, illegal street vending, intense work ethic, lack of property ownership, lack of credit and our endless position of struggle were shared by unseen brothers and sisters at home and around the world.

I began to articulate my values about family and togetherness, eldership and care-giving in an atmosphere where they were recognized and supported, and where my struggle to care for my mom was viewed as resistance and heroism, or just plain normal. It was here that I started to claim my own voice.

Everything began to redefined, rooted out and examined,

especially notions of mental and community health. I re-examined my own organic decision to stay with my mom within new contexts: from a Western psychotherapeutic perspective, my mom was severely phobic and I was her support person. But from the perspective of other almost every non-Western culture from Asia to Africa and all in between, nobody is *ever* left alone the way they are in the United States. Here, aloneness, "independence," is valued as a virtue, a strength, a form of normalcy, a barometer for sanity, whereas in other cultures togetherness, the group, the collective, is the norm. So, from a non-western belief system, or "deep structure" analysis as they say in Black Psychology, did my mama really have agoraphobia, was there even such an "illness" I wondered, or did we as a society have an insane and twisted notion of what sanity was? Perhaps my mother's worst problem was that she had no extended family.

All of these insights came to me in flashes, like light searing through a dark tunnel. My political consciousness was being born. Now if I could only get a minute away from survival mode to process it all.

I began writing more. All of my stories were written in a personal narrative format meant to be literary advocacy, and I submitted them to all kinds of publications, local and national. With the wide submissions came an ever-growing pile of rejections. Of course, all writers get rejections, it's part of the process, but my rejections came with a disturbing twist that continues to this day: as a journalist focusing almost exclusively on poverty and racism, I have confronted the intentional disinterest in poverty as a subject in most corporate newspapers and national literary magazines. "Too much misery," was one reply I received, or the advice to write about something else, "perhaps a current affairs story."

But I had little time to focus on this issue. Sales were worse than usual, we were facing eviction again, our car had just been towed, and with that we had nowhere to live and no way to make any money. It was during this last bout of hunger and homelessness that my mother and I decided I should apply for welfare.

A 25-page application, six different documents proving homelessness, three documents proving income (or rather, lack thereof), at least two documents proving residence in California and six intake appointments later, I received a whopping $279 check and $60 in food stamps. In order to receive this "free money" I had to wake up at 5:00 A.M. two mornings a week to sweep the streets. This was called "Workfare," the seldom-mentioned job required of all welfare recipients nationwide in order to receive their meager cash grant—which, of course, shouldn't be called a "grant" at all, since in reality it's a below-minimum-wage salary paid for work that used to be done for a living wage.

But this labor-intensive, hard work is not called *work*. Instead, to continue the mythology of the lazy welfare recipient who doesn't want to work, this work is called Workfare, and instead of receiving a living wage you "earn" your monthly cash assistance. Workfare jobs can vary from cleaning buses to sweeping streets or doing maintenance work at a county hospital, and depending on the city, they pay an equivalent in cash assistance of less than $2 per hour. Considering the unsafe working conditions, the lack of respect and the fact that these jobs were previously paid at a living wage, Workfare is viewed by many economic justice advocates as modern-day slavery.

Applying for welfare had taken several days away from any money making or apartment searching, and even with the infusion of cash we were still on the brink of immediate outsideness. Since I was now doing most of my unlicensed vending in different locations in San Francisco, and on many days I could barely afford public transportation to even get there from Oakland, my mother suggested that we seek out new housing frontiers.

A newer, updated, slightly hipper version of the rent-starter suit was assembled, and out I went. The stakes were higher than ever; we absolutely had to find a place or we would end up on the street, without even a car to hide in this time. I had 15 days from application to deposit to move-in. But this time something was different.

"You don't have any credit cards?!" After the tenth rejection I realized I was encountering a not so subtle, very powerful form of classism. It wasn't that these San Francisco landlords didn't buy the *innocent-suit-wearing-working-person-who-will-pay-their-rent-on-time-and-is-a-stellar-tenant* act; it just wasn't enough.

In my whole history of rent-starting, I had never lied about having credit. No one had ever offered me a credit card, sent me letters of solicitation for loans on cars or houses. I had nothing except a delinquent phone bill in my name, which stood out, alone and proud on the otherwise blank pages of my credit report.

So with the exception of my dental and rental crimes, when I said that I had no credit, good or bad, to all of the landlords in Los Angeles, Berkeley and Oakland I had been completely honest. But in San Francisco it wasn't okay to just be credit-free and hard working with a good story; it was necessary that one be "established," with credit cards, a car loan, or at least wealthy relatives in order to actually attain the coveted Lease. And so, on the tenth day of my search I still had no apartment and not much hope of getting one.

I was walking through the Tenderloin district of San Francisco scribbling down numbers from every possible For Rent sign in my path when I saw it. It wasn't obvious, almost obscured by a dust-blurred window, FOR RENT with a tiny printed reference to an obscure realty company. The same information was also printed in Cantonese.

"Hello, I'm calling about the apartment for rent."

"Who is it for?"

"Myself and my mother. She's disabled, and I'm her sole caregiver. I'm a hard-work—"

"Oh, you are a good daughter, that's wonderful. Why don't you come by tomorrow so we can talk? Your mother is very lucky to have a good daughter like you."

"Okay," I said quickly, baffled by my new title. A Good Daughter, is that what I was? No one had ever recognized my sacrifice to help my mom at all, much less recognized it as something "good."

I met the diminutive Laura, property manager and friend to the even more diminutive Mrs. Chin, an 83-year-old monolingual Chinese elder who owned and resided in a tiny two-unit building in the Tenderloin. Within minutes of our meeting, I was laughing a genuine laugh, not the fake sycophantic landlord laugh I employed at most of these interactions. Within a few more minutes I was telling her *everything*. Well, almost everything. She was still a realtor, after all. But I told her about most of our struggles, I told her hard I worked to keep us both alive. I told her how we didn't have any family to turn to because my mom was basically an orphan. And I told her that I would work as hard as I could to pay the rent, as I always did.

At the end of my story Laura hugged me and told me about her own struggle with her daughters, how only one of them was a Good Daughter, how she had done the same thing with her own mother. She told me about the tradition in all Chinese families for the children to take care of their elders. She told me how scared she was about the new generation of American-born Chinese children who wouldn't even consider working with their parents, and their parents who wouldn't insist, how she feared that the breaking down of traditions would lead to the breaking down of the Chinese community.

I later found out that what Laura was referring to was called "eldership" by Ethnic Studies scholars. And how that eldership was key to the health of not only the elders, but the children and everyone else in the community, for that matter. I also learned that capitalism does not support eldership, since people aren't as free to be good capitalists when they're worried about being good daughters and good sons. They aren't as likely to go out and rent their own apartments to live separately from their families; they aren't buying their own furniture, their own cars, their own food. In effect, the intact, multigenerational group sharing of resources, goods and land just isn't as good for business.

Eight months passed. With my mother and I doing nonstop assembly-line screening and painting sessions and no new crises thrown in our path, we had paid the rent on time, every month like the good tenants we strove to be. I wrote whenever I could, the beginnings of a novel taking shape in one of my many notebooks. Knowledge about collective banking, micro-economics, the struggles of poor women and families in the third world, and the scholarship of Trin Minh-ha and others were rolling through my mind, courtesy of my appropriated education at SF State, consistently informing my experience now. And perhaps most importantly, I was making very tentative inroads into organizing little piles of my belongings. I was slowly unfurling from a mountain of Hefty bags, in what was now the longest stretch of time I had ever inhabited any space. And then the shoe dropped.

I got really sick. So sick that I couldn't go out and sell on the ice-like winter streets. I was bedridden for ten days. That was more than enough to ruin us.

Although my mother was always involved in the vending, it didn't happen without me. It was only after I had set up the space and worked it for half the day that she would arrive, "ready to sell" for the remaining two hours. It was extremely difficult for her to get out of the house on any given day because her often depressed and always anxious mind was easily waylaid by too many thoughts, scattered goals and the urgent tasks of survival. But once there, unlike me, she actually really enjoyed selling because of the inherent community, immediacy and tangibility of the experience. Still, without me, selling did not happen.

Within days of my illness, we got the shut-off notice for an overdue water bill.

"Realty Company, can I help you?"

"Hi Laura, this is Lisa."

"Oh Lisa, how are you?"

"Not so good, a lot of bad things have hit at once, mostly that I got sick and then we got behind on everything, and now we don't have this month's rent."

"Do you need some time to pay the rent, dear?"

"Well, yes, if that's possible 'cause we don't have it right now, but I think I'm getting better, and I've been selling more than ever, and I'm sure I'll be able to get caught up by the first of next month."

"No problem dear. Just call me on the first and we'll see how you are."

"Okay, thank you so much Laura, and please thank Mrs. Chin for me."

"Its okay Lisa, just get well."

Things didn't get better by the next month. In fact, things didn't get better for several months because when things go bad they aren't easily made better when you have very little resources to begin with and even less left for the aftermath. But for the first time in my life, thanks to a kind and empathic landlord steeped in old-school Chinese culture, a financial crisis didn't mean we were facing homelessness. And this, perhaps, was the most important intervention of all because had it not been for the kind-hearted Laura and Mrs. Chin, I would never have had the chance to rest, to think, to dream, to conceptualize, to breathe. Or to unpack my clothes.

CHAPTER 30

my sister

It was during this time, with our first glimpse of stability, that my mother began the lengthy process involved in realizing a long-cherished dream to increase the size of her family. My mom's search for family and community was relentless and insatiable and it was a constant topic of discussion, her optimism about how we could achieve it and her mourning of the loss of the community we'd had in Venice Beach and Fresno, and she'd had in Camarillo and Hawaii. So as soon as she had half a second to think because of our newfound homefulness, she knew she had to pursue her dream.

My mother had also nurtured a lifelong dream of helping a child like she had been, a so-called "special needs child" or "older child" adoption. Her own experience as a child who was considered too old for adoption and languished in foster homes and the orphanage like an unwanted pet, watching other kids, cuter, smaller and younger get adopted, had galvanized this hope in her long ago. After endless amounts of paperwork, several home visits and interviews that spanned over four months, my mother legally adopted a nine-year-old mixed-race girl. A girl almost exactly like she had been as a child.

My sister walked through the door of our house with trepidation. Who were we? Did we really love her or was this just another stopping off point? She was quiet and thoughtful and full of natural distrust. Her parents had dealt with poverty and homelessness, and her mother, from what I could deduce, was another casualty of poverty, abuse and multiple foster homes. She had lost her mom in a tragic highway accident, another sorrow piled on a lifetime of sorrows, too many for her young shoulders to carry.

Taking care of a child, especially one who supposedly had "special needs," would be very difficult as we were barely dealing with our own survival on the little bit of money that I made, and then there were my mom's needs and all the other basic survival stuff that we always had to do. We both knew that. But my mother had taught me that nothing was ever too hard to do when it came to people, community and advocacy; as a matter of fact, *nothing* was ever too hard to do in life. Period. If it had to be done then it must be done, unless you were deathly ill, and even then it was somehow accomplished. This unrelenting work ethic and refusal to accept defeat or failure was one of the crazy wonderful things that my mother infused into me. Survival was just something you always did, no matter what.

Sadly, as much as my mom wanted to give love and receive it, in some ways she was even more afraid and distrustful than this little girl. Nonetheless, we all tried very hard to be a family, spending a lot of joy-filled time creating art, stories, music, and having in-depth political discussions, mixed in with plenty of old-school, hands-on child raising. My mom believed in being very present in a child's life and fought hard to get my sister her rightful access to services in an under-funded California public school system. She dispatched me on big-sister duties, which included picking her up everyday at school and taking her to as many activities and classes as my mom could find for free.

All of this familyness continued until my mom and sister's problematic relationship blew up once and for all four years later in a late-night, drama-filled, gut-wrenching crisis call. Their decline into nonstop contentiousness had begun when my sister hit fourteen and started trying to "hang out," wearing make-up and tight clothes and exhibiting other manifestations of teen behavior. Their fighting increased and became more desperate.

It all ended in an impossible slide down the slippery slope of Child Protective Services who accused my mom of not allowing my sister to "act like a normal teen," and cited the fact that we lived in a "low-income neighborhood" as part of the condemnation of our bad home. The whole experience was, as my mom described it, another little murder of the soul. Due to the horrendous nature of child abuse and its inevitable serious-ness, CPS is run like a mini-feifdom, with a lot of subjective, non-restorative family planning and punitive discriminatory policies, leaving countless families damaged. My mother had little recourse in her fight to keep my sister, and the authorities remained unconvinced of her merit as a "proper" parent.

CHAPTER 31

POOR is born

"The Kuna of Panama are one of the few indigenous tribes who control their own wealth, their own production of goods, and their own land. This is why they have successfully fought off multiple attempts at colonization." One of the last and most brilliant instructors I had the privilege to learn from was a teacher by the name of Mina Caulfield. Over the course of one short semester she illuminated the ways that several peoples had resisted the oppression of colonization by being in control of their own monetary systems.

That semester's selection of inspiration, education and consciousness—the powerful resistance of the Kuna people, the words of Toni Morrison and Mumia abu Jamal, courtesy of Professor Chinosole, and the haunting voice of Puerto Rican poet Piri Thomas—filled my slightly-less-tense mind. After months of living in Mrs. Chin's apartment, tasting at least a tiny bit of what stability might actually feel like, my mind was finally freer, at least somewhat, to think beyond daily survival. It was in this period that the birth occurred.

One of my best friends had just had a baby boy, and I had some time to kill before going to the hospital for a visit. I opted to go into a nearby bookstore, where I browsed the magazine section, soaking up all the specialty magazines. It seemed there was a glossy, high-production monthly for just about any interest or hobby. As I stood there, blinded by their collective multicolored sheen, I realized there was something glaringly absent. In a textual river of titles including *Money, Artforum, New Yorker, Atlantic Monthly, Cars, Cigars, Guitars, Artweek, Newsweek* and *Golfweek*, where was the word Poor?

Later, as I rode the elevator down from the maternity ward to the lobby, I suddenly felt a lightness; a strong breeze filled with floating ideas struck me all at once, almost lifting me off my feet. "That's it!" I shouted, "That's what's missing!" I was addressing a stain on the strip of industrial carpet that lined the elevator wall. "Why shouldn't poor folks have a beautiful magazine all their own, filled with literary and visual art, from people unseen, unheard, something so fine and glossy that it would reach across the great divide of class and privilege?" Bits of conversation, poetry, the shared search for solutions, opinions on issues ranging from shelter food to life in an SRO, the knowledge and talent of my homeless friends, many of whom were unrecognized artists in their own right, all of whom were poverty scholars, some of whom were just like I'd been a year ago, barely holding on and in desperate need of hope. All of whom were in need of some recognition, some love and beauty. I knew what I must do.

The elevator doors flew open, small children and animals looked on in awe. My flowing white beard and orange caftan waved softly in the morning breeze.

From that day on I was filled with the kind of unstoppable motivation one must have to attempt the impossible. What I was setting out to do would potentially cost a sum of money that I couldn't even imagine, and it would take several designers, editors, writers and artists to bring it all together, not to mention the biggest commodity of all: time. I had no backing, no secret friends in the publishing industry, no computer, no cash, no credit and most of all no spare time.

"Law offices."

"Hello, Osha, it's Tiny. Do you have a minute?"

"Yeah, what's up?"

"Well, I have a big idea, and I'm gonna make it happen no matter how hard it is," my words flew out in a nonstop rush. "I want to create a literary magazine dealing with issues of poverty and racism, stories, not a 'zine or newspaper but a glossy, intentionally high-end magazine like *Artforum* or the *New Yorker*. It would be nationally distributed and it would contain the writing, art and knowledge of poor and homeless youth and adults, their stories and what they think about trying to survive, stay alive and be heard. And it would be solution-driven, addressing the root causes of poverty and racism, and with information on how people could help themselves out of homelessness and how folks with privilege could help folks who need it. Anyway, the only missing link is someone who would print it. You know I have no credit or money or, well, you know. So do you know any printers who might do it for free or maybe on credit?"

"Whoa, well, that's a cool idea but the only printers I can think of are Inkworks, here in Berkeley. They do a lot of movement stuff and they're a union shop. I don't know if they'll give you credit, but you can tell them about your project and see what they say."

"Thanks for the tip! I'll check it out right away. Talk to you soon, bye."

Click. Dial.

"Inkworks, can I help you?"

A few seconds later, I was talking to a sweet-voiced man in their production department. I explained my idea to him, and after a few minutes he said, "Well, we can't do it for free, but we could give you our best reduced price."

"Okay, what would that be?"

"Well, a rough estimate based on the page count and quality of paper, I'd say approximately $6,000."

"Okay, thanks. I'll call you when it's ready to go."

I had just heard the most preposterous amount of money that I had never had my hands on and didn't expect to any time soon, but it didn't matter. I was on a roll. No obstacle seemed too great, no problem insurmountable. And in the process, oddly synchronistic events began to collect in my life, moving things forward and keeping me filled with hope.

On one of the rare occasions that my mother and I decided we could afford the gas and time away from selling to drive out of town, my sister, my mom and I piled into our car and started driving north toward Marin County. Once there we happened upon one of the little boutique coastal towns common to Northern California. After we parked my mother decided she needed to use the restroom, and the only bathroom for non-customers of the over-priced local restaurants was in a little bookstore. In we all trotted, instantly marked for shoplifting by our unsightly, oversized backpacks and dangling plastic bags.

The store was lined with coffee table books in large format color, none selling for less than $50, so I only looked on in admiration, noting their fine printing and binding quality, something I was now obsessed with. After I finished soaking up the array of literary delicacies, my eyes traveled nonchalantly over the check-out desk, and there they locked onto a tiny card announcing a gallery opening. There it was, one of the most frightening, beautiful and haunting images I had ever seen, and I knew immediately that it was the only image befitting the cover of Volume 1 of the as yet unpublished *POOR Magazine*. The title of the painting was printed in tiny type under the image: "The Hammer" by Evri Kwong.

The painting's background was film noir black-brown, a spotlight at the center shone on a very sad young girl, seemingly made of clay, lying on the ground outside of a toy house and toy car. Above the whole tableau was the oversized head of a giant, foreboding hammer. I asked the woman behind the desk if she knew of the artist or how I could get in touch with him, but she knew nothing about it; a previous customer had accidentally left the card on her desk, and the opening it advertised had long since passed.

When we got home I made several futile attempts to reach the gallery, but it was closed for an extended period of time and in a few weeks I gave that up. But I vowed that I'd find the artist since I was convinced that nothing else would do for the cover.

One day a few weeks later, I was driving with my ex-boyfriend on our way to get coffee — we were casual friends now, no more drama, no more pain, only mutual art and caffeine appreciation. As we talked, I suddenly noticed on his dashboard a small gallery opening card. I grabbed it.

"Do you know him?" I screamed.

"Oh, you mean Evri? Of course, he's a great friend; do you want to meet him?" he said this in the blasé style he'd been perfecting in order to seem painfully sophisticated.

"Do I want to meet him?! That's the cover of my magazine, that and nothing else!" I was pointing at the card as I shouted.

The next weekend, I had the pleasure of meeting the prolific Asian American painter Evri Kwong. We became instant soul mates. He immediately understood and believed in my vision for *POOR*, and I was startled and deeply moved by all of his work. He said that he was more than happy to allow the use of his image and pledged his support in any other way we could see fit.

After the magical meeting with Evri, I began conducting a series of what I called Extreme Outreach writing workshops, holding them in every place I could access where poor folks sought services, including the General Assistance (welfare) and Social Security offices, food stamp delivery centers, in shelters, group homes, and on the streets where we lived and died.

In the shelters they would allow us to convene in the community rooms, and in the GA and SSI offices the groups were very informal, a gathering of hard plastic chairs in a corner of the waiting room, away from the security guard and service windows. With the youth in group homes it had to be a formal agreement, created by an letter of inquiry and a series of calls and proposal letters.

The workshops were led by me, or me and my mom, and grew to include a core leadership of poor folks that was starting to build, culled from each workshop. They were organized in various ways, from simple drop-in meetings to a structured ten-week series of workshops. The locations were important in the success of the process, since they were *our* places and spaces and we weren't some outsiders coming in to colonize or patronize the "poor people," "poor youth," "homeless people," "welfare recipients," "old people," "those people." In fact, the first thing we addressed in each workshop was the necessity of discarding those marginalizing titles and personas and replacing them with experts, scholars, artists, poets and writers.

I had no formal experience or education to be a teacher, but I deeply understood the ways in which people could access their voice, and I intuited styles of getting at it that included creative writing exercises, sensory exercises, and consciousness-raising sessions. It was the result of a natural and long-practiced inclination to advocate and inspire people in crisis, which I had done for my mom for years. I was, as my mom would tell me, an organic intellectual.

I also knew that like me, these folks needed a new way of seeing their own situation, that more often than not they were not viewing their life through a politically conscious lens. They were caught in the wheel of shame about who they were, what they had not achieved, who they were supposed to be and how they had been taught to feel about their poverty and/or their family's poverty. More often than not, they didn't value their own experience and scholarship, and they rarely, if ever, claimed or represented their life experience and knowledge with pride.

And finally, from the core of my heart, I knew that everyone who wanted to write, who wanted to make art, who wanted to be heard but who didn't have the access to education, time and/or resources, should be given that space, that ability, that voice, so that they, like me, would be given some hope.

The workshops were life-changing for most folks who got

involved. Once people were given that space and empower-ment, the ideas and scholarship flowed. It wasn't just writing that we were doing, it was visionary problem solving: How do you solve homelessness in a capitalist society where the housing and land are owned by people with no accountability to their community? What are the roots of poverty and home-lessness, and how do you articulate those findings?

We led each workshop focused on actually creating a tem-plate for the solution to the problem that we put forth. To solve homelessness we went to the scholars like ourselves who had lived through homelessness. We did extensive research on the issue, and together we developed several different templates for long-term change, culminating in what we proposed as a solution. Our solution to homelessness was Homefulness, which became the title of *POOR Magazine*, Volume 1. The idea was to create an arts-based, sweat equity co-housing project that included a school for kids and adults, available on a sliding scale depending on what you could afford, and pro-viding everyone with that elusive thing that would ultimately take them out of homelessness on a permanent basis: equity.

One of the early expectations that I placed on the partici-pants in the workshops was that everyone needed to try their best to write well. Not just write, but write well. Also, they were encouraged to write about their truths from a first-person perspective: "I," not "they" or "them." And finally, it was stipu-lated that there should be no table-pounding, preaching or edi-torializing, that the same power can be communicated by a good metaphor.

The "I" requirement served several purposes: it required folks to be honest about their personal positions of oppression, their disability, their incarceration, their homelessness, police harass-ment, eviction, job-loss, their substance use and/or abuse, and by the very act of claiming these things it required them to stop the shame that surrounds them. This was never easy, and it usually required several sessions for each group to get at the root causes of that shame, both societally and personally.

The table-pounding was equally complicated. People who have been through a lot often feel the need, as I did, to yell about it in their writing, to indict the systems and/or the people that played a role in oppressing them. We had to show by example, with reading and writing exercises that demonstrated why, for example, a stronger case for welfare reform policy could be "shown, not told," by a well-written story about a homeless family on welfare.

In addition to these workshops, I also initiated some of POOR's early collaborations with several grassroots nonprofit arts organizations in the Bay Area that served very low and no-income youth and adults, such as Sixth Street Photography, the Luggage Store Gallery, the Coalition on Homelessness, the Suitcase Clinic and WritersCorp. We would run workshops with their participants or publish content culled from their own innovative projects. And looking toward a national/global solution, we established similar contacts with groups across the nation and in other parts of the world who were doing work on issues of poverty and racism. We learned about innovative solutions such as sweat equity housing projects, "squats" that had become permanent housing in New York, micro-economic initiatives and savings circles in Bangladesh and Haiti.

It was from these very successful workshops and collaborations that the voices, poetry and art were gathered to make up the content that became Volume 1 of POOR Magazine. While I and an ad hoc group of other organic intellectuals, houseless poverty scholars and writers were facilitating the grassroots production of a large body of literary work, Evri was helping me to reach across the divide of class privilege and into a pool of artists with expensive art school educations who were willing to have their artwork published in the first literary magazine on poverty.

Although it was our belief that POOR should be led by, created for and provide innovative resources to very low- and no-income youth, adults and elders, it was also our belief that the only way we could accomplish some of our media resistance goals—such as creating a new understanding of communities in poverty, fostering societal empathy rather than sympathy—as well as our personal, organizational goals—like flipping the poverty shame script, addressing the daily police harassment and abuse of poor people and people of color, achieving educational equity and real affordable housing for all, giving media voice to poor youth and adults—would be by reaching across the race and class divide, informing, raising awareness and making change happen through a collaborative effort of wealthy and poor, white and non-white, youth and elders.

My belief is that all of these forms of separation are like national borders, false and inhuman. Discrimination based on class, race, age and culture feeds into a capitalist system of separation and, as Dr. Wade Nobles stated in an article he wrote with my mother in Volume 4 of *POOR*, things that are separate from me are easier to harm. So we based our whole structure on a sliding scale policy in an effort to break down the walls of separation, and it was from this perspective that we also asked the established artists with gallery connections to donate work to our fundraising efforts, and in so doing facilitated the launch of *POOR*.

POOR

Volume 1, 1996
$3.95

MAGAZINE

HOMEFULNESS

Cover of *POOR Magazine*, Volume 1, "Homefulness". Original art by Evri Kwong.

CHAPTER 32

one year later

Being homeless ain't the thang for me.
Walking around with beat up clothes it's a catastrophe.
Can't take a shower I'm all funky and hot,
Staying in a old building sleeping in a cardboard box.
Living in this world it's a big struggle.
Trying to do jobs awarding myself with scratches on
my knuckles.
Being poor is like a maze,
Being in one place locked up in a cage.
No water, no food, no place to move,
Being poor is not nothing to prove.
It's like getting stabbed in the heart with a knife,
I need to get up and change my life.
Serving people saying Ma'am or Sir,
Getting out of this hell hole I'm my own answer.
— by Timothy Holden (age 16)

A year of street vending, shirt painting, workshop leading, art curating, copyediting, writing, outreach, administration and a desperate, underground form of fundraising passed without a hitch, or almost. Everything went right and everything went wrong, but nothing deterred me, no matter how impossible things might seem.

As the submissions of poetry and stories began to trickle in, culled from our multitude of workshops and workshop partners across the country, a new, unforeseen and seemingly impossible problem began to take shape: I had no computer, no access to one and no knowledge of how to use one even if I had it. Then I discovered the computer lab at Kinko's.

It started out as a search for a makeshift office to enforce my own form of writing discipline. There was no extra space in Mrs. Chin's tiny place, no painting closet that could double as an office for writing, so after roaming the streets in search of some kind of place to write that had a typewriter, I found the magic that was Kinko's. I could go there twice a day for my regulation two hours that I had set aside for writing and sit unbothered at the now unpopular typewriter. I would write, first in longhand, and then edit on the typewriter.

One day, I tremulously climbed the winding stairs that led up to the inner sanctum of the computer lab. A large sign demanded the toll to access: $.60 a minute. That meant it could potentially cost thousands of dollars that I could never attain just to word process all of the writing for the magazine. I sat down, momentarily discouraged. And then it came to me: there had to be a system, everything from welfare to jail to banking was based on some kind of system.

Within minutes of covert observation I had cracked it. It was all about access codes and who you knew.

His eyes and skin were a deep brown hue and he sported a small goatee. He was the computer lab attendant for Tuesdays and Thursdays. I launched a week-long assault of focused sexual politicking until I finally attained the access hook-up. Tuesdays and Thursdays were my favorite days.

Now the work began. Hours upon hours of time—stolen, as Trin Minh-ha said, away from the time it took to earn a loaf of bread—were spent in Kinko's. Early in the morning and late at night I tapped away, sorting through submissions that had come in on notebook paper, the backs of old envelopes, paper bags and even slices of cardboard boxes. My self-taught, too-slow word processing only skimmed the surface of the volume of work that had to be done, and the remainder of it was only made possible by the help I received from one of my best friends, Jennifer Harris, copyeditor and transcriber by day, visual artist extraordinaire by night. She was barely supporting herself on a part-time job, working from her home as a transcriber, which meant that she had a computer, and she helped us in every spare minute she could.

From that conundrum I moved to the next one: layout. I recruited the help of Eduardo Paulo, a talented artist and graphic designer, friend of another artist friend, who took the entire pile of poetry, prose, visual art and resource lists and transformed it into a coherent document ready for publication. Eduardo, and later David Baal and Kristen Bouvier (who worked on later volumes) were all graphic designers who'd had the privilege of an art school education and had launched their own businesses, but who also believed in what we were doing enough to donate several hundred hours of their time to this effort.

And then finally we were there. All 75 beautiful pages were safely nesting on a thing my digitally divided self had never seen before, called a Zip disk. The only problem was, we still didn't have any money to print. It was at that moment that I dreamt up my first fundraising project: Fun-Ding would be an art performance, auction and all around night of pure fun to raise money for the printers.

Getting a turnout for the event was the result of a concerted effort of time, foot power and name recognition. In collaboration with the Four Walls Gallery who hosted the event, Evri's artist friends and *POOR Magazine* founders and volunteers, we flyered the whole city with a card emblazoned with the planned cover of Volume 1, Evri's beautiful painting. The night was hosted by the wild and crazy Michael Pepe and me, a weave of salsa dancing and auctioneering, and it was a huge success. We had artwork for sale and performance by Barry

McGee, RIGO, Barry Schwartz, Michael Brian Foley, Chico MacMurtrie, Scott MacLeod, and the amazing Evri, who donated the proceeds of one of his large paintings. The art flew off the walls and the dollars flew in, and it was truly a Fun-Ding event. But despite our success, we only raised $2,100 and still needed $2000 more.

One thick-aired day in July I was standing in my favorite unlicensed vending spot, trying to sell at least one t- shirt so I could buy lunch, when a woman wearing a beautifully tailored ensemble came rushing down the street. I recognized her immediately; she was on the board of an organization that helped women get small business loans. Years before I'd embarked on *POOR*, we had tried to get a loan through this organization but were turned down because of prohibitive requirements, such as the necessity to organize your project into a business plan, which required regular attendance in classes on how to write a business plan, the ability to "show a profit," and the requirement for some kind of collateral to secure the loan. Anyway, she knew we were turned down for the loan, because of course my never-take-no-for-an-answer mom had caused a big stink, and she had felt bad about it and vowed to help us out in the future if she could. I stepped in front of her, reminded her who I was, and began my breathless pitch, determined to win her support for *POOR*.

"I and a whole group of very dedicated folks have worked all year to get this done. We started with nothing, as you know, but now at the end of the year we have raised $2,100, which is great, but it's not enough because we need at least $4000 for the printer to even start the job. Do you have any ideas, do you know of anyone who might lend us some money? We only need $2000. We could pay it back. I'm teaching myself to write grants, and one from the San Francisco Arts Commission looks really promising, or it could be an emergency grant or . . ."

My pleas floated down that busy street in the financial dis-trict, weaving in and out of cars and sailing above our heads into the windy afternoon. I couldn't hear myself; I only felt the sheer desperation of being that close and yet that far away, knowing that after all my struggle there was no other solution to turn to.

"Call me tomorrow in my office and maybe we can work something out."

Two days later, with $4,100 in my backpack, I stood at the front counter of Inkworks. My trembling hands held the Zip disk as I awaited the production representative with the oddly appropriate name of Lincoln.

Six weeks later

The day had a sweet smell, a just after rain smell, even though it hadn't rained. The clouds floated in the Bay Area sky like boats in a calm ocean, large, silent, almost unmoving. Today was the day. I had gotten the call, "Ms. Garcia, your magazines are ready for pick-up." It felt hard to keep my breath in my lungs. It was everything and everything, and it was ready. For pick-up.

I drove across the bridge, alternately blasting Tupac, Little Richard and Celia Cruz, and then I pulled into the driveway of Inkworks. Normal things like walking and opening doors, sitting down, licking my lips and swallowing all rolled into one dream-like movement.

"Because you don't have the balance of the cost, we can give you half of the magazines now and we'll keep the rest until you can pay for them." As the accounts person was describing their payment plan, Lincoln emerged from the back room with a copy of the magazine. He was rubbing his hand over the cover as though it was a kitten or a soft rug.

"Here it is." My hands reached out and everything became golden. A sane, more logical me continued to stand there and discuss when I would get them the rest of the money. The golden me was screaming and dancing and running outside. When the logical me was done, we opened the door and made it as far as the front stairs, where we both collapsed into a huddle with the magic that was *POOR Magazine* Volume 1, "Homefulness."

I sat there for many minutes, my hands catching the tears pouring from my eyes before they could buckle the fine glossy cover adorned with Evri's beautiful painting. My fingers caressed the pages, the stories, the solutions, the poetry, the resources.

As I stood to leave, I looked up at the sky. They were there, the flying words from Osha's office, floating on one of the ocean liner clouds. *"I feel good! I feeeeel good!!"* they were playing James Brown again. But this time something was different; in the middle, between all the R's, S's and E's for rent, eviction and sorrow were four letters standing together in neat order, spelling one word with so much meaning, simultaneously empowering, degrading and full of resistance in its directness, its possibilities and its pain: *POOR.*

CHAPTER 33

hard realities

So now,
they rename us . . .
to
members of the lodging tribe
and
remove us from the land
for having to sleep
there . . .
—*from "Arrested Artistry," a poem by Ken Moshesh*

After the unbelievable wonderfulness of *POOR* Volume 1 happened, a new kind of schizophrenia was birthed.

"How much is this t-shirt? Excuse me. Hey, how much is this t-shirt??" The day after receiving our first boxes of magazines and stuffing them in every spare corner of our broken-down car, I was back hustling t-shirts on the street for that day's lunch.

In the year of extreme outreach and writing workshops leading up to the publication of Volume 1, I had squirreled away $10 a month to pay for a voice mail that acted as *POOR's* message phone. That and the six boxes of as yet undistributed magazines was the sum total of *POOR's* assets, and if I didn't sell a t-shirt, I still didn't eat lunch.

Nothing had really changed, and yet everything had changed. Between vending, painting, silkscreening, helping my mom and my little sister, I was planning and leading workshops and outreach efforts in juvenile halls, elementary, middle and high schools, on the streets, in churches and community centers all over the Bay Area.

I had also begun to teach myself to write grants, beginning with an individual artist's grant offered by the San Francisco Arts Commission. After a painful and rigorous process of learning how to construct a "businesslike" sentence with my sixth-grade education in grammar and basic composition, I actually wrote a rather decent proposal and got the grant. That $10,000 allowed us to pay off the balance to Inkworks and pay the poor folks a small stipend for their submissions. This was very important to me, as I believe that it is critical to create access for poor artists by lessening, if at least temporarily, one of their primary problems, their poverty. Any remaining money went to the endlessly challenging Dee & Tiny rent fund, and I was still vending every day just to eat.

The word "hard" does not do justice to the layers of struggle that filled my plate while juggling the parallel realities of working on this extremely valuable project while also trying to survive and support my family, to keep us housed and keep the utilities on. My life was a mix of inspiration and struggle, hunger and hope, resistance and reality, but I was way too hopeful to ever get completely discouraged. Nothing was impossible. I had proven that, at least temporarily.

Many years later, after we'd won struggles to achieve powerful acts of media resistance—such as founding a multimedia publishing arm to produce youth poet/spoken word projects, instituting a teaching program in Poverty Scholarship, community organizing that prevented shopping carts from being seized from poor recyclers and African American elders from being evicted, and on and on—successful efforts that were met with discouraging losses of funding for the organization, I eventually lost the ability to be blindly hopeful. I had to recognize the inherent nature of philanthropy which, barring the support we received from the Catholic Campaign for Human Development, was all fraught with an element of patron/pimp mentality. I realized sadly that most "successful" nonprofit organizations are run by Executive Directors or board members who have an independent source of funding such as family money or trust funds, and poor folks aren't the ones deemed "best suited" to determine and service our own needs.

But this was the beginning and I didn't know that yet, so nothing could hold me back.

Members of the Po' Poets Projekt of *POOR Magazine* (l to r): Mari, Tiny, Dharma, Po'Poet Laureate A. Faye Hicks, Jewnbug, and JR from the *SF Bayview Newspaper* after one of their "extreme outreach" workshops.

CHAPTER 34

POOR practices

From the beginning, *POOR* practiced an indigenous organizing model, which meant that the key leadership of the organization would consist of family, elders and friends, in that order. Logistically what that meant was endless discussions among all concerned until we reached a unified organizational voice. After things were cleared and argued between Dee and myself, they were then cleared, conceived, built and organized with *POOR* elders and poverty scholars through a process of discussion, analysis, group critique and learning.

None of this is easy to do, but it is a common practice of indigenous communities and also many families (mostly from the third world) who have businesses or enterprises together. If one family member gets rich, "connected," or has an opportunity to build something, it's incumbent upon them to create access and/or a job for the other members of the family. Also, if a business is to be started with little or no financial capital it's imperative for families and communities to work together and help each other out with human capital as a way to come up together out of poverty. For very low-income, at-risk families like ours, barely making it in a capitalist society, we felt that intentionally adopting these non-capitalist principles of interdependence, collectivity and co-habitation was a key element of our survival.

We began to form the core leadership of *POOR*'s staff: Dee and me, Ken Moshesh, Jennifer Navarro, Deshawn Hollins, Joseph Bolden, Eddie Camacho, and Roxanne Trade, each one a poverty scholar and a poverty survivor, from Oakland, San Francisco, Santa Rosa, Costa Rica and beyond.

Ken Moshesh was homeless at that time, a former Black Panther, an artist, percussionist and videographer. He was the elder statesman of *POOR*, and in his tenure with us he co-authored several journalistic pieces, took a leadership role in the launch of the Oakland "Jerrification" Project, which was instrumental in the launch of Oakland's Just Cause Ordinance (Oakland's first form of rent control) and founded an organization with that same name. At the tail end of his leadership at *POOR* he launched and won a landmark legal challenge against California's Penal Code 647(j), which is the law used to cite houseless folks for sleeping outside, one of many Quality of Life citations.

Joseph Bolden, a photographer from the Sixth Street Photography Workshop, was a formerly homeless, SRO hotel resident, low wage and workfare worker, one of the first contributors to *POOR Magazine*, and then a regular columnist and one of the first paid staff.

Roxanne Trade, a formerly homeless workfare worker, artist and contributor to *POOR Magazine*, was also a proud member of People Organized to Win Employment Rights (POWER).

Eddie Camacho, cartoonist, Costa Rican immigrant, poverty scholar and artist and *POOR Magazine* contributor, collaborated with me to create the mythical "poverty superheroes" El Mosquito and Superbabymama.

Jennifer Navarro, one of my best friends, was a young, mixed-race raza activist, organizer and youth writer-facilitator who later worked as *POOR*'s first development director and grantwriter.

Deshawn Hollins, my mama's pretend son and my pretend brother, helped us in and out of homelessness in Oakland, and was a staff writer for *POOR Magazine*'s food reviews

All of these people are still with *POOR* in different capacities, and our staff has grown to include other amazing leaders, formerly homeless poverty and race scholars, and staff writers such as KaPonda, Leo Stegman, Anna Morrow, Aldo Della Maggiorra and Giovonna Barela. Our relationships grew and changed as we lived through each other's personal poverty and family dramas. My mother and I held down the core of *POOR* while the t-shirts and the teamwork flowed, the poverty continued, and a whole lot of hope and energy fueled the process.

In the first year of our organization, we developed the notion of poverty scholarship, which was inducted into *POOR*'s core practices with the clear realization that poor folk had to flip the power of media, voice and authorship. Poor people are inherently denied a voice in the media, and they're also denied a voice in the creation of legislation and academic scholarship. Consequently it became *POOR*'s goal to intentionally listen, to conceive of policy and reassign authorship to the folks on the frontline of the experience of poverty and racism.

In our formal workshops and leadership meetings, we established our radical notions of poverty journalism, which institutionalized my ideas about the hierarchy of authorship: if a poverty scholar at *POOR* was living outside, suffering with mental illness or dealing with assorted issues related to a life lived in poverty, and therefore could not steal the time, energy or clear thoughts necessary to write "their story," or due to a lack of literacy was unable to construct a clear sentence or paragraph, they were assigned a writer/facilitator who would listen and transcribe their stories, struggles and concepts into a piece of prose or journalism. I had launched this concept with the inclusion of my mother's name on the byline of my first essay published in the *East Bay Express*, believing that if you have lived through an experience and are, therefore, the subject of a story, you should get authorial credit. I also believed that it was a collective, non-individualistic way of thinking and acting.

We also expanded the narrow definitions of what journalism might be. For a youth of color speaking from his or her perspective about their experience, spoken word, hip hop and rap counts as journalism. Grafitti is journalism. Murals are journalism. Music is journalism. For an African American elder such as *POOR*'s Po' Poet Laureate, A. Faye Hicks, poetry is journalism.

And finally, we tackled the notion of journalism as defined by the mainstream media, which, we believed, was essentially a form of voyeurism. Take, for example, the mainstream media's headline: *Activists protest as an 86-year-old African American woman is evicted from her residence of 22 years.* The radio, TV and print reporters come out. They take some pictures, they point the cameras at her, they film the protest and then they leave. At best, you might get a "human interest story," following mainstream media standards that "represent all sides," so you'd hear the supposed side of the evicting landlord and maybe a quote from the activists. Rarely are the root causes of the eviction — such as the gentrification brewing in that neighborhood and the landlord's profit margins if he sells without a "problem" tenant in residence — written into the reporting. You will never hear directly from that woman at all, only one sad picture of her, saying nothing, and at worst, you won't hear from the activists, either.

POOR's rule from the beginning was to break down the myth of objectivity and the implicit "other" stance of journalism. We accomplished this through the integration of self, the use of the "I" in every story; no Dickensian positivism here. We were the subjects: the incarcerated, the welfare moms, the working poor, the disabled, the homeless, the low-income youth of color, the evicted tenants. We were the "insiders," seizing media and creating resistance with every article, statement, story, photograph. Every story was written from the first-person perspective, integrating creative writing techniques and opinions.

In later years, as we developed our Poverty Studies program, which was created for college students and professionals, we taught them the same thing: they were not sent out to cover a story only to report, but to support the activism, the resistance, the family, or the person. They were required to reveal themselves in their writing, their own relationship to the pain felt by the subjects of their stories. They were taught to have empathy, not sympathy.

We also decided that poverty journalism must include an attempt at solutions. For example, in the Homefulness issue (*POOR*, Volume 1) we discussed the problems that poor folks have staying housed—as a result of gentrification, displacement and crisis, people without means can easily become homeless. The solution developed by the poverty scholars (inspired by my community-centered mama) was to address those obstacles, along with the danger of isolation and disenfranchisment, with the strength of the "village" and the importance of equity to create long-term economic self-sufficiency. We proposed a sweat equity co-housing project and, in fact, realized it in a small apartment in the Tenderloin, using a small slice of the Arts Commission grant.

It was as utopic as it was planned to be, hosting poetry readings, community dinners and child care, and housing two single-parent families. It was over as quickly as it started when the funding ran out, but the good thing was that it opened our eyes to the viability of the concept and its application to poor folks.

A few years later, I took on the insane task of applying to HUD for funding for that same idea. I actually got the grant, but the federal requirements were so impossibly difficult to fulfill for a small organization with limited funding that we finally had to give it up. It's a model I still hope to carry forward.

POOR
MAGAZINE
Volume 2 1997 $3.95

HELLTHCARE

Cover of *POOR Magazine*, Volume 2, "Hellthcare". Orignal art by Michael Slack.

CHAPTER 35

hellthcare

"But it *is* an emer . . . gen—" the last part of my sentence was cut off by my own saliva, draining into my throat at a rate that felt like three gallons per second. It had been several months since I'd had an asthma attack quite this bad, and when I had the last one I vowed never to go to an emergency room again, after having sat for no less than 16 hours before receiving any treatment.

"No, Miss Garcia, I don't think so," the admitting clerk mistook my choking pause for uncertainty, and began shaking her head from side to side while she filled the silence with her persistent rant, "We can only see you if it's a life threatening emergency, and of course, that's only if there are no other county facilities available."

"I'm . . . tell . . . ing . . . you . . . I can't . . . breathe . . . . It *is* an emer—" She was still shaking her head. I managed to spit out one last sentence. "Can you ask your sup . . . ervis . . . or?"

She made a small snort of frustration and walked away.

Unfortunately, illness is a beast that strikes unexpectedly when you're least prepared. As an uninsured, very low-income person I had struggled on and off for all of my adult life with the impossible choices of 1) standing in line or sitting in the waiting room of a county health facility for innumerable hours; 2) fighting with a clerk about my right to emergency room care in a "private" nonprofit hospital; or 3) remain ill, hope to get over it, or who knows, maybe even die. Because my mother never allowed any illness to go unchecked, she would insist that I seek immediate care, usually forcing me into choice number two, and in my struggle to "prove" the emergency nature of my illness I stumbled upon the little-known piece of legislation called the Hill–Burton Act.

The Hill–Burton Act forces acute care clinics, hospitals and other medical health facilities to provide free services to people, whether or not they have the ability to pay. The illness has to be deemed of an "emergent nature," and there is a screening process that admitting clerks must follow in order to determine that someone is, in fact, in an emergency state. The problem is, even when they do decide that your problem is an emergency, and even if you tell the clerk very seriously and clearly that you are indigent, and/or otherwise unable to pay, the hospital's billing department will harass you mercilessly until you agree to pay or sell your debt to a credit collection agency that proceeds to ruin your credit, forcing many people to file for bankruptcy.

If you're an undocumented worker, many county facilities, acting under the guise of "reporting," use the billing and collection process as a way to feed information to the INS, thereby terrifying the potential undocumented patient and keeping them from ever seeking care.

Due to the highly punitive nature of health care policies for poor people, I and many of the *POOR* staff were in constant fear of becoming sick, and as we planned our next issue of *POOR Magazine* it seemed only logical that we should focus on this extremely dangerous problem plaguing poor folk.

As was *POOR's* standard, we set about looking at not only the problem, through investigation as well as the creation of literary and visual art, but also at possible solutions. Our goal was to create each issue of the magazine as a resource for poor folks, as well as a resource for empathic and creative-minded providers who might be seeking to be part of the solution.

We began by questioning western notions of mental and physical health and the ways in which poor people and poor families are pathologized, as well as the lack of mental health services for uninsured folks and the impact that lack can have on community survival. We also investigated the ways in which providers might actually provide services for poor folks on a real sliding scale, providing dental and medical care starting at Free.

In the end, we published *POOR*, Volume 2, the "Hellthcare" issue, but it was never truly finished, because the hellish experience of poor people attempting to access care continues today, changing, worsening and endangering lives, while budgets are cut and cities around the world grapple with an ever-increasing number of people in severe need.

POOR Press Catalogue

Publications of Very Low and No Income
Youth and Adult Literary and
Visual Artists

A Project of POOR Magazine

Cover of the POOR Press catalogue. Poor Press is a publishing access project dedicated to publishing the work of very low and no-income youth and adults. Photo featuring youth scholar David Smith by Barry Schwartz, cover design by Marissa Kunz.

CHAPTER 36

youth at POOR

Pain is in my head
It's in my art
It's in my body
It's in my life
Like the time I got hit by a car
It was like a hit
From a shot gun
— by Kevin (age 15)

In the year leading up to the release of the Hellthcare issue we conducted a series of six-month-long workshops with very low-income youth aged twelve to seventeen who were interned in group homes and closed mental health placements. With the help of a friend who was a youth counselor, we launched a formal collaboration with a Bay Area agency that ran locked placements and schools inside and outside the public school system for severely emotionally disturbed youth. Unlike our previous workshops for youth, these spanned a semester and included a series of literacy exercises that tied in with the kids' curriculum and were part of their school day.

Prior to these we had done several workshops for low-income youth in the local public schools and community centers, as well as conducting several very successful, one-time workshops at the Youth Guidance Center (juvenile hall). Those workshops all incorporated art and story as a way to get at issues of class and race, and the kids loved them. This was a new opportunity; it would be the first time that we had a whole semester in which to teach and enlighten, inspire and awaken poor youth, mostly of color, who had in many cases, lost hope for themselves and their families.

My motivation to work with youth was simple: if I hadn't had the opportunity to understand my life from a conscious perspective and hadn't been given the chance to be "heard" by being published, I wouldn't have made it. And if I had had that sooner in my youth, I know my life would have been different. If I could pass on any of that life-changing process and access to these kids, I believed that they, too, would have a chance to begin the process of resistance and hope.

It was at this time that we instituted *POOR*'s multi-generational learning and scholarship model. Our belief was that all members of the community—children, youth, adults and elders—needed to learn, grow, resist and heal together, overcoming our collective experiences of broken school systems and/or broken or disempowered families that had been impacted or destroyed by the crime of poverty and/or racism.

Each workshop included a media literacy and social justice component that questioned the unjust society of haves and have-nots, raising awareness of the system that most of these youth were caught in, and the mythologies of capitalism they were being spoon-fed by the corporate media on a daily basis. We integrated hip hop, spoken word and grafitti into every lesson, redefining what journalism is and could be, what writing and art are and could be, talking about how some of the best art and journalism is on the walls of our neighborhoods and in rhymes and raps. As Eduardo Galeano has so eloquently said, "The walls are the publishers of the poor."

"Who do you think makes your shoes?" I would call out to

the class. "Do you think the workers at Nike are getting paid fairly?" These questions would open the discussions, which would inevitably lead to a critique of media messages and corporate product-pushing, opening the students' minds to other forms of survival and success.

"Who would call themselves poor?" Perhaps the most important thing we dealt with was the shame inherent in the life of a poor kid. A shame so powerful that a kid would shoplift or take part in some form of unsafe underground economy just to attain the right clothes, right shoes, or right computer accessories. A shame that would make a kid lie about being homeless so they wouldn't be "the homeless kid" in their school.

After an intensive discussion that allowed a safe space for kids who had been the abused and the abusers, who had bullied and been bullied, who were so confused about who to be and what to be, caught up in trickle-down MTV references of what's cool and how being a "playa" and a pimp is the goal of any self-respecting "gangsta," we proceeded to create a series of images and stories that paralleled what the adult participants of *POOR* were digging into.

We began by asking them to describe through image and a story what "poor" is. Most of them described everything but themselves. Everyone who had experienced poverty was everyone else; this is oddly like adults, never realizing their own colonization, always finding it easier to act as though it's happening to someone else. Those stories opened up the discussion further into more specific explorations of the issues we were dealing with, such as healthcare. For example, how were their mother or father treated when they tried to get medical help at a county emergency room, or how did their parents get their teeth fixed, and so on.

In another class we asked the question: What is "work"? This led to a fascinating examination of underground economies and economic survival through alternative means. The kids knew very well that if you had to live on welfare you would need to do some kind of "alternative" work.

The youth aced *POOR*'s empathy exercise, one that college students are routinely stumped by, a two-part question that asks, "What has been your worst financial crisis?" and then sets up a virtually impossible scenario, one faced by most very low-income parents: *You are a single parent with three children aged one, three, and five. You just acquired employment, which was very difficult for you to obtain because you have no high school diploma and it's a very competitive job market. It's a 40-hour-a-week job but you can only get free child care for 15 hours a week. This means you will only end up with enough money to cover the cost of your child care and utilities, but not enough for rent. What would you do?*

"There is no 'legitimate' solution," the kids would immediately blurt out at every version of that quiz. "The only thing that mama can do is something that isn't legal or 'acceptable.'" The kids were poverty scholars and survivors. They had been there with their poor parents, making those impossible choices, diving into that vicious cycle. They knew that you did what you had to do to feed yourself and your children, and that might mean committing crimes of poverty.

That year and a half of workshops inspired me, terrified me, and brought me to endless tears. These kids needed us there for a lot longer but the limited funding we'd gotten from a grant for the workshops ran out and we had no money to stay on for free. In our last group of classes, they each gave us a book with their pictures and pages filled with promises to keep on writing, resisting and caring for their communities and families, and then from many of the kids a heart-breaking promise to take care of us, Dee & Tiny, forever and ever.

Boxes so large
Spaces so small
These are the things
that make up my walls

240

Cement so cold
Covers so dirty
More boxes around me
Keep my house sturdy

Begging for money
Finding old clothes
Looking for something
to cover our toes

Giving donations
of a quarter or more
Some hesitate
Because they think they know what it's for

Living like animals,
Hardly ever clean
People look and laugh
Because they don't understand what they have seen

Walking down the streets
with nowhere to walk or run
Material things your people have
me and my people have none

Crying for all of your help
in the midst of our own tears
Searching for someone, anyone
to calm us of our fears

These cries for help we ask from you
You act like you can't hear
Because we are the homeless
and we will continue to be for years
— by Jennifer (age 14)

Cover of *POOR Magazine*, Volume 3, "Work," featuring "El Mosquito: Panhandler by Day, Superhero by Night." Original art by Eddie Camacho, concept by Tiny.

Cover of *POOR Magazine*, Volume 4, "Mothers" Original art by Evri Kwong.

CHAPTER 37

work

As *POOR* was gaining more and more momentum, the vending continued. Day after day, I would trek down to the financial district where I was now vending, many times not making anything as the tired office workers streamed by. The money for rent would come in fits and starts, and still Laura and Mrs. Chin didn't resort to "normal" landlord behavior. Whenever we did manage to get a booth at a street fair, or got a grant, or had a good weekend of sales, it would almost entirely go to the rent fund, leaving us with little or nothing for food and other needs.

Meanwhile, my mother fought for and received a subsidy for my sister so that she would always be fed and clothed, albeit not in the newest brand-names, but better fed than me or my mom, with everything she needed always provided.

But then the rains came and sales dropped off entirely. I was applying for grants in every spare second, and the rent hadn't been paid for over six months. Laura and Mrs. Chin began to gently hint that "something had to happen soon."

"You are just lazy." I sat on a hard plastic chair perched on the edge of the tiny cubicle that was my welfare worker's office.

He officiously stacked a pile of papers together and pushed them across his faux wood desk in my direction.

I let him tell me that and I just sat there and gulped. I was conscious, aware and understood the wrongness of what he'd said. And yet, I felt small and idiotic. I was nothing. I was almost homeless.

I was there to learn about a new welfare program, born from the loins of the Welfare (de)Reform Act, legislation signed by President Clinton in 1996 that was about to impact many of the POOR staff. There were many punitive aspects of the "reform," but the main thing it did was to put a cap on the amount of time a person could receive the little bit of nothing that constituted cash assistance from the government. The papers I was signing told me that I had a limited time to "transition" off of cash assistance and that I had to enroll in a job training program within a few weeks or I would stop receiving food stamps and cash aid immediately.

"Would it be possible for me to go to school? I'm a writer, and I'd like to pursue a career in media," I ventured.

"That's great but you need a job, any job, as soon as possible, so that's not practical," he dismissed me without looking up.

"But I can eventually get a job in that field that would pay me more," I tried again.

At this point he scrunched up his face even smaller than it already was, like someone who was peering at a bug they were about to step on, and pronounced my laziness with an exasperated stare.

I left his office with a punched-in-the-stomach feeling. I kept my eyes focused on the soiled tile of the welfare office floor until I reached the outside.

The next morning I donned my orange jacket and went out to fulfill my twice weekly Workfare requirement of cleaning the streets.

"Excuse me, you should come to our next planning meeting about Workfare wages," a small woman also wearing an orange jacket was handing me a flyer as I toiled over my last load of trash.

"You know these jobs used to be done for decent wages by union employees," she added.

"Yes, I know."

"So I hope you come," she said, and then disappeared down the street into the early morning fog.

I looked down at the flyer: POWER, People Organized to Win Employee Rights. Steering Committee Meeting.

"What do we want?"

"JUSTICE!"

"When do we want it?"

"NOW!!"

I sat tentatively at the edge of a small, stuffy room for my first POWER meeting. That morning I'd sold shirts until 12:30 and then, fraught with guilt and fear over possible lost sales, I raced over to the 1 P.M. meeting where I was met by a group of folks chanting for justice, a stack of steaming pizzas and an array of butcher paper signs lining the walls, listing in red the mythologies of Workfare and the action steps needed to attain a living wage.

Everyone there had experienced the oppressions of the racist and classist welfare system, and they were organizing together to fight back. After a few more meetings stolen away from rainy days, I became a proud member of the very powerful POWER.

Meanwhile, we were trying to raise money for the creation of *POOR*, Volume 4 but had received an onslaught of "no's" from private foundations that require that you come up with a new, "sexy" project each grant cycle in order to fulfill what they have determined to be the designated need that year. Even though Volume 3 had been about as "sexy" and innovative as any literary project could be, that didn't seem to matter.

I had attained a grant from the San Francisco Arts Commission and one from the Vanguard Foundation to produce Volume 3. Those funds, in addition to a small loan from our partners-in-struggle at the Coalition on Homelessness and some individual and in-kind donations from friends, artists and subscribers, had enabled us to barely scrape by with enough cash to publish one of the most revolutionary and powerful issues of *POOR*: Volume 3, the "Work" issue.

> POOR Magazine *would like to propose in this issue that "work" must be defined by the worker. We believe that the concept of work itself should be broadened to include unrecognized labor, or what some mainstream researchers refer to as "outlaw subculture," which is a marginalizing title for what we at* POOR *consider work and workers.*
>
> *Additionally, in this issue we are dealing with the concept of the "new slavery." This concept defines prison labor, sweatshop labor, workfare work and any other labor in which someone does work that receives less pay or benefits for their labor than those performing the same work in another setting.*
>
> — Excerpt from the *POOR Magazine* editors' statement in Volume 3

The Work issue examined unrecognized forms of work and workers, including Dee's revisioning of panhandlers and recyclers as micro-businesspeople, Workfare and prison workers as low-wage workers, and sex workers as, well, sex workers. We also claimed mothering (parenting) as a legitimate form of labor. The issue featured the work of over fifteen street artists from Berkeley to Venice Beach, showcasing their products and providing their contact information, and it featured a fascinating array of food reviews, which focused on everything from the best shelter food and free coffee places to a restaurant dedicated to making soups. It included pages and pages of literary and visual art, as well as video and book reviews, an amazing resources page and a feature story on a micro-business enterprise in Haiti. The cover and full-color centerfold featured a new superhero that the talented youth artist and poverty scholar Eddie Camacho and I had created together: El Mosquito, a multilingual, polyracial panhandler by day, superhero by night.

We went to grant meeting after grant meeting showing Volume 3 to the funders and encountered the dreaded, "No," in response to our request for support to produce the next volume. In one grant proposal meeting, five members of the *POOR* staff laid out all of the projects we had launched surrounding the creation of Volume 3, including workshops focused on an exploration of labor, the commission of a first-person feature story on micro-business in Haiti and Bangladesh, book and video reviews by houseless artists, artwork by houseless and very low-income youth and adults, journalism and photography on welfare reform written by the folks suffering under that system, and the creation of a list of local and national resources. At the end of our presentation, the response was, "That's all wonderful, but how are you really changing the world?"

This experience and future ones I would have with "philan-thropists" soured me on the strange world of charity. The whole funding process mirrors the consumer culture, with each new granting season/fiscal cycle treated like a sale at Macy's: whoever is working on the newest, "sexiest" issue is the one that will be supported and even courted to solicit funds. Rarely, if ever, are organizations granted sustaining support just for doing great work, just to keep them going. Most grants are project-based, and organizations are under the gun to speed through to their completion and then to create "newer and better" products/projects for the next grant cycle. And even when you accomplish that, which *POOR* was consistently doing, it's still often about who you know, if you have friends in foundations, corporations, government, etc., and most small grassroots organizations are rooted in the community and just barely getting by, and like us, have no such friends or connections.

There were some exceptions over the years, such as the Catholic Campaign for Human Development, which awarded *POOR* a three-year grant and supported us in all of our endeavors, and our individual donors who, although none of them are wealthy people, truly cared along with us and tried

247

with their small donations to keep us paying the phone bill and, in some cases, even the rent.

But in the end, what really kept us going was my mom's and my sheer determination to keep *POOR* alive, through drama, through eviction, through our organizational and personal poverty, through our discouragement. We believed—and still believe—that our voices, our scholarship, our media and our advocacy is vital, that it has, in fact, kept many people housed and heard, resisting and fighting race and class oppression, and that it must not end.

CHAPTER 38

welfare deform

YOU MUST APPEAR ON THE BELOW LISTED DATE OR YOUR BENEFITS WILL BE SANCTIONED.

As I read and re-read the most recent dispatch from my friendly welfare worker, I was struck by the irony of its punitive tone. Although I had never missed an appointment and had only been late once in the two years I'd been receiving benefits, all of my case workers had been either rude, indifferent or downright hostile. I can't blame them; I know that they're just cogs in the wheel that was set up to criminalize poor folks for just needing help, a system that accuses a poor mother of fraud if she lies about who she's living with on her welfare application, and God help her if she manages to make any money, even $5 on the side, and not claim it, since that would be punishable with ankle bracelets and a two-year probation.

"How much is this t-shirt?"

"Fifteen dollars."

"Oh well, thanks, maybe later."

My stomach was growling with hunger and yet there was no t-shirt "hustle" left in me. I fingered my welfare appointment letter under my display table. I knew that this appointment would be the intake for the "job, any job," training program that my worker had set up for me. I knew I had to do something. And then I heard a faint noise.

"Get Up, Stand Up! Stand up for your rights . . ."

I looked up and there they were, the words in the sky, dancing and singing. This time they were rocking to Bob Marley, and their flying carpet had morphed into a tiny black stage rolling through the sky.

And then it came to me. "Of course," I shouted into the sky. "That's it!"

I threw all of my shirts and the elaborate galvanized steel racks onto the dolly and raced home to our Tenderloin apartment. I searched desperately through my welfare documents until I found a pink piece of paper stuffed among the other hundreds of superfluous forms they handed me each time I visited the welfare office. I had picked this one up at a satellite office for my food stamps. It was meant as an internal document to service providers: A Request for Proposals for Welfare to Work Job Training Programs. Due Date: November 1st, 1998.

For the next three nights and early mornings I taught myself how to operate Excel, creating an elaborate budget and learning the meaning of terms and acronyms that were completely foreign to me, and then I constructed a four-page narrative about a job training program, replete with corporate service provision concepts like intake, orientation, hard skills, soft skills, placement and retention.

On the morning of November 1st, I walked into the Private Industry Council (PIC), which was the corporate entity who would facilitate the Welfare to Work dollars for the City and County of San Francisco's Department of Human Services. I had managed to organize all of the literacy and education programs that *POOR* was already doing into a full-fledged Welfare to Work job training program in journalism and multimedia digital technology, calling it the New Journalism/Media Studies Program at *POOR Magazine*. It was structured as a six-month program, which in and of itself was revolutionary, since most of the WTW programs were set up to "graduate" folks into jobs in 30-45 days. It had two tracks: 1) writing, journalism, media content development; and 2) digital technology, graphic design and web development.

Within thirty days we received a phone call. It was Joyce Crum and Amanda Feinstein who, although they were working inside the system, were thinking "outside the box" on that rainy Thursday in December.

"We think your program is interesting," Joyce gingerly started the discussion that day after we had all introduced ourselves. I had received a tentative "yes" to our proposal. We spent the next two hours working out some of the details, and within ten days *POOR* got a check for start-up funds of $18,500.

Christmas came and went that year without so much as a glance at the streets near Macy's. My mother whined sadly at the loss of "all those holiday dollars." I agreed with her; it wasn't like we were rich or even had money for the rent, and we could definitely use some of that fast cash that flows in over Capitalistmas. But I didn't relent. I wasn't going back. Ever. Dee and Tiny had made it out of the rabbit hole, finally.

Po' Poets Projeckt members (l to r) A. Faye Hicks, Tiny, Dharma, and Mari conducting the "equity performance protest" in solidarity with Right To A Roof.

Top row (l to r): Carol Harvey, Resistance Award winners Johnny Spain and Marie Harrison, Diallo McLinn, Tiny, *SF Bayview* editors Mary and Willie Ratcliff, and Dee; Middle row: Mariposa; Bottam row (l to r): Jewnbug and Charles Pitts at the Resistance Awards dinner sponsored by *POOR Magazine* to honor folks who have resisted poverty and racism.

CHAPTER 39

POOR takes off

With that little droplet of water, we soared. The day I received the check I ran over to Joseph Bolden's SRO hotel room in the Tenderloin (because he didn't have a phone) and told him to get off welfare and come to *POOR* to be our first employee.

Together, Dee, Joe, Ken Moshesh and I began to set up the next phase of *POOR*; beyond the magazine, we were now growing into a full-fledged, multifaceted, grassroots community arts and advocacy organization.

With the help of in-kind donations from our webmaster and designers, we launched PoorNewsNetwork (PNN), an online version of *POOR Magazine* and a news service focused on issues of poverty and racism. We began the Community Newsroom, a radical, community-based news-making project that met weekly and integrated the voices and scholarship of low and no-income youth, adults and elders in the making of news. We inaugurated a monthly radio broadcast of PoorNewsNetwork on KPFA radio, which also included a media training program to teach *POOR's* students how to write and produce their own radio segments. We started the Po' Poets Project, a multicultural, multigenerational program that used poetry and spoken word to heal, educate and share wisdom on how to survive, thrive and stay alive in the face of race and class oppression. We formalized the Media Education Institute, our journalism/multimedia training program for low and no-income folks, as well as the Poverty Studies/Media Activism Institute, our internship training program for college students and media professionals who needed to learn how to translate the stories of low and no-income communities without perpetrating the usual "other" positions. We launched the YouthinMedia/Digital Resistance Project, a media and journalism training program for very low and no-income youth. And we started up POOR Press, our publishing arm that published books and CDs featuring the powerful scholarship of our poet/journalists, and which also published Dee's hilarious political allegory, "The Po' Cats," as well as "The Poverty Hero," an anthology about a new literary superhero.

While all of this amazing growth, productivity and wonderfulness was happening, the relationship between my mother and my sister was getting more and more contentious. My little sister's entry into adolescence had sparked a crisis between the two of them, a battle of wills, and within the year they would have a fight over some bit of minutia that resulted in the removal of my sister from our house forever.

It was a brutal and difficult split, played out against the backdrop of our increasing success with POOR, and it's telling of our own pathology and ghetto reality that there was no way the success could or would prevent the trauma. No rise for poor folks is ever that simple or clean, and we almost always have drama.

The whole process was extremely painful for my mother, since she was on the frontline dealing with the punitive Child Protective Services system. As a result, she launched the powerful Courtwatch program, an advocacy project that provided support for parents being abused by the CPS and the Juvenile Dependency Court. We uncovered the information that there is a monetary incentive of over $12,000 every time a child is removed from a home, and the hypocrisy of a foster care system that pays everyone but the parent up to $4,000 to care for a child, while it penalizes the parent for being poor.

Courtwatch's innovative advocacy and investigation provided a voice for thousands of unheard stories of abuse at the hands of CPS, such as Mina, a single parent whose children were taken from her solely because she was houseless, or Charles, a poor single dad, whose own father had turned against him and testified that he was unfit to keep his child. There were problems in the lives of all the Courtwatch parents, but the "solutions" coming from the government administrators of "social service" were always reflective of the separation mindset; there was no eye toward family restoration, and usually no attempt to encourage the extended families to support each other, only an odd, hateful fight fueled by money and separation. In the tradition of *POOR*'s solution-driven problem solving, we promoted a model for non-punitive family and community restoration, based on the work of the Family Rights and Dignity Project of the Coalition on Homelessness, who had worked hard to create a community/village model where elders helped low-income mothers and fathers parent their children.

And finally, we cemented our collaborations and launched projects with Media Alliance, *Street Spirit*, Families with a Future, the Homeless Prenatal Program, the Applied Research Center, the Coalition on Homelessness, Hospitality House and with the wonderful family of the *San Francisco Bayview*, a community newspaper that provided job training and placement support for the graduates of our journalism program.

With that little droplet of water, we drank deeply, we organized, we gave voice to unheard elders, youth and adults, and communities facing gentrification, we helped stop evictions, we formed partnerships, we made change happen.

We were the subjects of our stories, the incarcerated, the mothers on welfare, the working poor, the disabled, the homeless, the low-income youth of color, the evicted tenants. We were the "insiders," seizing media and creating resistance with every article, statement, story and picture.

Tiny speaking while *POOR Magazine* staff, Joseph Bolden, Laure McElroy and Ingrid DeLeon hold signs next to members of LIFETIME and California Tomorrow at a *Poor Magazine* protest held at Laney College in Oakland on the first day of school, to demand the re-opening and stabilization of the Infant and Toddler Care Centers at community colleges state-wide. Photo by Mike Malacek for PoorNewsNetwork.

CHAPTER 40

media resistance

As *POOR* hit the streets of the Bay Area, something else was hitting, a modern-day gold rush unlike anyone had seen for many years before or since, a movement that spurned a new form of urgent colonization. It was 1999 and as the dot.com gold rush hit with full force, everyone who owned any slab of property, commercial or residential, was ready to cash in. No neighborhood was safe, no renter was exempt from the fear of gentrification and eviction.

One of the largest struggles was played out in the Mission District of San Francisco, where elders, youth and families, many of them immigrant, mostly Latino, were being evicted from their apartments right and left. Entire neighborhoods were being decimated, and while we fought to stabilize them, their allies and advocates, the nonprofit organizations who supported them in their neighborhood were being threatened with eviction from their offices as well. For the entire span of 1999-2001 we worked non-stop in collaboration with the other grassroots community organizations that were barely holding on, trying to keep our organizations afloat and keep the communities housed. It was a time of utter craziness, unchecked, greed-driven capitalism at its most frightening.

One of the powerful groups that we collaborated with was

the Mission Anti-Displacement Coalition (MAC), which actively worked to get at the root causes of this massive displacement, confronting the city's planning commission that was aiding and abetting the hungry landlords.

We employed a multilevel media strategy: we began with one voice, the insider who felt the experience personally, the tenant, the victim of police harassment, the elder, the family. Once that story was told and heard, assigned and strategized in *POOR's* Community Newsroom, we crafted and published the first of a series of stories on the subject on PoorNewsNetwork's radio show on KPFA, and in PNN's online magazine. Then we moved outward, creating a network of independent, proactive media, working with independent media partners such as KPFA, KPOO, the *SF Bayview*, and Indymedia. And as an outgrowth of our commitment to reporting and supporting, we actually peopled the protests, advocated for the tenants and did outreach into the community. From there we launched a full-scale media effort to bring the larger society's attention to the issue.

One such effort was waged to save the shopping carts of houseless people in San Francisco, an action that brought together the worlds of art and activism, corporate and independent media, and sheer creative brilliance. In the drive to get rid of the poor people, immigrants and houseless folks who convened in San Francisco's Civic Center, then-mayor Willie Brown had issued a mandate to seize the shopping carts from recyclers and houseless people.

My mama, ever the brilliant conceptualist, decided that we would "transform the shopping carts into art" by adding a small strip of colored wire and then give each houseless person a deed/manifesto for each shopping cart that told of its origins and properties, explaining how it was a piece of art that they owned. We worked closely with our colleagues at the Coalition on Homelessness, who had done extensive work on the civil rights of houseless folks in the Bay Area, asking them to act as our legal advisors and partners.

It was a raging success, as corporate media trucks followed

the *POOR* "change-agents" and houseless artists around as they transformed the shopping carts into "ArtCarts." Finally, due to intense media and community pressure, the Mayor backed off from the shopping cart seizures.

Another creative combination of media resistance, art and activism that *POOR* carried out was the Jerrification Project. We began with the articulation of the unheard voices of those who were most affected by the impending gentrification of West Oakland (one of Oakland's largest low-income neighborhoods, which was under extreme pressure from then-Mayor Jerry Brown's open-armed welcome of real estate development). We published and broadcasted the voices of the poor communities of color being pushed out with illegal evictions and rent raises, and we also worked to connect the dots with the white, middle-class gentrifyers-by-default whose formerly cheap lofts were also being threatened, and who were being discarded along with the poor communities of color. We helped these two otherwise disconnected yet neighboring communities to join with each other in a tent city and art action in the Oakland's Civic Center Plaza.

It all culminated in a press conference and a 30-minute show down with Mayor Jerry Brown. We got him to admit on camera his belief that rent control and affordable housing would lead to the slummification of Oakland, and this helped to launch the efforts of a fledgling project called Just Cause Oakland, which would later usher in Oakland's first rent control ordinance.

The grassroots connections and actions continued, and more projects were birthed. We applied for and received a grant from the Catholic Campaign for Human Development, which allowed us to purchase a full-color printer so we could launch our own small press. We applied for and received a Creative Work Fund grant to create a new literary hero, The Poverty Hero, which became a narrative radio piece and allowed us to collaborate with one of my first heroes and personal advocates, Osha Neuman and his Community Defense,

Inc. We brought advocacy and art together by providing legal advocacy along with literary workshops for very low and no-income people, honoring the unheard voices of people who had struggled unnoticed for years.

We launched another publication entitled, *The Houzin' Project: Words, Art, Resources on the Diaspora, Gentrification, Displacement and Homelessness*, and we created the Resistance Awards, where we honored several famous resistance leaders in the Bay Area like Piri Thomas, Boona Cheena, Ida McRay Robinson and Marie Harrison, alongside people's family members (in my case, my mother), mama's, cousins and aunties who had survived race and class oppression.

Toward the end of 2000, the Private Industry Council put out a request for proposals, and again we had a radical idea. We wanted to create living-wage jobs in media for poor people. We would teach them the skills of writing and reporting, basically what we were already doing but at the same time paying them a living wage ($10 per hour!) and having the city underwrite it as a paid internship. We called it J.O.B.S. (Jobs Organized to Break Stereotypes) in the Media. I taught myself to write even more complicated government grants, and we applied. In early 2001, we were granted the funds to do the JOBS program, an actual solid amount of income that would cover our staff, rent and utilities. We were ecstatic!

It was almost unreal; the money we applied for actually flowed in. We applied for and received grants from the Schwab Family Foundation, the Tides Foundation, and the San Francisco Arts Commission. Projects were completed and, for the first time in my life I earned a paycheck; albeit tiny, it was a pay-check nonetheless. Meanwhile, I had created a job, a real social work advocacy job for my mother, and she was thrilled. I was thrilled. She ran the case management aspect of the program and co-led the Poverty Studies internships. She felt safe enough to drive to and from our office everyday. She was on time. She was achieving her first bit of autonomy; she was for the first time in many years, truly happy, and that meant that I, for the first time in many years was truly happy as well. Nothing could stop us now, or so we thought.

One year into the JOBS program, after doing an extensive series of insider reports on the problems with the welfare system (while getting paid by the welfare system to do the program, therefore, biting, swallowing and spitting out the hand that was feeding us), the inquisition began. We went through a series of gut-wrenching audits that were supposedly an attempt to insure that we were doing the paperwork "right."

After three painful months, sixteen live testimonies from community leaders, a seemingly endless paper trail and eight appointments, the money stopped. Even though we had done everything by the book—we had an accountant, no one had flown to the Bahamas with their meager salary—we were no match for them. They killed us with paperwork, we hadn't dotted an "i" or crossed a "t" somewhere, and nothing anyone could say or do could help us. The beautiful JOBS program was over, the Welfare to Work formal program was over, and the money was essentially gone.

Another project we'd been steadfastly working on unraveled abruptly at this point as well. We had spent almost two years fighting for accreditation for our Journalism curriculum through City College, and when I called to check on progress, we were abruptly informed that, "Sorry, the provost had changed the rules for accreditation. Your class won't qualify now."

Somehow, like a weird kind of waterfall, all of the funding streams seemed to fall apart and drop away, dwindling down to nothing. And with the money went the short-lived stability that Dee and Tiny had achieved.

CHAPTER 41

life in the face of death

In August of 2002, spiraling down the same bad luck waterfall, my mother began to have trouble breathing. She had always had allergies; like me, she had always had asthma, but she said, "This is different, Lisa," grabbing my hand with hers in a rare moment of affection. "I'm scared."

The fight to get a diagnosis as a Medi-Cal patient began. We went to doctor after doctor who could tell us nothing, and then, finally, we found out.

The wind whipped and swirled around us. My mom had to walk very slowly up the hill. She was weak and had hardly had any sleep over the last several weeks, unable to breathe every time she reclined.

"You have cardiomyopathy," the doctor's words were like ice on a stove. They burned and hissed and spit back and forth over both of our heads. He spoke them casually, like he was asking for a haircut or a cup of coffee, as if they were just words. "This is a fatal illness; life expectancy ranges from two to five years," and then he looked at us like we were supposed to thank him, his eyes like ice cubes, static, grey pools of nothingness.

My mother's hand shot out again for mine, and mine for hers, our hearts stopped in full terror. Everything—life, sound, movement—all of it stopped. And we stopped. Stopped thinking clearly, doing anything, functioning.

Before we left, Dr. Ice gave my mother a nine-pill cocktail, each pill promising more frightening side effects than the last. Each one less likely to be ingested by my terrified-of-medicine mama.

We went home to begin another sad series of actions. Between crying and screaming and crying and screaming we would search online for the origins of this illness, the roots of its cause, and an alternative, some alternative to the death sentence that this man had so coldly pronounced. She did try one pill on one fateful night, and was so terrified by how it made her feel that she never tried one again. Six months ensued of trying to get answers, some answer that was different from what he had said, from someone, anyone.

Meanwhile at *POOR*, everything stopped. What little resources we had left, we spent on a move to make *POOR*'s office accessible, since my mother couldn't make it up the stairs anymore. We brokered a deal for an overpriced office that ended up costing more than we'd ever paid before. I was only able to go into the office during off hours when I wasn't caring for my now immobilized and terrified mother. Somehow, we managed to keep a couple of our programs going at half-mast.

Under the influence of an insurmountable terror of losing the only family I'd ever had, I began an urgent push for something that I'd been planning and talking about with my on-and-off-again partner, the idea of having a child. As someone who had never had an extended family, who had been summarily rejected by my father and his new family, who had inherited my mother's sorrow and desperation over her own lack of family to care for her, it was my long-time dream to bring a grandson to my mama, a son to me and my partner and another generation to all of us. I believed that in this way I would be "growing community" and really having a family, and in the face of losing my mother, it must be now or never.

I began to try to get pregnant, which turned out to be harder than I'd thought it would. It took time and commitment and multiple visits to a gynecologist, paid for by the health insurance provided by my partner, which was on the brink of being canceled. With two months of insurance left and a tear-stained face and tear-blurred mind, I sought out the option of a sperm donor clinic. I chose a mixed-race man whose profile said that he, like me, was a political artist, and who was close to his family of Mexican and Asian immigrants.

Six months later, on the eve of the move to our new office, I found out I was pregnant. I had no idea what I was doing, but I was completely delirious. Things were getting really out of control but it didn't matter; I was going to have a baby. The only problem was that it wasn't my partner's biological child, and I didn't have the courage to tell him.

For a brief period of joy my mother, partner and I celebrated the impending birth, until the class, race and consciousness differences among us began to collide in the choosing of what would become my son's name: Tiburcio. Though important, the arguments over the baby-to-be's name were only a surface-level manifestation of the problems between my mother and my partner. These feelings would erupt later, in a painful and almost permanent break initiated by my mother.

Meanwhile, my stubborn and determined mama had saved every cent she had to seek a doctor who would give her a prescription for an exercise program. After much research, she had learned that her illness was very likely the result of her childhood of starvation and lack of care, and that short of getting a heart transplant, which we could never dream of affording, there was really nothing to be done about her condition. Considering her inability to take any medication, exercise was the only thing that might offer her any kind of physical help. So after a lifetime of never doing any kind of formal exercise, my mother dutifully went to this exercise program, twice a week. And we settled into a sort of schedule that laid the foundation for what became the most difficult four years of both of our lives.

In the year that followed we managed to publish several of the previously granted books we had planned out for POOR Press. We hosted a book release party that was a big success and we conducted several internships and Digital Resistance programs. We continued to do our work, but we weren't happy and there was little or no hope. My mother was dying. I knew it, she knew it, and everything had changed.

I did my best to make her happy in any way I could, but she was depressed and angry a lot of the time. She began lashing out at me with much more severity, and it seemed nothing I said or did could make her feel better.

In August of 2003 I had my beautiful baby. My mother, who was the only person who knew it wasn't my partner's biological son, chose to tell him, driving a wedge into their already contentious relationship and setting off a time bomb in ours, which blew up into a domestic violence drama within five months of my son's birth. To my partner's credit, for those five months he was an extremely careful and loving father to our son. But between his anger at what I'd done and my own guilt at my lie, coupled with my confusion, depression and sorrow and my mom's endless assaults, we were all doomed.

I had entered a new kind of hell, that of a very low-income single parent, who from time to time, depending on how angry my mom was, was also homeless, since she would threaten constantly to kick me out of the house and several times made good on the threat. And even when she wasn't threatening me, we all faced a new terror of impending homelessness when Mrs. Chin passed away and her family's lawyer began to lose patience with our now constant "rent problem."

I was still my mother's sole caregiver, doing her shopping, taking her to her doctor's appointments and cardio rehab sessions, taking care of all of the details of her life while also taking care of my infant son. It was unbelievably difficult; I hadn't realized how hard all this was going to be. And in the midst of it all we had to move out of our new office. We had to let go of all of our paid staff, and only a scant group of dedicated volunteers stayed on. But we held on. Somehow. I was determined to keep *POOR* alive.

My mother and my son got along beautifully and she loved him in a way she had never been able to love me. But she was really too weak to care for him by herself, so I was unable to get a break from full-time, multigenerational caregiving. I was becoming completely overwhelmed, and the final straw of my almost-breakdown occurred when I tried to apply for welfare. A stipend that my mother was receiving for in-home support services made it look like I made too much money on paper: a whopping $750 a month. Although all of that money was needed for my mother's care, and I was supporting myself and my baby as well, $750 was $50 too much to qualify for welfare or food stamps. The only reason my son and I were able to eat throughout that time was because of the little bits of money I earned writing stories for the *SF Bayview* and the intermittent eggs and cheese I got from WIC.

Days were a blur of writing, caregiving, driving, yelling, writing, caregiving, cooking, cleaning, shopping, caregiving, with little or no sleep. I tried in vain to get a job, thinking that would allow me to hire someone to help with my mom's care and my child's care. But I couldn't get a job to save my life, even with all of my experience. I had no degree (no formal college, not to mention high school). At one point of extreme desperation, I decided I would try to enroll in school, thinking I could get financial aid and somehow get a degree, and then maybe I could get a job and everything would be okay.

I discovered new obstacles placed in the paths of all poor folks, such as the fact that if you don't have a high school diploma you can't qualify for financial aid without passing an extremely complicated assessment test. Another shock, something I already knew about but which now really hit home, was the complete lack of subsidized childcare for working poor parents, and the substandard wages paid to the caregivers of those on welfare. Parents and families aren't supported in the U.S., and poor parents are demonized, disrespected and dishonored.

I also discovered real heroes for poor parents in California who are trying to come up and out of poverty: the Family Resources Centers at community colleges. Specifically, I found the Betty Shabazz Family Resource Center at City College of San Francisco, where poor mothers and fathers are given nine hours of free childcare in exchange for volunteering for the center. It was the beginning of my salvation—two days a week, for two hours each day I could learn and think and read, developing what would become my long-range goal to carry poverty scholarship into academia on my shoulders and eventually to launch a Poverty Studies program at the college level. And so, even if for a very short time, I was able to help my mom and keep my son happy, and for a minute I could feel hope for something else, something more.

Against the backdrop of this personal struggle, *POOR* received yet another blow to its organizational psyche when a grant we had received was rescinded at the last minute. We'd planned to use the money to make our first movie, "A Walk of Resistance through Poverty, Homelessness and Homicide," which would focus on the high homicide rate of youth of color as well as other issues of poverty and racism affecting four neighborhoods in the Bay Area. We did the project anyway, unfunded, thanks mostly to the dedication of two of our volunteer teachers, who then volunteered even more time to make it happen. As hard as it was to carry it off, it was also extremely inspiring, and we went on to use the film in our curriculum with youth of color affected by the issues addressed in the film.

In August of 2005, on my son's second birthday, things started to change. I always say that the goddess must have known that I was about to completely crack and realized she'd better do something to help me quickly, because the change was swift and strange. First, after joining forces with other poor parents and advocates from Coleman Advocates and the Coalition on Homelessness, I received one of the rare subsidies granted by the City to working poor parents. At the same time, I was actively looking for work non-stop, and lo and behold, I got a call back. Within weeks I was hired as the communications director (right up my alley) for Justice Matters, a nonprofit research and policy organization that works on racial justice in education policy. Suddenly, I could taste a little bit of stability.

My having a job was going to be hard on my mom, since for her it signified true aloneness, and we both were afraid about who we could find to replace me during the daytime. At first, she resisted my efforts to look for work, but when she saw that we were facing homelessness again she relented and even encouraged me. Once I had the job she still needed to communicate with me constantly, calling me several times throughout the day, alternately yelling at me about one thing or the other that I had done that she wasn't happy about and telling me how depressed or sad or discouraged she was. But I know, even though she refused to admit it, that she was proud and happy that I had gotten a job.

The money I made, although not that much, allowed me to pay our rent to the Chin family's attorney, who by now had begun formal eviction proceedings. It also allowed me to get a little part-time place of my own, for the very first time in my life.

CHAPTER 42

mommahouse

I didn't move out completely—I would never do that to my mother. I started MommaHouse, a home for low-income single moms who, like me, needed each other's support to help raise their families. Having learned from my mother that one of the most important things poor parents can have is community, the two other mamas and I designed it as a community space to foster art, activism, community and mutual support.

One of the most dangerous conditions of being a poor single parent in the United States is the deadly isolation. Isolation can kill you, or at the very least kill your spirit. It can lead you into destructive behaviors like attaching yourself to hurtful people just to avoid being alone, consuming substances to ease the pain, and/or becoming abusive to your own children. I resolved that I would not get into the same predicament that I had watched my mother suffer from. I would change the pattern.

MommaHouse was a dilapidated building in the Mission district owned by a slumlord, so in San Francisco terms that means our rent was a little below market rate. The place was filled with non-paying guests like roaches, mice, and pigeons, but we all pitched in to clean and fix it up to the best of our limited financial and physical abilities. My son and I shared one of the smallest rooms and we only stayed once a week, so it was cheap for us. It was only one night a week, but it was a blissful night of away-ness, a peaceful moment to think and dream. It was here that I was able to conceive of the project that brought POOR back to life: the welfareQUEENS.

I started welfareQUEENS intending for it to become a play, a movie and a cultural change project that would bring voice to all of the much maligned, rarely heard, poor mamas (and papas) who were struggling, unsupported, to raise children in America. It would be a tribute to my mother and myself, and to all the other poor families we'd worked for and with at POOR. We began to have monthly production meetings at MommaHouse; they were designed to be, unlike most production meetings (or any meetings, for that matter), user-friendly for families, with meals and childcare provided, gas and/or bus stipends to get there, resource sharing and emotional support.

The outreach began with our own core group of poverty scholars at POOR, like Jewnbug, po' poet and graduate of POOR's Digital Resistance Program, Lauri McElroy, poverty scholar and writer for POOR Magazine, as well as some powerful immigrant sons from POOR's youth program who wanted to honor their mother's struggle to raise them. Beyond that core we reached out to our comrades at LIFETIME, Homeless Prenatal Program, POWER, Parent Voices and the Family Resource Centers that had saved me when I was trying to go to school. It became one of the most powerful groups I've ever had the honor to launch and be a part of, and as of the writing of this book, the welfareQUEENS has finalized a script and is in the first stages of producing our debut in San Francsico, with the goal of taking our play on tour across the country.

It was also in MommaHouse that I began a slow reconciliation with my former partner, who had decided, no matter who the biological father was and what drama had occurred between us, that he was committed to being the father of our son.

My time at MommaHouse, even though it was only one day a week, was seen as a horrible breach by my mom, and I'm sorry to this day that I couldn't be constantly with her, seven days a week. But I had no choice; I desperately needed those moments of silence. I hired a friend of hers to stay with my mom on the nights that I was gone, and though my mother couldn't really admit it, they would actually have a blast together. And in spite of how weak her illness made her, she continued to work at *POOR* as much as she could, yelled as much as she wanted to and still went to as many movies as she could afford.

Dee in our miniscule *POOR Magazine* office, surrounded by pictures of poverty heroes and poverty scholars.

CHAPTER 43

dee's last campaign

"But we have to save John Swett! It's not just a school, it's a whole community, and it's just a crime if they close it . . ." my mother's voice trailed off into the car's whir.

The campaign against the closing of John Swett Elementary School was the last media organizing my mother worked on. Ever since she'd heard about the pending closure of the school, located in the heart of San Francisco's Western Addition, a historically African American neighborhood that had been destabilized by redevelopment-induced displacement in the 1960s, she had insisted that POOR's staff must unilaterally dedicate our time to save it.

We visited several John Swett classrooms, talked with teachers and students, had conversations with the school principal and a supportive school board member, and perhaps most importantly, with the tireless advocates and parent leaders, Anitra and Dwayne Baker. As we pursued our comprehensive research, our sense of urgency increased; this was one of the most real examples of the "village" we had ever seen in action.

The school was an unbelievable mix of classes, cultures and languages. Families were truly integrated into the running of the school in a way neither of us had ever seen. The school actively practiced the indigenous tradition of eldership, and they didn't follow scripted, packaged curricula, instead creating an innovative arts-based curriculum that drew on the scholarship of the school's diverse families and communities.

John Swett Elementary was slated for closure and merger with another school in 2006 as part of the school board's response to declining enrollment in the San Francisco Unified School District, even though this school was running at 81% enrollment. After a huge outcry from the parents, grandparents, students and teachers of John Swett, several members of San Francisco's Board of Supervisors decided to support the community's effort to save the school, resulting in the approval of a measure to award John Swett $650,000 in emergency funds. The money was rejected by the school board.

"Well, then we'll just have to work on John Swett as our only media campaign this month," I concluded with an annoyed, disrespectful tone in my voice, at which point my mother almost slapped me upside my 35-year-old, attitude-having head.

I regret every moment that I gave my mama "lip," especially that last time about John Swett, because she was right: nothing else we were working on mattered as much right then, no matter how important, because if this school was closed, a community would fall apart. The elders would lose their important role in the raising of our youth, and a whole community and its future generations would suffer.

CHAPTER 44

mama dee's road trip

As chips of ice fell from the sky, my mama, Mama Dee, mixed-race
orphan from the streets of Philly, passed away.
Mama Dee, co-editor of POOR Magazine, disabled artist,
conceptualizer and storyteller.
Mama Dee, media critic and media producer, singer
and dancer to all rhythms.
Mama Dee, torture victim, fighter for social justice.
Mama Dee, grandmama to Tiburcio, mother of Tiny,
the one without whom there would be no me.

On the snow-laced San Francisco night of March 10th, 2006, Mama Dee toiled on a segment for PoorNewsNetwork's monthly radio show at the *POOR* office. At 7:19 P.M.—atypically, she had only called me once in the previous two hours—she called to say she was heading home. We laughed together about what she called Dick Cheney's new scam to sell America to Halliburton. That was the last time we spoke. She drove herself home and then, taking a catnap on our couch, she died suddenly at 8:45 P.M.

One of the things my mother had adamantly told me for many years, at first facetiously and then with a certain amount of sardonic determination, was that she never wanted to be buried in the ground. Her own mother, Helen Jo hadn't had the money for a burial plot, and she'd had to lie and pretend that she was married to a man she'd had an illicit affair with for many years just so she could "squat" his burial plot. And my mother, who had never had money to buy land for her life, considered it wrong to buy it for her death. But beyond that, she thought it was simply way too linear and plain boring just to be buried, and so, in a post-modern hindu-cum-live-art-performance, my mama decided that she wanted her body to be attached to the top of our car and driven around for a year.

The struggle to come up with a ceremony/tribute that would please my mama's spirit was crucial. In order to be consistent with our lifelong practice of indigenous-style family values of interdependence, collectivity and eldership, the next step was ancestor worship and ancestor veneration. I believe this to mean that it's important to listen to your ancestors and follow their instructions, as their contentment in the next life is as important as their contentment in this one.

After discussing mummification with Jewnbug, co-mama and co-daughter who also ascribed to these values, and a few other options with some of my mother's closest friends, I was convinced that my mother's spirit would be okay with cremation as long as her ashes were taken on a road-trip laced with art, humor and the wildness befitting my crazy artist/activist mama. I asked my former partner to create a kinetic sculpture that incorporated all the wonderfulness of my mama and the things she would want to take with her to the Other Side. We would place her ashes in that sculpture and attach it to the roof of our car. This was the Lucky Po' Cats Urn.

Once the urn was finished, we scheduled the official San Francisco road trip send-off at UN Plaza. At 6 P.M. on March 24th, *POOR* subscribers, community support members, conscious politicians, Poverty Studies interns, Po' Poets and poverty scholars alike huddled under a drooping blue tarp affixed to the lift-back door of the *POOR Magazine* van.

The rain pounded down on the red bricks of an eerily quiet UN Plaza. As befitting my mama, it was a multimedia, interactive ceremony, including some video clips from her powerful Media in Action pieces, spoken word and poetic testimonies from several of her students and mentees, as well as words of solidarity from POWER members and Po' Poets. The night concluded with Tiburcio and me singing a song in honor of my rhythm-, music- and song-making mama.

"Whether you're a brother or whether you're a mother, you're stayin' alive, stayin' alive. Feel the city breakin' and everybody shakin' and we're stayin' alive, stayin' alive. Ah, ha, ha, ha, Stayin' alive. Stayin' alive . . ."

It had been raining for literally 40 days and 40 nights in San Francisco. Drops of icy water glided down the soft windshield, the fleshy rubber wipers caressing its surface. If you only looked quickly, the 4-foot tall golden lucky cat urn that held my mama's carefully wrapped cremated remains seemed to be gazing down from its mount on top of the van. It was 9 A.M. on Friday, March 31st, Cesar Chavez day, when Tiburcio and I and a couple of my mother's friends embarked on El Espíritu de Mama Dee Road Trip.

In honor of my mother's pondering of Pea Soup Anderson's as a possible place for us to live all those years ago on our trip up from Los Angeles, I decided that it must be a stop on the road trip down. After we pulled into the store/restaurant/motel conglomerate and sat down to consume a pea-filled lunch, my son jumped out of his chair and ran off to see some random thing in the dining room. In the process, he bumped his head on a chair and began bleeding profusely from his forehead. I rushed him to the bathroom where a nurse just happened to be standing with her adult daughter, who proceeded to create a butterfly bandage out of paper towels and saved my son from an emergency room visit.

Once we had sort of recovered, we and the lucky cat urn re-entered the highway. Within minutes we heard a loud knocking coming from the roof, and then I watched in the rearview mirror as a piece of the urn seemed to suddenly jump from the roof and land on the freeway's grassy median strip. Mama Dee always did want to see how it would be to live at Pea Soup Anderson's.

A hundred and twenty miles later down Highway 5 as we coasted out of the Grapevine, we heard a deep, scary sounding knock—this time it was coming from the engine. We barely made it off the freeway and into a town called Valencia. It was late afternoon on a Friday, and we were supposed to be arriving in Los Angeles in one hour for Mama Dee's ceremony on Venice Beach. It didn't look good.

Within minutes we were told that the van was irreparable, and that's when we met Sal. "Hey guys," he said as he approached the car, "do you need help?" For no good reason at all except that he knew we needed help, Sal agreed to drive us the 45 miles to Los Angeles so we could carry out Mama Dee's ceremony. We found out later that Sal was a friendly "coyote," helping families and friends across the border just because he thought he should help as many people in the world as he could. Sal was the kind of direct service provider my mother would have loved.

We didn't arrive in Los Angeles until close to midnight, so that night's ceremony was canceled. After much debating about what to do and whether to abort the whole project, I realized I had no will in the process and again consulted with some of my mother's friends. They urged us to keep on going. So at midnight, with Sal's help, we attached the lucky cat urn to a rented car and drove to Venice Beach.

The next morning the sun was out, the first day of sun after so many days of rain. In the morning glare, attached to a discount rental car, the lucky cat urn pulled into the Venice Beach parking lot where my mother and I had lived—housed and un-housed—and had made art and community for a few years of our lives so long ago.

CHAPTER 45

a message from my mama

When I returned from our journey, I constructed a living altar at one of my mother's favorite places, the *POOR* office, and my son and I continue to honor her almost every night by singing one or more of her favorite songs. He always ends the song by calling out her name into the sky.

One evening I was working on the last draft of this memoir, with my mama's picture watching me from the corner of the office. The picture had a clip-on light that would not turn on no matter how many times I changed the bulb, the extension cord—I had even changed the entire fixture, still with no luck.

On this chilly night in August, at approximately 6:30 P.M., the fire alarm suddenly screamed throughout the entire eight floors of the building. Everyone was evacuated onto the windy, wide sidewalks of Market Street. I waited, confused and annoyed that my last edit on the book was being held up when I had very little time left to complete it. After 30 minutes, two fire trucks, and three inspectors later, we were told to re-enter the building; "the alarm was inexplicable," they concluded.

As I walked back into the office, grumbling to myself about time lost, I noticed a strange glow emanating from the corner, and then I looked. The light was on, my mother's eyes glistening in the 40-watt glare.

"What do you want to tell me Mama Dee?" I screamed into the black night. The answer was not made clear to me that night, but it became very clear the next day that my mother was trying to tell me that I was not ready to finish the book. There was something else I needed to know.

I had scheduled the next day for the very sad job of going through all of my mama's things, her art, her post-homeless, pre-emergency pile-up of stuff that she had collected, mostly in plastic bags, after we'd become homeful not so many years back. Underneath the pile of Kleenex boxes, band-aids, towels, blankets and enough socks to warm the feet of a thousand shoeless children, sat a torn-up, dark brown folder, filled with yellow legal paper covered with cursive handwriting and some sheets of onionskin paper filled with neat type. It was the folder containing her original records from the orphanage, on all of those pages were the notes of her social worker, notes that I had seen, notes that I had heard about, reports that my mother had shared with me, details that I already knew, and yet I didn't know. Apparently, I hadn't really seen all of the records; apparently, my review of the folder had been edited.

Mary Jo's mother put an ad in the Philadelphia Inquirer *asking someone to "take Mary Jo." From that ad she got over fifteen responses. Mary Jo was shipped off to these homes, each one more abusive than the next, including significant sexual abuse. At two years old, Mary Jo was taken to the hospital because she was unable to void her urine due to the sexual abuse she received at one of the homes.*

The final home belonged to Marguerite Leland who, after losing her husband, became severely depressed and allowed Mary Jo to be used sexually by several of the adults who came to "visit" at her house.

The passages stared back at me in violent black courier font. My legs buckled; my eyes filled with tears. I fell to the floor, unable to move, devastated that I couldn't hold my poor unprotected, unwanted mama.

The last paragraph was an assessment of her "termination from the home" and referral to a mental institution and/or youth lock-up because she had made several "sexual overtures" to girls in the orphanage, behavior that would now be clearly diagnosed as that of a child who had been sexually abused and was acting out what had been done to her. And then the final, horrible passage:

Mary Jo's mother, upon hearing about Mary Jo's sexual behavior, became visibly revulsed by her own daughter, unable to even look at her, touch her or speak to her.

I already knew that my mother was abused and tortured, I already knew she was an unwanted child, but what I didn't know about was the severity of the sexual abuse, and that these sexual violations of her person were so horrible, so intolerable, that even she, as angry, conscious and powerful as she had become, had never been able to face this, the worst of all abuses. I screamed into the air and wanted so much to hold her and all the unprotected girls and women, boys and men that have ever been unwanted, uncared for, sexually and physically abused, unwatched and thrown away.

After this, the last and most painful revelation from my mother, the one so painful that she had never been able to speak of it, I was filled with a sorrow and pain that I'm not sure will ever really heal. I'm not sure I can live comfortably knowing there was something we couldn't talk about, knowing that she lived with that pain silently and alone, and there is nothing I can do now to make her feel better. I can't hold her hand ever again, hug her and tell her just one more time that it will all be okay.

Students, parents and members of the welfareQUEENS and LIFETIME standing in *POOR*'s F.A.M.I.L.Y Project classroom, in front of the "Inter-DEPendence Day" mural (l to r): Mahasin Moon, Gladys, Dianna Collier, Tiny, Dawn, Jamal Abdul-Musawwir and Tracey Faulkner. Photo by Mike Malacek for PoorNewsNetwork.

CHAPTER 46

FAMILY

So much of my life stopped making sense after my mother's passing, and one of the only things that gave me the strength to go on was the memory of her tireless work alongside me in pursuit of media justice and social justice. I realized that I must continue in her tradition at *POOR* and so, even though we had no funding except for a small contract with the Tenderloin Housing Clinic for a program to teach journalism to the residents of SRO hotels, I decided to make it happen, supporting it with the small salary I received from my job, hours of volunteer work and pure hope.

Since that time we have blossomed into a new and improved 21st-century *POOR*, including the formal launch of the Race, Poverty and Media Justice Institute, a bilingual column on immigration rights written by immigrant reporters, a welfareQUEENS media segment, as well as starting up new classes for digitalResistors and POOR Press writers that include a mother-daughter, formerly homeless duo who remind me of me and my mama and bring me to tears every time they're in class.

But perhaps the most important development of all is Family Access to Multicultural Intergenerational Learning (with our) Youth (F.A.M.I.L.Y.), the true manifestation of

POOR's belief in multigenerational learning. FAMILY is a collaboration with a project started by *POOR*'s own Jewnbug called Artistikal Revolutionary Teaching [ART], and our collaborative goals include an arts-based, intergenerational, multilingual model of teaching and learning that includes social justice, media critiques, world music, film studies, storytelling and writing, movement, dance, cooking, gardening and community health and survival for children aged two to eighteen. Our tuition is on a holistic sliding scale, free for low-income families and then up from there depending on the means to contribute, and with the added asset of childcare provided for poor parents who are enrolled in *POOR*'s adult programs.

FAMILY is part of a larger dream originally inspired by my mother: the Homefulness Project, a multipurpose building that would include three to five units of permanent sweat-equity co-housing for homeless and formerly homeless families, an on-site location for the FAMILY project, a café, community space and a permanent office for *POOR Magazine*, all of this providing stability, protection, community and equity for poor families so they never again have to face what I and my mother, and her mother and all the other poor and homeless mamas and papas face every day, here and around the world.

At *POOR* we hope to start publishing the hard copy of the magazine again. We hope to get accreditation for our Race, Poverty and Media Justice Institute and by doing so bring more poor students of color into colleges and universities. Alternately, we hope to take our Institute into the university setting in order to provide that scholarship and those scholars to the more privileged students who need that knowledge. We hope to gain more media access and media affiliates nationwide to syndicate our powerful writers and journalists. We hope to secure solid funding for our innovative education and advocacy programs, and above all we hope to keep providing access to unheard and unrecognized youth, adults and elders.

As the poverty dots come even closer to connecting, as poor folks worldwide, from China to Los Angeles, get pushed out of their housing, we must resist and relearn how to house and educate ourselves. As economic apartheid deepens everywhere, our families, our elders, our children and our communities remain confused, in motion and under attack. And to survive and thrive we must take back our strength, reclaim our indigenous cultures and practices and, as we continue to do at *POOR*, learn from and listen to our elders and our ancestors, stop allowing ourselves to be separated, colonized and incarcerated. And above all, we must actively resist the increasing destabilization, gentrification and criminalization of poor folks and poor communities everywhere.

Tiny and Tiburcio at a protest against California Governor Schwarzenegger's official endorsement of an Arizona Minutemen patrol of the California border.